Reading Greek Tragedy with Judith Butler

Classical Receptions in Twentieth-Century Writing

Series Editor: Laura Jansen

Each book in this ground-breaking series considers the dialogue with Mediterranean antiquity in a single writer from the 'long' twentieth century. From Virginia Woolf to Judith Butler, Walcott to Soyinka, and Calvino to Foucault, the modalities and texture of this modern encounter with antiquity are explored in the works of authors recognized for their global impact on modern fiction, poetry, art, philosophy and politics.

A distinctive feature of twentieth-century writing is the tendency to break with tradition and embrace the new sensibilities of the time. Yet the period continues to maintain a fluid dialogue with the Greco-Roman past, drawing on its cultural ideas and claims, even within the most radical thinkers who ostentatiously question and reject that past. Classical Receptions in Twentieth-Century Writing (CRTW) approaches this dialogue from two interrelated perspectives: it asks how modern authors' positions on the ancient classics open new readings of their oeuvres and contexts, and it considers how this process in turn renders innovative insights into the classical world. Interdisciplinarity is at the heart of the series. CRTW addresses some of the most profound shifts in practices of reading, writing, and thinking in recent years within and beyond the arts and humanities, as well as in the poetics of reading antiquity that one finds in twentieth-century writing itself.

Also new in this series

Derek Walcott and the Creation of a Classical Caribbean, Justine McConnell
Fellini's Eternal Rome, Alessandro Carrera
Foucault's Seminars on Antiquity: Learning to Speak the Truth, Paul Allen Miller
James Joyce and Classical Modernism, Leah Culligan Flack
J.R.R. Tolkien's Utopianism and the Classics, Hamish Williams
Tony Harrison: Poet of Radical Classicism, Edith Hall
Virginia Woolf's Greek Tragedy, Nancy Worman

Reading Greek Tragedy with Judith Butler

Mario Telò

With an Afterword by Judith Butler

BLOOMSBURY ACADEMIC
LONDON • NEW YORK • OXFORD • NEW DELHI • SYDNEY

BLOOMSBURY ACADEMIC
Bloomsbury Publishing Plc, 50 Bedford Square, London, WC1B 3DP, UK
Bloomsbury Publishing Inc, 1359 Broadway, 12th Floor, New York, NY 10018, USA
Bloomsbury Publishing Ireland, 29 Earlsfort Terrace, Dublin 2, D02 AY28, Ireland

BLOOMSBURY, BLOOMSBURY ACADEMIC and the Diana logo are trademarks of Bloomsbury Publishing Plc

First published in Great Britain 2024
Paperback edition published 2026

Cover design: Terry Woodley
Cover image © Collier Schorr

A catalogue record for this book is available from the British Library.

Library of Congress Cataloging-in-Publication Data
Names: Telò, Mario, 1977– author.
Title: Reading Greek tragedy with Judith Butler / Mario Telò.
Description: London ; New York : Bloomsbury Academic, 2024. |
Series: Classical receptions in twentieth-century writing ; vol 8 |
Includes bibliographical references and index.
Identifiers: LCCN 2023053362 (print) | LCCN 2023053363 (ebook) |
ISBN 9781350323384 (hardback) | ISBN 9781350323421 (paperback) |
ISBN 9781350323391 (pdf) | ISBN 9781350323407 (ebook)
Subjects: LCSH: Butler, Judith, 1956– | Greek drama (Tragedy)–History and criticism. |
Literature–Philosophy.
Classification: LCC B945.B884 T45 2024 (print) | LCC B945.B884 (ebook) |
DDC 191—dc23/eng/20240124
LC record available at https://lccn.loc.gov/2023053362
LC ebook record available at https://lccn.loc.gov/2023053363

ISBN: HB: 978-1-3503-2338-4
PB: 978-1-3503-2342-1
ePDF: 978-1-3503-2339-1
eBook: 978-1-3503-2340-7

Series: Classical Receptions in Twentieth-Century Writing

Typeset by RefineCatch Limited, Bungay, Suffolk

Contents

Illustrations

Acknowledgments

My warmest thanks to Laura Jansen, the formidable editor of the wonderful series "Classical Receptions in Twentieth-Century Writing," in which this book appears. After asking me to write this book, she oversaw the writing, peer review, and production with unique generosity, kindness, and care. I feel deeply indebted to her for her vision—and I eagerly look forward to working on other projects together. Many thanks to the three anonymous referees, who provided important guidance. Alice Wright, Lily Mac Mahon, and Zoe Osman at Bloomsbury were, as always, the best editorial team. My dear friends Ella Haselswerdt, Sara Lindheim, Ramsey McGlazer, Paul Allen Miller, Dan Orrells, and Jim Porter read the manuscript, providing encouragement and stimulating feedback. Jim and Ramsey also participated in "Reading with Bespaloff, Butler, and Sedgwick: Homer, Sappho, and Greek Tragedy," an event organized by the UC Berkeley Rhetoric Department, which also featured Melissa Mueller and Ramona Nadaff. Penelope Deutscher showed much support and enthusiasm at a public discussion of chapter 1.

Judith Butler has enriched my life not only with their endlessly inspiring work, but also with the gift of their friendship. The afternoon in which JB hugged me because they sensed, even before I did, that I wanted (or needed) to hug them was a professional and personal *Wendung*. Reading, hearing, seeing, thinking with JB is an energizing experience that helps me and so many others keep going, in spite of this world's unceasing challenges. This book is a small tribute to what their existence has done for all of us. Alex Press is my pillar. Thank you, Alex, as always, for your intelligence, patience, and love.

Unless otherwise indicated, I follow these editions: Lloyd-Jones and Wilson 1990 for Sophocles' *Antigone*; Seaford 1996 for Euripides' *Bacchae*; Podlecki 1989 for Aeschylus's *Eumenides*.

Introduction

Breaking Apart: Greek Tragedy, Judith Butler, and Critique

> *Consider . . . that laughing and crying both disrupt the very conditions of communication and open up modes of expression and intervention that go beyond the sphere of communication. One starts to speak but breaks out in laughter, at which point the laughter interrupts speech; one cannot finish the sentence. One can hardly catch one's breath. Or one starts to tell a story, and one breaks out in tears and starts gasping for breath. Something somatic is happening that interrupts the course of speaking. The sounds of the body exceed that form of vocalization called speech. Something else is making itself known; the body erupts, the body interrupts its own speaking and announces itself as insistent, graphic, audible, and unavoidable. I do not know, but I don't believe that people die from laughing or from crying, and yet, it is possible to say that both laughing and crying indicate a crisis for the human subject, one that is to some extent ordinary.*[1]

In this extract from the lecture "Out of Breath: Laughing, Crying at the Body's Limit," delivered in Mexico City in 2019, Judith Butler poetically lingers on the relation between "break" and "breath," on the sensory emergence of the body through its being torn apart in a moment of affective dissolution, its grasping for relief amid the eruption of its own undoing, a serendipitous self-interruption. Crying and laughter do not pit tragedy and comedy against each other; coexisting and blurring in the aesthetic domains of both genres, they are disruptions that spread the social and political sense of *drama* ("doing, action"), a word in which the initial rhotic vibration (*dr. . .*) enables a vocalic opening (*a. . .a*) for *action*, *acting*, or—to take the Latinate etymological constellation in a different direction—*agitation*.[2] They offer an opportunity to experience the affective and cognitive perception that as a coming apart the brokenness or breakability of a notionally individual breath or body manifests a projection toward, or an implication with, an other-than-oneself-ness.[3] The exceeding of boundedness is what makes the subject's life possible, producing a self-loss, a de-subjectification, that is unavoidable but can be embraced (rather than disavowed) in the *being with* that being always entails.[4]

Breakability is central to the aesthetics of Greek tragedy and to an array of distinctive, influential, and deeply tragic critical-theoretical Butlerian ideas: gender and kinship trouble, precarity, interdependence, grievability, and vulnerability in resistance, among others. The goal of this book is to illuminate these affinities through an analysis of what I call Butler's tragic trilogy—a phrase I use to group together a book and two essays devoted to three classics of Greek tragedy, one for each major tragedian: Sophocles' *Antigone*, at the center of *Antigone's Claim: Kinship between Life and Death* (2000); Euripides' *Bacchae*, in "Breaks in the Bond: Reflections on Kinship Trouble" (2017); and Aeschylus's *Eumenides*, in "Fury and Justice in the Humanities" (2023). Butler's trilogy does not trace a developmental narrative, nor does it outline a dramaturgical enactment of the Hegelian dialectic's tripartite movement, as the *Oresteia* has been read to do.[5] It is both like Sophoclean and Euripidean trilogy—which, as far as we know, offered no narrative through lines—and the *Oresteia* itself, in which diachrony, teleology, and resolution after tension are replaced or un-dialectically problematized by unexpected thematic intertwinements and disruptive synchronies.[6] In Butler's trilogy, as we will see, "improvisational solidarit[ies]" and "sliding identifications"[7]—to use their phrases—are formed between Antigone, the Maenads, Agave, the Erinyes, and also Niobe and Iphigenia. The anti-narrative triangularity of the Butlerian trilogy—unplanned, "improvisational"—goes along with the *Oresteia*'s thickly imagistic, intricately intratextual plot or anti-plot, an alternative mode of connectivity that, like laughing or crying, "interrupts speech," breaking the imperative to "tell a story."[8] Exceeding narrative's "own speaking," the drive to move on, anti-narrative connectivity bids us to linger; it makes room for critique, alternative "modes of expression and intervention" that turn affect's and form's power of undoing into a theory and praxis of politics.

Modern and contemporary thought is bound up with Greek tragedy—a major point of reference and an inexhaustible archive of dialogue for the likes of Hegel, Kierkegaard, Nietzsche, Marx, Freud, Benjamin, Heidegger, Lacan, Arendt, Sartre, Derrida, Foucault, Irigaray, Kristeva, Deleuze and Guattari, Cixous, and Nancy, as many studies have illustrated.[9] However, unlike Butler, none of these thinkers ever dedicated an essay or a book to a close reading of a play; their various engagements with Oedipus, Antigone, Dionysus, Prometheus, Niobe, the Erinyes, and other figures were folded into their theorizations, published and unpublished. Different, as well, from Sartre's *Les Mouches* (1943) and *Les Troyennes* (1965), Cixous's *Le Nome d'Oedipe* (1978), and Cixous's translation and production of Aeschylus's *Eumenides* (1992),[10] the three works of Butler's trilogy are not deliberate remakes of the Greek originals but rather disruptors, in the very modality of writing (about) tragedy, of dichotomies between literary-criticism and philosophical speculation, scholarship and creative adaptation, that have built a model of writing (about) tragedy seen, for example, in the interventions of another major thinker of our times, Bonnie Honig's *Antigone, Interrupted* (2013) and *A Feminist Theory of Refusal* (2020).[11] While remaining attentive to linguistic texture both in the Greek and its translations, Butler's trilogy gives us an invigorating alternative to the deep-rooted tendency to detach the classical past from the present and, in the guise of respect and responsibility, to otherize it, monumentalize it, and archive it away.[12] The trilogy models an experimental way of approaching ancient tragedy that demonstrates and embraces the impossibility of separating the interpreter's historical situatedness from the ancient object's own temporal stratification, from its impenetrable layeredness, which we disavow every time we decide to take fifth-century Athens as our primary (or exclusive) frame of reference, giving in to the normative fantasies of purity, unmixedness, and self-identity—the hierarchical forces that Butler's ethico-political reflections have repeatedly helped us resist and contest.[13] Even though I place this trilogy in dialogue with a number of other contemporary thinkers, my "reading with" Judith Butler is not meant to paint an intellectual-historical picture. My goal is to enact Butler's mode of intimate engagement with the tragic imaginary by reproducing it, extending or expanding it, letting it exert its rich and liberating power of impression, heeding its generative capacity and its generous excess, its fecund ability to envision and stimulate a beyondness. For me, this entails explicating and continuing the legacy of Butler's hermeneutic provocations in the form of an open-ended, impromptu metacommentary that encompasses the three ancient plays; Butler's textuality itself; the unpredictable adjacencies and mergings between them; and the resulting contributions to radical politics—intended, in Butlerian fashion, as an imaginative inscription of the impossible within the realm or the regime of the possible.[14]

What I propose is thus an experiment, a Butlerian reading of Butler's reading of tragedy sustained by the impetus, in their writing and my own, to break apart, come undone in pursuing tentative, dispossessive intertwinements, disruptive intimations of meaning.[15] I construe my approach as Butlerian not in the customary sense of a reading à la—but, instead, in the commitment to a politics or, in Denise Ferreira da Silva's term, a *poethics* of interdependency.[16] Overcoming the borders between "I (me)" and "you," "my/mine" and "your/your(s)," practices of close reading and critical thinking perform vertiginous polyphonies;[17] intense processes of unreconstructable deindividuation; continuous motions of folding, unfolding, and refolding— experiences of the undoing, the breaking apart (that is, the impossibility of self-sufficiency) that underlies and contradicts every self-affirmation, every egological exercise.[18] Reading *with* Butler is thus the opposite of reading *according to*, or à la Butler; it does not mean taking on a bounded, recognizable mode of thinking, adhering to a distinctive intellectual brand, but instead self-reflexively dismantling the territoriality, the proprietary logic that shapes and constricts academia, and opening up possibilities of productive unintelligibility, unrecognizability, and indistinction.[19] Reading *with* Butler can, consequently, help us locate and enact, through the *agitated* affect of interpretive *activity*, the modes of self-critical being (of *being* as *being in crisis*) that are crucial for addressing our urgent planetary crises.[20] To be Butlerian in being non-Butlerian is to evade the reinscription of possession and sovereignty while aligning oneself with, even being cathected to, the theorist who has most powerfully contested the tyranny of identity, autonomy, and self-sufficiency.[21] This being in non-being is the paradox that ethically and aesthetically frames my engagement with the inexhaustible imaginative potentialities of Butler's critical-theoretical readings of Greek tragedy.[22] To exemplify my methodology of *co-reading* and unveil the tragic aesthetics informing Butler's writing even when it is not focused on tragedy, I return now to the initial citation to muse on the relation between breath and laughter in the three plays of the trilogy: *Antigone*, *Bacchae*, and *Eumenides*. This sample of the kind of interpretive intertwinement I practice in the course of the book—reading Greek tragedy with Butler, reading Butler with Greek tragedy—will then lead me to consider the phenomenology of the "unbearable" and the "unlivable," two generative Butlerian concepts that illuminate the critical-theoretical richness of tragic form.

Breathing, Laughing, Politics

> One laughs or one cries, which is another way of saying that one is bound to the body as living process precisely at the moment in which the body breaks open or breaks into an involuntary heaving, catching its breath, becoming intimate with the threat of no longer being able to breathe. Both laughing and crying do not merely interrupt the body's functioning in everyday life, but bring that functioning into crisis, nearing the condition of physical emergency, miming, without full control, that reaction to being imperiled.[23]

The sudden appearance of a laugh at the beginning of Aeschylus's *Eumenides* solves the crisis of the Erinyes' stalled movement—the movement of rage that the plot needs to renew in order to arrest it once and for all, allowing us to breathe in the mirage of civic harmony, the "neoliberal fantasy" of democracy.[24] Something laughs at the Erinyes, but laughter is a convulsive emotion homologous to the "fury," the rage that, as I discuss in the third chapter, Butler enables us to conceptualize not as the alternative to, but as the propulsive energy of, justice, a *dikê* liberated from the normative constraints of judgment. Here, the Erinyes are assaulted by a remainder of the enticement that feeds their death-driven fury, their tragic impetus, which breaks them apart while keeping them going (253):

> *osmê broteiôn haimatôn me pros-gelai*
> The smell of mortal blood is laughing to me.

The brilliantly synesthetic line that tortured Francis Bacon, that made him feel exhilaratingly pursued by the Erinyes, like Orestes,[25] resounds with the laughter of a sensation—having dissolved, the dismembered or self-dismembering face of the laughing subject has in turn evaporated into the more-than-human agency of an odor.[26] Just before this line, tragic *poiêsis* inscribes the Erinyes' canine panting and wheezing as they resume their chase with effects of phonosymbolic mimeticism that make reading a process of becoming Fury, of "becoming intimate with the threat of no longer being able to breathe" (245–49):

> Follow the signals of the voiceless (*aphthenktou*) informer; like a dog, we are tracking the wounded (*tetraumatismenon*) deer, by blood and drip. *With much man-killing toil, my innards are gasping; the land's* whole space has, in fact, been explored by our flock (*pollois de mochthois androkmêsi phusiai / splanchnon; chthonos . . .*).

A displacement of the speaker's respiratory congestion onto the clotted blood of matricide, the consonantal occlusion in *aphthenktou* (245)—the adjective modifying the "informer" that is blood—and the hexasyllabic, hyper-stretched participle *tetraumatismenon* (246) mimetically "interrup[t] the course of speaking." The vocalization that calls itself speech is overwhelmed and stalled by the eruption, the coming into rebellious being, of its own medium, breath and saliva, which, like laughter and crying, interfere with "the sphere of communication," refusing to be domesticated. The verbal rendition of the panting—*phusiai / **splanchnon*** (248–49)—coincides with the expectorating aggregate of a sibilant, a labial, and a liquid consonant, a "buccal" crisis,[27] which extends into the syntactical micro-unit opened by ***ch**th**on**os*, whose *ch* (χ) and "*on*" sounds, attracted back into the phonetic substance of the preceding word *splanchnon*, further clot articulation, generating "an involuntary heaving." Language does not stutter,[28] but alternately cries *or* laughs, or cries *and* laughs, "nearing the condition of physical emergency." Tragic language invites a formalistic analysis, a micro-practice of critical phenomenology, an approach heavily influenced by Butler.[29]

The respiratory contraction of the Erinyes, the hunters, seems then to prefigure and merge with their target's modes of appearance, the ghostly, intermittent feel of the smell of blood, the visceral sensation of laughter or panting. The synesthetic, Baconesque line that closes the Erinyes' speech supplies the image of the Other mocking the death-driven looping around the *objet petit a*, teasingly feeding the *jouissant* quest that occupies the living subject, that catches it in a restless immobility. Beyond this Lacanian schema—emblematized by the Antigone of *The Ethics of Psychoanalysis* (1992), the main target of *Antigone's Claim*—another reading is possible. The internal resonance, a quasi-rhyme between *osmê* ("odor") and the objectified subject *me* underscores the atmospheric breaking apart of a breathless subject, the subject's receiving air, finding respiratory relief, taking in enlivening substance through the very process of giving up its boundedness, of participating in the social ecology[30] that causes it to become a diminished yet heightened version of itself, an *osmê* rather than a *me*.

Laughter and crying can effect a breaking apart of the status quo—a political change— through the very physiology of these motions, that is, even despite the intentions of the laughing and crying subject, of the subject losing itself in laughing or crying. As Butler continues:

> I do not lose myself entirely, but I discover that I am a creature defined in part by this very capacity for self-loss. When I am laughing or crying, I am not usually acting deliberately in a situation to impart an idea or effect a change, although some forms of acting can follow this plan. Rather, some embodied dimension of who I am is at once departing from a situation and reacting to it. I am still the one who is laughing or crying, but this I is becoming undone, physically.

In Sophocles' *Antigone*, after the discovery of Antigone's transgression, Creon chastises her for her double hubris: not only did she violate or, more literally, "overstep" (*huper-bainousa*) the established laws (*nomous . . . tous prokeimenous* 481), but after having done so (*dedraken/dedrakuian* 482–83) she "laughed" (*gelan* 483) at the deed. Differently from Creon, we can read Antigone's laughter not simply as a display of defiance, a self-gratifying backward glance at her "act," but as *drama* itself, a "doing" that consists, in fact, of "becoming undone." An instant of death that provokes a gaping hole in the face,[31] Antigone's laughter is an "overstepping" of the limits of the corporeal "given": what is allotted to human embodiment, the contours of enfleshed individuation, the line that notionally separates one body from another, the fantasy of impermeability or immunity.[32] This is the immunitarian illusion that, in *Bacchae*, Pentheus clings to in attempting to drive away the stranger Dionysus, a rejection expressed by his mockery of, his laughing at, the god's trans-birth. This mockery is epitomized by the triple occurrence of *dia-gelais* ("You mock," that is "you laugh through" 272, 286, 322), Tiresias's *j'accuse*, which foreshadows Pentheus's *dis*memberment, bodily *dis*persal as the extreme consequence of his cathexis to self-possession, of his refusal of the self-interruption, the self-breaking that is brought about by laughter, by Dionysus, the "laughing god."[33] The "split" that breaks Pentheus's laughing face (*dia*- "through"), that opens up *Di*onysus's own face in it, is an image of the self-loss at work in anti-Dionysian immunization—of the failure of "laughing at" to put distance between self and other. It is also an image of the break in the bond between the cousins Pentheus and Dionysus, of kinship in and as a break, which, as we will see, Butler locates in Euripides' play. When Pentheus laughs, the cutting through his face suggested by *dia*- projects the split into the final scene.[34] The master Dionysus, facially co-implicated or intertwined with his cousin, does not entirely escape the latter's permanent separation of head from body.

We can say that the "capacity for self-loss" in Antigone's laughter "impart[s] an idea or effect[s] a change," "form[s] of acting" that are part of her "claim" for expansive relationalities, for breaking the givenness of (heterosexual) embodiment and kinship. In the same essay on crying and laughter, Butler discusses the practice of *escrache* in Spain and Latin America:

> The tradition of *escrache* makes this clear: the judiciary fails to punish the torturer, and the crowd assembles outside his home at night, chanting and drumming and calling his name. Noise, yes, but also political expression, an intervention into the everyday: he will not sleep at night; there will be no rest.... Extra-judicial punishment ... takes the form of unwanted sound—not quite torture, but its reminder.... In these instances, sounds break the law, but they also demand justice.... That register ... is the one that belongs to bodies in alliance in public space, asserting weight and presence, becoming a differentiated mass, talking at cross purposes and so producing sounds that cannot be avoided and from which there is no exit and which take us to the edge of language itself.

Butler's characterization of the *escrache* brings to mind the first appearance of the Erinyes in the *Oresteia*, as a *kômos* (the source of the word *comedy*),[35] a band of rowdy revelers seeking to burst into a house after a drinking party: "after having drunk mortal blood (*broteion haima*), the revel (*kômos*) of the Erinyes is remaining in the house" (*Agamemnon* 1188–89). The obvious intratextual echo between this passage and the synesthetic line of the *Eumenides* allows us to see the inebriated Erinyes as dogs keen on bursting in, to construe their panting, materialized in rough consonantal obstruction, as laughter, like scratching at a door—*escrache* is, in fact, cognate with the English *scratch*.[36] The door is, like Antigone's body itself, the barrier of the (human and non-human) given, which the Furies, as symbols of tragedy, dogs but also a "flock," seek to break or scratch through, performing the enfleshed self-breaking, the crisis, of crying or laughing, or laughing-as-crying, as in a nocturnal carousal. This enraged and aggrieved laughter activates the space of the "unbearable," where Butler situates the emergence of tragedy's political force and its convergence with critique.

The Unbearable and the Unlivable

In a review of Anne Carson's *Antigonick* (2012), significantly entitled "Can't Stop Screaming," Butler refers to Carson's answer to the question of "Why does Greek tragedy exist?":[37] "Because you are full of rage. Why are you full of rage? Because you are full of grief." Commenting on the emotional chiasmus of Antigone and Creon, Butler continues: "Antigone rages forth from grief, causing new destruction, and so, too, does Kreon; they mirror each other in the midst of their opposition.... The reader is *implicated* in this recurrent alternation of grief and rage, subject to the destruction she or he is capable of inflicting, if there is no timely intervention."[38] This bond of grief and rage runs through the moving writing of perhaps the most tragic of Butler's books, *Precarious Life* (2004)[39]—a reflection on the "unbearable vulnerability" that "was exposed" by September 11[40] and on "grievability," the enduring inequality in the distribution of the right to grieve and to be grieved (in Israel/Palestine and many other parts of the world), which has, directly or indirectly, influenced classical scholars' approaches to Greek tragedy's politics of mourning.[41] In response to Bonnie Honig's critique of Butler's "grievable humanism" as ultimately anti-political,[42] Andrés Fabián Henao Castro has pointed out that in the transition from *Antigone's Claim* to *Precarious Life* Butler "does not move away from politics and towards ethics" but rather "to a more radical critique of the more violent disqualification of speech-acts from the public sphere under geo-political conditions of settler colonialism."[43] In other words, "Butler's ethical-political frame of grievability" is a way "of addressing the speechlessness that prima facie disavows the Palestinian claim to equality by coding"

Palestinian mourning "as an act of vengeance against the colonial order." Butler's reflection on Walter Benjamin's treatment in "Towards a Critique of Violence" of Niobe, a tragic symbol of the bond of grief and rage, is tellingly folded into *Parting Ways* (2012), in which Butler observes: "One hears, time and again in Israeli public discourse, that a single Israeli life is worth more than countless Palestinian lives. Yet only when such obscene calculations definitively fail, and all populations are deemed grievable, will the principle of social and political equality start to govern."[44] "The differential allocation of grievability"[45] is the most radical inequality, since "grievability is a presupposition for the life that matters." Commenting on Israel's "implementation of a genocidal plan" in response to Hamas's massacre of 1,400 Israelis on October 7, 2023, Butler remarked that "Palestinians have been labeled as ungrievable," and their loss has been considered "not . . . a real loss." In this urgent and fraught context, "mourning and carrying the dead and honoring the dead" has become—once again—a policed, at times forbidden, mode of political gathering.[46] In *Frames of War* (2009), the ethical politics of Greek tragedy and the fundamental contribution that Greek tragedy can make to understanding our time of global crisis from the perspective of critical-theoretical activism[47] are reflected in the observation that grievability is "a condition of a life's emergence and sustenance" that "precedes and makes possible the apprehension of the living being as living, exposed to non-life from the start."[48] In the display of public mourning after police murders of countless Black people, the right to grieve and be grieved vociferously claimed in Greek tragedy—a right that the status quo seeks to curtail—is indissociable from enraged demands for livability and rebellion against thanatopolitical enforcement of racist inequality in the US and other Western countries.[49] In *What World Is This?* (2022), polluted air made even more precarious by a global pandemic is cast as the tragic epiphany of the world, the materialization of differential measures of mattering, of differential breathabilities, of unequal rights to breathe caused by the disavowal of shared vulnerability. Butler writes that "the Movement for Black Lives is . . . a form of public mourning . . . of gathering and nongathering . . . that crosses borders," adding that "in marking and mourning these lives, even if we did not know them, we are insisting . . . that the police or other perpetrators should be held accountable or . . . that the police force itself should be dissolved."[50] In the third chapter, I will connect Niobe, in her endless mourning, with the Erinyes—

the agents of the critical Fury that Butler prescriptively sees as animating the humanities—and read this bond against the dismissal and suppression of Black rage, barely distinguishable from Black breath.

I am struck by the intratextual co-implication that the verb "implicate"—that is, "enfold," "entwine"—establishes between the aforementioned review of *Antigonick* and the passage in *Precarious Life* in which Butler notes the inability of "liberal versions of human ontology" to "do justice to . . . grief and rage, . . . which tear us from ourselves, bind us to others, transport us, undo us, *implicate* us in lives that are not our own, irreversibly if not fatally."[51] The aesthetic relationship between tragic character and tragic reader/spectator is mapped onto Butlerian social ecology, onto the ethics of intertwinement—in this light, Aristotelian catharsis, attentive to mimetically protecting the subject from the contamination of "grief and rage," to safeguarding it from the irreversible contagion of "unbearable vulnerability," comes to mind as an ancient predecessor of "liberal versions of human ontology."[52] In a 2014 lecture entitled "On the Edge: Grief"— "a kind of mini-soliloquy of unrestrained intellectual *fury*"[53]—the bond of "grief" and "rage" in the space of the "unbearable" theorized in *Precarious Life* is tightened from the "implicated" perspective of Butler as a reader of tragedy, who, in their inescapable entanglement, is conscripted (or constricted) as a co-performer. This (co-)performer's aggrieved, enraged speech act furiously unfolds and folds back on itself until it finds itself tangled in the unbearable collapse of its own medium:

> The grief is unbearable, and from that unbearability, one kills, a killing that produces more grief. Have we yet figured out exactly how this works, the transition from unbearable grief to uncontrollable rage and destructiveness? . . . If we could bear our grief, would we be less inclined to strike back or strike out? And if the grief is unbearable, is there another way to live with it that is not the same as bearing it? We know the contours of this terrible circle—destroying to stop the unbearable grief, to bring an end to the unbearable, only to then redouble that loss by destroying again. . . . If the world is unlivable without those one has lost, perhaps there emerges a despairing form of egalitarianism according to which everyone should suffer this devastation. . . . Perhaps there is an effort to bring grief to a full stop through taking aim at the world in which such grief is possible, rolling over into a form of destructiveness that furiously proliferates more loss, wantonly distributing the unbearable. . . . With great speed we do sometimes

> drive away from the unbearable, or drive precisely into its clutches, or do both at once, not knowing how we move, or with what consequence. It seems unbearable to be patient with unbearable loss, and yet that slowness, that impediment, can be the condition for showing what we value, and even perhaps what steps to take to preserve what is left of what we love.[54]

Language here takes us to the edge, but it is also lyrically taken to the edge. As it nervously explicates the spiral of grief, the cumulative, unbearable logic of loss, it generously pushes itself into the spiral. It becomes tragically ec-static, seeking to convert itself into pure intensity, to overcome itself as the filter, the obstruction of the enraged grief or the aggrieved rage that it verbally expresses. The apparent medium, the support of the feeling that drives it, language strives to make itself *un-bearing*, surrendering to our desire for unmediated emotion, or, according to a different reading, language becomes exhausted—like the earth that we call "ours"—fatigued, worn out by its function as the surface, the support, the infrastructure that, like the air or the paper it itself depends on, never stops bearing, making itself almost un-bearing in the repeated effort to bear the unbearable.[55] Grief, which language bears, is, in fact, etymologically what is *grave*, a burdensome, aggravating heaviness.[56] In the moment of the collapse of language, the disavowed dependence on the supporting surface—human, inhuman, or both human and inhuman—comes to the fore. As I read Butler's words in conjunction with their discussion of *Eumenides*, the third play of their trilogy, I am reminded of the Furies' entrance song, which spreads the affective sensation of "unbearable" (*a-phertos*) againness while bringing this word's long journey throughout the trilogy to an end (143–46):[57]

> Iou, iou, popax! We have *suffered* (*epathomen*), dear ones.
> Indeed much I have *suffered* (*pepontha*), and in vain;
> We *suffered* (*epathomen*) a horribly painful *suffering* (*pathos*), oh popoi,
> An *unbearable* (*apherton*) evil.

The overarching trajectory of the *Oresteia* can be read as "an effort to bring grief to a full stop through taking aim at the world in which such grief is possible, rolling over into a form of destructiveness that furiously proliferates more loss, wantonly distributing the unbearable." Towards the end of *Agamemnon*, Aegisthus reconstructs the background, the *archê* of his revenge murder plot, the intrafamilial dispute between brothers, Atreus and Thyestes—

Agamemnon's and his own father, respectively. When Thyestes realized he was tricked by Atreus into eating his own children's flesh, he disgorged their remains or, more literally, "their slaughters" (*apo sphagas erôn* 1599)—an emetic undoing of the act—vowing "an unbearable fate" (*moron d'apherton* 1600) on the offspring of Pelops, his father. Even though syntactically modifying the curse, this "unbearability" reflects back on the anti-teleological rhythm of emesis and on the biological "impossibility," the "unintelligibility" of male pregnancy.[58] The "scandal" of trans-parentality[59] at the center of *Bacchae*, a dramaturgical reflection on Dionysus's trans-birth, will be discussed in the second chapter in light of Butler's responses to the global recrudescence of legalized anti-queer and anti-trans violence.

The emancipatory potentiality of "living with the unbearable" is tragedy's chief critical-theoretical attraction for Butler. Whereas for some the unbearable is a condition of material, economic unlivability, the normative voice of the status quo conversely dismisses the sharing of that unbearability as what is "unbearable," that which cannot be "realistically" borne, what cannot be (ethically, culturally) tolerated, (financially) sustained, (conceptually, epistemically) held, (legislatively) upheld.[60] This dismissal arises from a disavowal of dependence on structures of support that may become incapable of bearing even those who imagine their own self-reliance.[61] For those attached to their protection from unbearability,[62] living with the unbearable would be a step toward a sharing of unbearability—that is, a recognition of and participation in the human condition of "unbearable vulnerability." In "living with the unbearable," the comitative force of the "with" underscores the commons built on the discovery that one rests on, is (un)built on, the taken-for-granted givenness of a material and social base.[63] The Butlerian Antigone's claim for queer kinship and for radical deindividuation stems from her perception of heteronormative boundedness as unbearable; it is a striving toward the expansive relationality that the state finds unsustainable, intolerable.[64] To live with the unbearable Erinyes does not mean simply tolerating them by archiving them but, as we will see in the third chapter, striving toward a model of justice enmeshed, colluding with rage, able and eager to be undone by unbearable anger.

In *Agamemnon*, before Aegisthus, Cassandra—as alert to smell as a canine Erinys—verbalizes "unbearability," as other characters will do later in the trilogy, with a neuter form of *aphertos*, meaning "misfortune," "misdeed," "pain," "grief": "What is this novel pain? A big, big evil—unbearable (*apherton*) for the kin, unhealable—is being devised in this house" (1101–3). In this scene, Cassandra, the enslaved prophetess delivering unheeded warnings, deemed the bearer of ominous, improper messages, is the unbearable.[65] Forced to subject her voice to Apollo's prophecies, she acts as the despised surface, the support of the god's language, taken for granted by him and the humans around her, the dehumanized infrastructure bearing human and divine life, the unbearable more-than-human bearing the extraction that makes the human.[66] At the same time, the "radical *unintelligibility*"[67] of Cassandra's words forestalls interpretive extraction; they emblematize what, in "On Not Knowing Greek," Virginia Woolf refers to as the "dangerous leap through the air without the *support* of words" that in *Agamemnon* readers are caused to make when facing this "tremendous" drama in which Aeschylus "stretch[es] every phrase to the utmost, by sending" those phrases "floating forth in metaphors."[68] Appearing again in the neuter gender in *The Libation Bearers* and *Eumenides*, *aphertos* is a reminder of the human groundedness in various forms of other-than-itself-ness that make grief not bearable, but expressible, perceptible, repeatable.[69] It is a reminder of the collectivity, the commons, which is always involved in, and burdened by, notionally individual grief, and of the untenability of the marginalizing, racializing distinction, implicitly made, between "bearable grief" and "unbearable grief," grief that can (or should) be tolerated and grief that can (or should) not be sustained. The neuter of "unbearable" is a reminder of the non-human that makes humanity possible, bearable.[70] The "living with the unbearable" that Butler sees dramatized in Greek tragedy is tied to their investment in social critical ontology, a post-human social ecology, and a politics of interdependency, which respond to the white disavowal of precarity and vulnerability, to the individual's aggressive and illusory cathexis to self-possession and self-sufficiency, to the state's ultimately auto-immunitarian pursuit of bio- and necropolitical strategies of immunization.

As I read, in not-quite-post-pandemic times, in a context of escalating environmental catastrophe, Athena's worry that if the Erinyes do not win the trial, a poison (*ios*, cognate with "virus") "again will fall to the ground (*pedôi pesôn*), unbearable (*aphertos*), eternal disease" (478–79), I think of Butler's discussion of Covid-19 in light of Max Scheler's essay "On the Tragic" (1954) and critical phenomenology:

> Even as the tragic is occasioned by events . . . the tragic can never be reduced to the event which is its occasion; it persists, rather, as a kind of atmosphere. . . . Grief seems to pour out from the event into unlimited space. . . . "The remote subject of the tragic is always the world itself. . . . This 'world' itself seems to be the object immersed in sorrow."[71]

An "unbearable, eternal disease" that will lead to "unbearable grief" overlaps with a poison that, shading into our own pandemic virus, manifests the *escrache* of the worn-down ground, a surface no longer able to bear human attacks, much less sustaining crops.[72] When Athena ascribes to the Erinyes the power to make the earth sterile, the unbearable grief that *Eumenides* is tasked with repairing acquires a global resonance.[73] Reading "the tragic as a way in which the world leaves its impress and provokes a sorrow that exceeds the limits of experience,"[74] Butler contends that our exposure to the increasing unlivability only heightened by the virus should grant us

> a chance to grasp our relations to the earth and to each other in sustaining ways, to understand ourselves less as separated entities driven by self-interest than as complexly bound together in a living world that requires our collective resolve to struggle against its destruction, the destruction of what bears incalculable value.[75]

As in life, the unbearable in Greek tragedy is correlated with a sense of the unlivable, of a life that appears impossible to live yet pulsates through the very enunciation of its unlivability. "The unlivable is worse than death"—says Frédéric Worms in his 2023 conversation with Butler—"because even if this life goes on, [a] person cannot live it as their life but only as death within life."[76] A quasi-Antigonean drama of mourning and unbearable grief,[77] Euripides' *Alcestis* stages not only Alcestis's self-sacrifice for the benefit of her husband, but also Admetus's melancholic life, a life, as Butler might put it, lived "with the unlivable as a companion . . . an unbearable companion from which separation is impossible."[78] The Chorus advises against marriage, after observing the condition of Admetus, who "after having lost (*amplakôn*) this wife (*alochou*), the best one (*aristês*), will, from now on, live (*bioteusei*) an unlivable (*abiôton*) time" (241–43). These lines powerfully visualize the consequences of Admetus's attempt to shield himself from destruction by displacing it somewhere else. As Butler observes, "We cannot take distance from the destruction without aiding and abetting ... its reproduction, one that entails both heightened destruction and loss."[79] In a passage affectively dominated by the alpha privative of *a-biôton* ("unlivable"), the three remaining initial alphas in *amplakôn*, *alochou*, and even *aristês* morph into additional losses, a heap of mutilations and deprivations making life unlivable because they weigh down the bodily surface or the formal structure meant to bear them. "We have to develop," Butler says, "a collective practice of not looking away, or resisting conscious and unconscious collaboration with destruction."[80] The collaboration with destruction chosen by Admetus—a domestic *feminicídio*[81]—results in an illusory claim to self-preservation in lieu of the recognition of "common vulnerabilities." Alcestis's death does not replace his own death but is, in fact, his death[82]—a death projected into a life that becomes unlivable because it is deprived of a grounding in the relational support of reciprocal self-undoing, of parallel, complementary deindividuations, a support fetishistically recrafted through the statue that he imagines himself clinging to, in an excess of prepositional dependency, after the death of his wife.[83] Alcestis is like Eurydice, the character lost by an Admetus-like Orpheus, who, as Butler writes, "appears only in the moment in which we are dispossessed of her": she appeals to us because "there is something of our dispossession in her, the one by which we come into being, through another, as another."[84] The multiplication of pseudo-alpha privatives—proliferating losses that almost autonomize the phoneme *a*, liberating it from the burden of carrying the names of *A*dmetus and *A*lcestis[85]—also suggests a sense of unlivability that atmospherically spreads throughout the house, making not just the enslaved inhabitants and the guest (Heracles), but also the architectural structure barely capable of bearing it.

In Euripides' *Hippolytus*, a play whose emphasis on sexual repression, immunity, and dismemberment makes it a thematic prequel to *Bacchae*,[86] environmental unlivability is explicitly tied to the refusal of the social ecology of interdependency. This is the lament of Theseus, the king of Athens, after having discovered that his wife, whom he had abducted from Crete, committed suicide, ashamed, as the audience knows, of her passion for Theseus's son, Hippolytus, who has embraced sexual abstinence (818–24):

O fortune, how heavily have you pressed on me and this house,
an ineffable stain from one of the demons,
an unlivable (*abiotos*) destruction of life (*biou*).
And I see, wretched me, such a sea of evils
that it will never be possible to *swim* back *out of* (*ekneusai*) it
nor to *cross over* (*ekperasai*) the wave of this misfortune.

The marine metaphor patently looks ahead to the disaster orchestrated by Aphrodite to punish Hippolytus—a bull exiting from a surging wave, an image of troublesome sexual desire, scaring his horses, who will drag and break him on the ground.[87] In the reduplicated *ek-* compounds we glimpse a striving for self-preservation not just in the straightforward sense of survival, but in the pregnant sense of a refusal of social ecology, of intimacy, kinship, "intertwinement" with the marine environment, the liquid surface that allows Theseus and the Athenian state to project their power through mobility.[88] The state's extractivist impulse, the imperialistic use of the sea, is coterminous with an individuating, exclusionary gesture of self-differentiation from the liquid ground, which, in fact, bears the ships, sustains the weight of their aggressive presence even while they seek to subjugate it.[89] The unlivability alluded to by Theseus is linked with the dramatization of an infrastructure—a chariot—homologous to the marine surface, which violently becomes "unbearing," loses its ability to sustain a driver, in the apocalyptic tableau recounted by the Messenger in the following scene.[90] The consequence of the breakdown of the chariot is that "all pieces were confused (*sumphurta*)" in the wreckage, including the broken flesh of Hippolytus. Poetic form becomes unbearable in the gruesome description of Hippolytus's entanglement with the reins that have ceased to be at his disposal: "And the wretched one, ensnared in straps, / bound in an inextricable bind, is dragged (*desmon dus-exelikton helketai detheis*)" (1236–37). The alliterative phonetics of the last line—a tongue-twister that encapsulates the articulatory organs' intractability, their unresponsiveness to the demands of language, their unwillingness to bear the semantic burden—are supplemented by a chiasmus (*desmon* is attracted to the cognate *detheis* while *dus-exelikton* is inseparable from the thickly resonant *helketai*).[91] This is the rhetorical figure of Butlerian interdependence, the intertwinement (not just sexual in this case, but social and especially environmental) needed for conditions of livability, a formal removal of the bodily demarcations intrinsic to self-possession, which tragic language renders as moments of dense formal entanglement, of verbal deindividuation.[92] Broken, like the marine surface that no longer bears its burdens, launching, as though in pained laughter, the destructive bull onto the shore,[93] the language that renders the wave releases an imagistic excess that blocks the narrative flow, that disjoins signification from its formal ground, such that verbal ungrounding bespeaks environmental unsustainability. For Butler, "a more relational understanding of my life, your life, our life, the lives of others" means understanding that "we cannot set death and destruction aside as we think about life."[94] Hippolytus's self-possession, his precarious self-separation from the animal sustaining his body and his name,[95] is the unbearable that makes the world collapse; it is the disavowal of lifedeath, the death-in-life that is life. The breaking apart of the notional self, a breaking apart constitutive of being-with (or rather of being itself), may be precisely what is needed to ward off environmental disaster, deferring, if not preventing, extinction.[96]

Butlerian Tragedy and the Writing of Critique

> I read Modernist works—European Modernism. I read a fair amount of German and French twentieth-century writing. And I also read and teach Greek tragedy—I just love it. If someone wants to take me on a very good date, it would be to see a Greek tragedy. I don't know why my pleasure in it is so enormous, but I love Greek tragedy and I love adaptations. So I also need to see what people do with tragedy in their present historical circumstance.[97]
>
> I think that reading poetry is different from other kinds of readings, since you have to work with syntax and ellipsis in a different way. . . . I don't accept the prejudice against narrative, but I do think that a line break can be an ultimate linguistic experience. The point is not that it is like life, although one can say that and be understood. It is that the divergence between life and language becomes syntactically dramatic, and what is lost by way of comfort is surely worth the exhilaration and displacement from grammatical rule.[98]

There is a strong, deep bond between these two quotes. Butler's candidly expressed love for Greek tragedy is correlated, as I suggest, with their investment in the critical-theoretical possibilities of "displacement from grammatical rule." This correlation invites us to think about the metapolitical ramifications of syntax, of an ellipsis or a line break[99]—about the potential of the radical or resistant formalisms displayed by tragic languaging.[100] My re-reading of Greek tragedy alongside Butler's ethical politics and my reading of Butler's revolutionary interventions on gender trouble, precarity, vulnerability, and social ecology in light of Greek tragedy comprise the modality of co-reading, of hermeneutic intertwinement, that I privilege in this book. This modality is conceived as a political aesthetics of interdependency enacted through an unrelenting attentiveness to and over-analysis of microform, which tragic diction demands, and a corresponding recession of the interpreter's claim to self-possession.[101] In what follows, I briefly elaborate on the kinship between Greek tragedy's formal experimentalism, its intense, Antigonean call for modes of over-interpretive or post-interpretive lingering, and Butler's commitment to close reading and a praxis of writing that draws its metapolitical energy from its tragic texture, its self-undoing in the radical defamiliarization or deterritorialization of recognizable grammars.

The stretching of grammar and syntax that is integral to tragic diction (in Aeschylus, but also in Euripides and Sophocles) can be placed in dialogue with the issue of critical-theoretical "difficulty" and with Butler's ongoing commitment to philosophical writing as a form of undoing of grammatical structures, of the normativities of language. As Butler put it in a 2000 interview, "The critical relation to ordinary grammar has been lost in [a] call for radical accessibility."[102] When "accessibility" is divorced from the infrastructural adjustments that allow full participation by those obstructed by an ableist organization of space and rights, it can become a call for simplification and homogenization, aligned with the neoliberal impetus for "immediacy," which Anna Kornbluh has referred to as the style of "too-late capitalism."[103] The economy of "disintermediation"—which resides in disposing of the middleman, of what is in the way of instant gratification and speedy fulfillment—is, for Kornbluh, also integral to auto-theory as a self-made, self-liberating, spontaneous alternative to the complexity, layeredness, and mediatedness of critical theory. It is easy to understand that certain expressions of auto-theory are informed by the same disingenuous culture of hyper-authenticity, of unmediated access to "life" as such, promised by social media.[104] As the fabrication of this "pure," unmediated life expands exponentially, there is a corresponding acceleration of the bio- or necropolitical abjecting of the lives of those in the "middle," a precarizing elimination of the middleman and intermediate steps for the sake of fast production and easily accessible "content," goods, and services. The Indo-European root of "middle" and "medium" concerns betweenness: immediacy is, consequently, another facet of the self-defeating mirage of self-sufficiency, a self-destructive rejection of the infrastructure or of the supporting structure that makes life livable. In manifesting skepticism about "radical accessibility," Butler does not endorse "difficulty for difficulty's sake"; their point is rather that "there is a lot in ordinary language and in received grammar that constrains our thinking."[105] "Difficulty," the stylistic quality attributed to Aeschylus in Aristophanes' *Frogs* when he is asked "not to be grumpy," etymologically conveys an incapacity (or incapacitation) of "doing," or an unwillingness to "do" or "make"—as though non-doing, non-producing, undoing or un-producing placed one outside of the social, made them incompatible with the social recognition that individuates the subject. The Greek word for "difficult," *chalepos*, which informs the warning to Aeschylus, "Don't be difficult!" (*chalepaine* 1020), is rendered in Liddell-Scott-Jones, as "hard to bear." Not giving birth, the primary form of non-producing, is the chief manifestation of Antigone's "difficulty," of the situatedness that shapes her political statement—against political legibility, against the ordinary morphology and syntax of kinship. Antigone is the "trouble maker," a tragic character easy to map onto the figure of the feminist killjoy (or the Aeschylean "feminist Fury"?), whom Sara Ahmed has reclaimed, taking inspiration from the preface of *Gender Trouble* (1990): "We need to be in trouble or to be the trouble we are assumed to cause, to trouble the prevailing laws, the rules that tell us where we can go and who we can be, even if being in trouble is to risk being reprimanded, caught up in the same terms."[106]

In *Giving an Account of Oneself* (2005), Butler famously observes, "We must recognize that ethics requires us to risk ourselves precisely at moments of unknowingness, when what forms us diverges from what lies before us, when our willingness to become undone in relation to others constitutes our chance of becoming human."[107] Undoing the intelligibility, the immediate recognizability of language means preventing language from doing what it is supposed to do, from enacting the norms that it is meant to inculcate. "Calling into question ordinary language" through a writing that denies "radical accessibility," says Butler alluding to Heidegger and Adorno,[108] means performing "an analysis of the kinds of occlusions or concealments that take place when we take ordinary language to be a true indicator of reality as it is and as it must be."[109] "Through messing with grammar as it has been received,"[110] one bids the reader to stop; to gather, regather, and ungather the pieces; to face the political ethics of opacity and its critical-theoretical pressure on language; to revisit the parameters of what should be said and what should not be said, of what can be understood and what cannot; and to challenge the positivistic illusion of unmediated comprehensibility, clarity as a cognitive and affective perception that remains within the bounds of the given. The diction of Greek tragedy is permeated by formal micro-phenomena that appear to us a "messing with grammar," deformations or violations of linguistic expectations that may arise from our temporal and cultural distance from a dead idiom—which undo our aspiration to epistemic self-mastery every time we confront them—or that may be there because they were conceived as renditions of tragic collapse, as formal intimations of *diastêma*, of "the antinomy between conflicting laws that" for Derrida tragedy makes "non-dialectizeable."[111] (And, obviously, this distinction, which I am positing, remains murky.)

Reading Butler's prose, like reading Greek tragedy, is a process of immersion, of self-loss in the bewildering discovery of the unboundedness of intelligibility, of the possibility of reinventing (and never fully stabilizing) the very notion of intelligibility. Although philological scholarship construes tragic textuality as a minefield of "difficulties," that is, accidental corruptions of classical "clarity" introduced in the course of textual transmission, an aesthetics of syntactical *diastêma* is arguably distinctive of tragic *poiêsis*. As James Porter has noted in relation to *Agamemnon*, tragic diction defies the distinction between clarity and opacity. This play "does not travel an arc from riddling announcement to the revelation and clarification of unknowns, but only a lateral path of knowing resistances to knowledge."[112] Even though ancient criticism likes to dichotomize the "difficult" Aeschylus and the "clear" Euripides, placing Sophocles in the middle, my own experience of the three tragedians' language is that of a similar wrought density.[113] What I am suggesting is that the overdetermination of tragic language bids the reader to indulge in the exploration of alternative syntactical configurations, extemporaneous non-grammatical or para-grammatical associations, subliminal juxtapositions, jarring semantic adjacencies, and meaningful or non-meaningful phonetic attractions beyond established structures of meaning. In a corpus of texts that thematize the collapse of conventional kinship through a multifaceted queering—a queering that Butler, in fact, has crucially contributed to elucidating—the kinship between semantic units that makes language is subjected to a restless motion of deformation, to an oversaturated multiplicity of junctions and disjunction that becomes unbearable, that spreads the aesthetic sense of the unbearable.

In the close encounters that I will stage between tragic form and Butler's engagement with tragic form, I resort, as I showed in the previous sections' examples, to the imaginative possibilities of "messing with [tragic] grammar," dwelling on serendipitous moments of unbearable unintelligibility.[114] Creating the interpretive conditions for the emergence of these moments entails a critical-theoretical dramaturgy, an orchestration of unrealized verbal and metapolitical possibilities that diffuses a hermeneutic anxiety:

> What [critique] is really about is opening up the possibility of questioning what our assumptions are and somehow encouraging us to live in the anxiety of that questioning without closing it down too quickly.... Anxiety accompanies something like the witnessing of new possibilities.... As we approach the problem of what to change and how to change, we are already within the confines of a language, a discourse, and an institutional apparatus that will orchestrate for us what will or will not be deemed possible.... It does not engage the fantasy of transcending power altogether, although it does work within the hope and the practice of replaying power, of restaging it again and again in new and productive ways.... Taking for granted one's own linguistic horizon as the ultimate linguistic horizon leads to an enormous parochialism and keeps us from being open to radical difference and from undergoing the discomfort and the anxiety of realizing that the scheme of intelligibility on which we rely fundamentally is not adequate, is not common, and closes us off from the possibility of understanding others and ourselves in a more fundamentally capacious way.[115]

Anxiety is one of the tragic feelings that hold us tight when, in *Antigone*, we hear the Messenger reporting the discovery of Antigone's suicide. The translation of asphyxiation into affect, our anxiety is a ghostly, sublimated version of her self-suffocation: "we saw her hanging by the neck attached to a halter of threads of linen" (*tên men kremastên auchenos kateidomen / brochôi mitôdei sindonos kathêmmenên* 1221–22).[116] Not only life but also death occurs in the space of interdependency, at the unlivable edge of this chiastic intertwinement (accusative adjective, genitive noun, dative noun, dative noun, genitive noun, accusative participle). Entangled, like Hippolytus, in a web of threads almost functioning as a supplement or a surrogate of Haemon himself, suspended in the middle and at the same time at the edge of the line (*tên . . . kremastên . . . kathêmmenên*), Antigone trembles, oscillates, and hovers, like a deus ex machina, deprived of the ground beneath her feet.[117] The "standing" without a base perhaps looks ahead to the precarity of a "state" with no ground to stand on, hanging by a thread, borne, if only for the moment, by the unbearable.[118] At the same time, the phonetic resemblance between "we saw" (*kateidomen*) and "attached" (*kathêmmenên*), between "we" and "her," between our visual "anxiety" and her "hanging," between a finite verb form and a non-finite one, confuses us with her, our suspended gaze with her own hovering unbearability. Antigone's "stance" here, which we can glimpse by "messing" with normative grammar, perhaps returns us to the human after the human has been strained, stretched to its limits, undone:

> If the humanities has a future as cultural criticism, and cultural criticism has a task at the present moment, it is no doubt to return us to the human where we do not expect to find it, in its frailty and at the limits of its capacity to make sense. We would have to interrogate the emergence and vanishing of the human at the limits of what we can know, what we can hear, what we can see, what we can sense. This might prompt us, affectively, to reinvigorate the intellectual projects of critique, of questioning, of coming to . . . create a sense of the public in which oppositional voices are not feared, degraded, or dismissed, but valued for the instigation to a sensate democracy they occasionally perform.[119]

* * *

The three chapters are experiments in expanding, within a Butlerian framework, Butler's expansive readings of the three plays. While I try to disentangle Butler's thoughts from my own commentary and elaboration on them, the force of the intertwinement of my voice and theirs makes this disentanglement sometimes difficult if not impossible to achieve. In the first chapter, I re-read Butler's

Antigone's Claim in the light of infinite heterology, the idea of a proliferation of sliding identifications that is reflected in the dialogue I set up with Ana Mendieta, Saidiya Hartman, W. E. B. Du Bois, Sara Uribe, and Toni Morrison. What I call radical or infinite heterology, a deindividuation that is the correlate of the queer kinship demanded by Butler's Antigone, is, I argue, an ethico-political take on the Freudian death drive that can further contribute to rescuing Antigone from her confinement in the ultimately unpolitical space that she is relegated to by the Lacanian death drive, one of the polemical targets of Butler's book. Using the autobiographical scene of the Freudian death drive in *Beyond the Pleasure Principle* to connect the Underworld's temporal and relational ontology with Antigonean queer kinship, I show how the slide of identifications that, for Butler, turns Antigone into her brother, that makes her both brother and sister—just as Freud becomes a mourning mother or sister for his grandchildren—expresses a radical horizontality or even a self abolition that can be placed in dialogue with Blackness and neuroqueerness. This a chapter where Sophocles' *Antigone* is defamiliarized not only through *Antigone's Claim*, but also through various expressions, direct and indirect, of the reception and resonance of the first work in Butler trilogy.

In the second chapter, I analyze Butler's reading of Euripides' *Bacchae* as a dramatization of the exceeding of human kinship, a kinship transformed, recognized through becoming other than itself—through in-humanity, through the ever-repressed kinship with the animal, through the possibility (or inescapability) of humananimal kinship. While Butler construes *Bacchae* as a tragic instantiation of the posthumanist presupposition of their ethics of precarity— "wherever the human is, it is always outside of itself in the non-human"—they also help us recognize the disturbing topicality of Euripides' play, its resemblance to an ironization of the current paranoia surrounding abortion and trans-parentality. Chiasmus appears as the rhetorical trope that formally situates kinship, that is, Butler's kinship trouble, in the indeterminacy of "father" and "mother" in Zeus's trans-parentality, parallel to the collapse of "human" and "animal" in Agave's fantasy of feral cross-species becoming that follows the killing of Pentheus, an act reminiscent, I propose, of contemporary imaginaries of so-called "dismemberment abortion." For Butler, kinship bonds in *Bacchae* express kinship's constitutive predication on rupture, that is, on potential expansion, on potential decentering of traditional modes and structures of care. This expansion encompasses Zeus's trans-motherhood, parallel to the trans-paternity that, à la *Gender Trouble*, I see as melancholically introjected by Agave and then sparagmatically released; it also encompasses the elemental, as in a river's participation in Zeus's transing of pregnancy. The interchangeability of animal and human child—the equal grievability of the latter *and* the former—is the unbearable scandal, the ultimate "break in the bond" or "bond in the break" that transes kinship. Butler's reading of the finale of *Bacchae* helps us posit unexplored interpretive and critical-theoretical connections with the story of Iphigenia, apparently replaced by a deer, in *Iphigenia in Aulis*, which belonged to the same Euripidean trilogy as *Bacchae*.

In the third chapter, I approach Butler's *Eumenides* as a theorization of the ways in which justice can and should become Furious. Reading Aeschylean Erinyes alongside Walter Benjamin's Niobe and Butler's own Kafkaesque (and Benjaminian) Niobe, I make a case for a bond between the Erinyes' Niobean affect and the rage that the Black feminist radical tradition has regarded as an abolitionist instrument, the only appropriate response to the (racializing or racist) violence of the law. What the liberal status quo stigmatizes as (Black) "rage" is nothing else but "breath" itself, or the right to breathe, the Butlerian "breathability" denied to the Erinyes when their anger is suppressed. Justice (*dikê*), as I go on to say, can open itself up to, and be inflected by, the unbearability of rage after it has detached itself from what Butler would characterize as the liberal valorization of judgment as such, after it has supplemented *dikê* by roughening it into the adverb *dicha* ("asunder"). Stemming from an irruptive breath, the counterpart of a Furious spitting, *dicha*, as I suggest, confronts the law with its disavowed dependence on expelled air while sustaining the possibility of "insurrectionary" or "improvisational solidarity."

1

Infinite Heterology: *Antigone*

We may ask what would Antigone's claim be for the present. . . . It seems to me that in insisting on the grievability of lives, she becomes for us a war critic who opposes the arbitrary and violent force of sovereignty. . . . She, in some sense, becomes a figure through whom we can think what it means to understand certain lives as more precarious than others . . . [as] liv[ing] out a precariousness so that others can engage in the fantasy of their impermeability and omnipotence.[1]

Inspired by the collective being-in-mourning, sibling melancholy, and vulnerability in resistance in the time of AIDS, *Antigone's Claim* (2000) locates the critical-theoretical force of Sophocles' play not in escapist wishes, but in a demand for queer kinship that opens the possibility of bonds unconstrained by heteronormative imperatives. These bonds express a politics not of "oppositional purity (to the state, i.e., from the realm of kinship)" but of "the scandalously impure."[2] In the words of a reviewer, Butler's Antigone is "a figure that puts both kinship (and its related notions of gender and heteronormativity) and the state into question," standing "not for kinship as pre-political, but rather for the forms of kinship that have to be repudiated in order for the political to exist, forms that always threaten to return to disrupt state order."[3] This Antigone embodies incestuous desire not as the vehicle, through prohibitive negativity, of heteronormativity, but as the encrypted outside that threatens and undoes it, and the political as a desire for, even an erotic attachment to, the "impossible" that disrupts the givenness of the Symbolic, not simply a quietist if defiant withdrawal into the anti-Symbolic Real-ness of death. For Andrés Fabián Henao Castro, in *Antigone's Claim* "Butler extends the subversive capacities of queer mimesis . . . to the subversive capacities of queer families to do kinship differently, that is, against the transcendental assumption of heterosexual positions"[4]; emphasizing that Butler's Antigone[5] is "a heroine with no easily recognizable gender,"[6] Cecilia Sjöholm says that, "like a drag king, ... [she] performs the illusion of Creon's masculine authority."[7] Published before the legalization of gay marriage in the US and other Western countries—while already voicing a "radical critique of the naturalization of the military-marriage goal as the telos of equality for gay politics"[8]— Antigone's claim, as articulated by Butler, has taken on renewed urgency in the face of accelerating attacks against LGBTQIA+ people, whom authoritarian governments have been quick to use as scapegoats in the midst of the global socio-economic and ecological crisis epitomized by Covid-19. In the next chapter, dedicated to Butler's reading of *Bacchae*, I will explore its disturbing topicality—which eerily connects the 2020s to the early 2000s while retrojecting, I suggest, the Theban conflict between Oedipus's sons, the background of *Antigone*, to the struggle of his great-grandfather Pentheus with Pentheus's cousin Dionysus. In this chapter, my focus is rather on the Sophoclean and Butlerian Antigone's relation to what I call radical heterology, an ethico-political stance that places Butler's eminently tragic ontology of precarity and vulnerability[9] in dialogue with recent theorizations of Blackness and neurodiversity.

For David Eng "Antigone's acts of defiance," which "might ... be characterized as the anguished process of becoming human," generate "the occasion to redress the social violence that constitutes the human's political boundaries ... in order to create ... a new field, for the human,"[10] while showing that "the human cannot be considered ontologically pre-given, a universal entity, or a *singular* subject or form" (my emphasis). My concern is with extending the ramifications of Antigone's rejection of singularity, her plural singularity. As we will see in the last stage of the argument, where I juxtapose Butler's Antigone with Toni Morrison's Woolfian (and Faulknerian) Antigone in her unpublished Cornell M.A. thesis, Butler's theorization enables us to imagine a neuroqueer Antigone (an *Aut-igone*, in fact), whose radical heterology encompasses a relational horizontality, a collapse of biological and generational positions and determinations typical of the Underworld, of afterlife achrony. While resisting the anti-political consequences of the Lacanian association of Antigone with the death drive, Butler's Antigone invites us to reconsider the Freudian theorization of the psychoanalytic concept, to draw out its relevance to radical heterology, or relational horizontality. Butler's refusal of Lacanian anti-politics, I suggest, is integral to this horizontality. I will link Antigone's claim—the public call for "a socially survivable aberration of kinship in which the norms that govern legitimate and illegitimate modes of kin association might be more radically redrawn"[11]—with a foundational scene of the psychoanalytic theorization of tragedy, that is, Freud's enunciation of the *fort* and *da* principle in *Beyond the Pleasure Principle* (1920), in which he first conceptualizes the death drive. The autobiographical framing of Freud's discussion locates the death drive in a proto-queer zone that looks ahead to Butler's breach of the abstract impermeability, the structuralist fortress of the Lacanian Symbolic. In particular, it anticipates the valorization, in *Antigone's Claim*, of the "overdetermination" and "equivocation"[12] at the center of traditional heteronormative kinship, "a decidedly postoedipal dilemma, one in which kin positions tend to slide into one another."[13] Making a case for the idea of an Antigonean Freud—which renders impossible the Oedipal complex and undoes its self-styled Oedipal father—I will characterize Butler's anti-Lacanian Antigone as (neuro)queerly Freudian with the help of Derrida's reading of *Beyond the Pleasure Principle.* At the same time, I will re-read and perhaps defamiliarize Butler's reading of Sophocles' play through a plurality of intertwinements, a web of visual, critical-theoretical, and literary proximities, including Ana Mendieta, Saidiya Hartman, W. E. B. Du Bois, Sara Uribe, and Toni Morrison.

I take Butler's critique of Lacan as an entry point and a constant referent. (Though critiques of Hegel and Luce Irigaray are given equal prominence in *Antigone's Claim*, they will not be my concern here.) As Azille Coetzee has pointed out, Butler contests Lacan's idea that "kinship is a function of language rather than a socially alterable institution"—in other words, "because language is not a socially alterable institution, kinship is not either."[14] In *The Ethics of Psychoanalysis* (1992) Antigone is forced to occupy the anti-political space of the Real,[15] of the death drive, or death as such, rather than a movement or rushing toward it, because the linguistic constitution of the heteronormative Symbolic, of a kinship constrained by a structuralist vision of the Oedipal complex, by the fixity of pronominal and familial roles, does not leave any space for a modification of the status quo from within, for any emergence of the "unintelligible" that Antigone incarnates.[16] "Challenging the Lacanian reading that sees heteronormativity as a necessary corollary of the incest taboo," says a reviewer, "Butler proposes to decouple the incest taboo from heteronormativity, thus opening the door to alternative counter-hegemonic kinship arrangements."[17] For Butler, the Symbolic is the "sedimentation of social practices," which complicate the Lacanian picture, "demand[ing] a rearticulation of the structuralist presuppositions of psychoanalysis."[18] Counterintuitively, I propose that this "rearticulation," which enables the claim for queer kinship ascribed by Butler to Antigone, might be understood as a return of sorts to the Freudian death drive, but in this case not a regression to the inorganic—the backward movement that Antigone apparently pursues when she commits suicide in the cave (notwithstanding Lacan's customary contemptuous self-differentiation from Freud). A preoccupation in Butler's psychoanalytic and political-theoretical agenda,[19] the death drive might seem a purely negative presence in *Antigone's Claim*. The reader can detect it in the background of Butler's anti-Lacanian position,[20] as the psychic force that, for Lacan, energizes Antigone's anti-Symbolic self-positioning, as the libidinal negativity wherein he grounds her anti-political enjoyment,[21] or, as Mari Ruti might put it, her "ethics of opting out" (2017).[22] After *The Ethics of Psychoanalysis*, there has been no attempt to reconceive Antigone's figuration of the death drive against, beyond, or without Lacan.[23] In *No Future*, Lee Edelman faults Butler for shutting Antigone back into the Symbolic, for cultivating the "liberal" (as he says) fantasy of a space for radicality within the Symbolic, for (in his words) "[an] engagement with psychoanalysis all too 'American' . . . in its promise to provide the excluded with access to a livable social life."[24] In *Let Them Rot: Antigone's Parallax*, published in 2023, Alenka Zupančič presents the Lacanian/Žižekian perspective on Antigone. However, Zupančič observes that "to be able to say death," that is, to bring it into language, "you have to bring death to life; you have to make it part of life, give it a symbolic existence to which you can relate; you have to resurrect death from death, so to speak."[25] While *Antigone* is the only surviving play whose offstage space notionally slopes downward through the catabatic descent of Antigone and other characters to the cave, there is equally an upward motion of the underground: transported onstage, the corpses of Haemon and Creon's wife "bring death to life," make "it part of life," or at least of Creon's unbearable life.

In the analysis that follows, I will use the autobiographical scene of the Freudian death drive to find ground for a conceptual link between the

Underworld's temporal and relational ontology and Butler's Antigonean queer kinship. Butler says, "Antigone is the brother, the brother is the father . . .; for anyone living in this *slide of identifications*, their fate will be an uncertain one, living within death, dying within life."[26] Strongly connected with, but also exceeding, incest (Antigone's "impossible and death-bent incestuous love of her brother"[27]), bearing the insurrectionary mark of the "underlife,"[28] this "slide of identifications" expresses a Freudian-Butlerian death drive that approximates "self abolition" and shares affinities with current theorizations of Blackness, neuroqueerness, and their mutual interrelations.[29]

The sole appearance of the Freudian death drive in *Antigone's Claim*, which previews Butler's later preoccupation with the Furies, the topic of chapter 3, allows us to link the so-called "madness" of the Sophoclean Antigone with *Beyond the Pleasure Principle.* Discussing the relation between the Lacanian Symbolic and social norms, Butler explicitly refers to Freud with a phrase from *The Ego and the Id* (1923), "the culture of the death drive," which in that work "entrenches itself" in the superego. For Butler, the superego, as an enforcer of social norms and, in particular, heteronormativity is responsible for our perception of such norms as "intractable, punitive, and eternal."[30] In anti-Lacanian fashion, the "culture of the death drive" is an ally of the Symbolic—as Butler intimates when, in the sentence following the Freudian phrase, they say that "the very description of the symbolic as intractable law takes place within a fantasy of law as insurpassable authority."[31] It is significant that in the cited passage from *The Ego and the Id* a counterpoint to or a correction of the superego is located in the strikingly tragic condition of *mania*, which, as we will see, in *The Force of Nonviolence* (2020), Butler analyzes in the same context as their discussion of tragic and Freudian fury.[32] Freud writes:

> The destructive component has entrenched itself in the superego and turned itself against the ego. What is now holding sway in the superego is, as it were, a pure culture of the death drive, and in fact, it often succeeds in driving the ego into death, if the latter doesn't fend off its *tyrant* in time by the change round into mania.[33]

It is easy to see this dynamic—an anti-tyrannical *mania* safeguarding the subject from the super-egotic "culture of the death drive"—reflected in the language of Sophocles' *Antigone* if we track the occurrences of *a-noia* and related words.[34] Commenting on Antigone's intention to persist in her "desire for the impossible" (*amêchanôn* 90), in her "bad decision" (*dus-boulian* 95) to violate Creon's prohibition and possibly face death, Ismene says: "If it seems good to you, *go*! But please know that you are foolish (*anous*) in *going*" (99). Ismene uses the word *a-mêchanos* twice (90, 92) to emphasize the "craziness" of Antigone's desire (*eros*)—which, for Butler, carries the political force of longing for the impossible,[35] an *objet petit a* that upsets the conventional assessment of what should be deemed possible and what should not. An expression of *eros*—the quintessential agent of lifedeath[36]—Antigone's *mania* is the destruction (or the death) that disrupts death, a violation of political immobilism, of the tyranny of the pleasure principle that, protecting the status quo, enforces a "culture of the death drive." The deranged "going" that Ismene imputes to Antigone has the same kinetic force as the "rushing" of the death drive in *Beyond the Pleasure Principle*.[37] As Antigone is dragged onstage by Creon's guards, the Chorus opposes *mania* to *nomos* ("law"): "Don't they *drag* you (***ap**-agousi*) because you do not obey (***ap**-istousan*) the king's laws (*nomois*) and they caught you in folly (***aph**-rosunêi*)" (381–83)? The ambiguity between dative plural and third person plural activated by *ap-agousi*, which seems almost a participle modifying *nomois*, renders the laws as agents of "arrest" (*apagôgê*), of corporeal immobilization, the biopolitical violence empowered to reduce the live body to a corpse. At the same time, the aspiration in the initial syllable of *aphrosunê* adds some vital breath to the *ap-* in *ap-agousi* (as well as *ap-istousan* "disobeying"), encapsulating the liberating potential of *mania*, the "rushing" of a mind and a body seeking to break the constraints of the norm, to stretch themselves, subjecting the smoothness of the law to a roughening tension. In a later stasimon, Antigone is the Erinys acting through or as *anoia*, infiltrating the domain of *logos* in the latest iteration of Oedipus's ancestral curse (*logou t'anoia kai phrenôn Eri-nus* "the madness of *logos* and mind, an Erinys" 603). The Fury at the center of the third play in Butler's trilogy, the Erinys (phonetically corresponding to *Eri-nous*, not far from *Eri-nus*, that is, *eris* "dispute" and *nous* "mind"), can be understood as a contentious, rebellious anti-*nous*, an alternative to cognition, to the stability of the pleasure principle in its stifling psychic, social, and political expressions. Regarding an ancient scholiast's gloss ("she dared do that, having been stung by the Erinyes"), the author of a classic commentary on Sophocles' play, Richard Jebb, elaborates:

"an erinys of (or in) the mind: *i.e.* the infatuated *impulse* which urged Antigone to the deed is conceived as Fury that drove her to her doom."[38] For Jebb, the anti-*nous* of the Erinys-like Antigone is a drive (an "infatuated impulse") powered, we can add, by the desire (the *eros*) for the impossible. *Antigone* helps us understand that the *mania* that is ostensibly opposed to the death drive in *The Ego and the Id* resembles the death drive of *Beyond the Pleasure Principle*, a kinetic force contrasting with the tyrannical equilibrium, the immobility foisted upon the subject by the pleasure principle and the superego—an immobility that can coincide with death, that is, with the ever-delayed destination, not the restless motile orientation, of the death drive. This is just to say that inasmuch as we associate Antigone's death-driven dimension simply and exclusively with Lacan's specific take on the death drive—which, for Butler, is colored with quasi-metaphysical, Platonic tinges, as it ascribes to Antigone a desirous projection toward "pure Being" or "an impossible and pure ontology of the brother"[39]—we miss the importance of *Beyond the Pleasure Principle* for *Antigone's Claim* and the co-implication of queer kinship with a manic rebellion against the pleasure principle, which, already in Freud, is attached to the reproductive imperative, the foundation of heteronormativity.

In a 2009 interview, Butler seems to ground the political project of *Antigone's Claim* in the aesthetic experience of tragedy, its ineffable—and unbearable—mixture of pleasure and pain, which very much concerned Freud:

> The deaths by AIDS were not shameful deaths, but horrible deaths that deserved and deserve a public mourning. In a way, that point brought me to consider Antigone. . . . The politics of mourning within war is clearly linked to that question of the distribution and regulation of grievable lives. How do we think about who is grievable and who is not, who is allowed to grieve openly and who is not? And what kind of public speech, *parrhesia*, is needed to call attention to the horrifying way that our capacity to feel horror is differentially distributed and naturalized?[40]

Although "horrible" and "horrifying" evoke Lacan once again—he discusses Antigone's aesthetic "splendor" as a possible cathartic counterpart of her sublime "horror"[41]—we are also reminded of the central scene of *Beyond the Pleasure Principle*, where the autobiographically charged enunciation of the psychic circuit of *fort* and *da*, which contains the kernel of Lacanian *jouissance*, results in a fraught interrogation of the aesthetics of tragedy, in the wake of (yet in contrast to) Aristotle's theorization of a catharsis engendered by tragedy's affective mimesis of "pity" and "fear" (a close cousin of "horror").[42] The thoughts of public mourning during the AIDS crisis, which Butler retrospectively casts as the *archê* ("origin") of *Antigone's Claim*, can be juxtaposed with the atmosphere of familial grief looming over Freud's account of his grandson's death-driven game. Just as mourning those killed by AIDS deterritorializes the individual experience of grieving—for the collective trauma inevitably pluralizes the singular loss, expanding (and, thus, annihilating) the contours of bounded lives and deaths, eliding the distinction between "us" and "them," "kin" and "non-kin"—Freud's doleful cathexis to Ernst, his grandson, and his daughter Sophie, occasions an effect of radical deindividuation that, as will become clear, renders his conceptualization of the death drive (and his own investment in it) resonant with the Butlerian Antigone. A posthuman pun activated by the word *aphros-unê* encapsulates the *mania* of deindividuation, which, as I will suggest, makes Antigone into a conceptual bridge between *Beyond the Pleasure Principle*, on the one hand, and converging critical-theoretical approaches to Blackness and neuroqueerness, on the other. In a play centered around the elemental imagery of dust, Antigone's cathexis to dust, even her becoming her brother through dust or becoming dust itself, "dust" is an image of becoming and mimics the cycle of water.[43] Could it be significant that Antigone's *aphrosunê*, her madness, contains a cryptic *aphros*, the word for "foam," perhaps another figuration of the social amorphology, the anarchic being-with, the self abolition stemming from a compulsive "slide of identifications"?[44]

Butler and "Antigone" Mendieta

I begin the analysis of Butler's *Antigone* (the notional Antigone play that *Antigone's Claim* constitutes) by considering the cover image of the book and its relation with the subtitle, *Kinship between Life and Death*, which I will connect with Derrida's reading of *Beyond the Pleasure Principle* in *The Postcard* (1987) and *Life Death* (2020). By coincidence, the late Ana Mendieta's work, which we see on the front cover of the Butler book, part of her *Silueta Series*, dates back to the same year, 1975, as Derrida's seminar at the École des Hautes

Études on which *Life Death* is based.[45] In these installations, feminist and animistic earth-body sculptures, Mendieta carves the silhouette of her body into soil, sand, and stony surfaces in Iowa and Mexico as a way to reconnect with the land as a birthplace, to "become one with the earth," as she puts it, or an ancient chthonic goddess.[46]

Visualizing scenarios that evoke the Freudian return to the inorganic, or Antigone's forced yet voluntary descent into the cave, Mendieta's work programmatically signals that "there is no original past to redeem." As she puts it, "There is the void, the orphanhood, the unbaptized earth of the beginning, the time that from within the earth looks upon us. There is above all the search for origin."[47] Mendieta's "memory traces," in Anne Raine's phrase, recall the Freudian mystic pad, which, in *Archive Fever*—a theorization of the death drive in its own right—Derrida sees as emblematic of the loss that generates and compromises every technique of archivization, foreclosing the possibility of a distinction between the (lost) event and its trace, between the trace and the structure designated to preserve or contain it.[48] In *Writing and Difference*, Derrida calls the mystic pad "more complex than slate or paper, less archaic than a palimpsest," though, he says, "compared to other machines for storing archives, it is a child's toy"—an observation that evokes the psychoanalytic child's toy par excellence, that of Ernst, the *fort/da* player in *Beyond the Pleasure Principle* (1920).[49] The deformed contours, the bare yet thick markings of corporeal survivance, the containers becoming content in a limbo of distinction and indistinction, of appearance and disappearance, that we observe in Mendieta's work exemplify *auto-thanato-graphy* or *auto-bio-thanato-heterography* (see figures 1 and 2), terms that Derrida employs in *The Postcard* and in the "Freud's Leg(acies)" section of *Life Death* to indicate self-inscriptions of life, death, or rather the overlap of the two (lifedeath).[50] I will return to these terms later to discuss the relation between the death drive and heterology by way of Butler's notion of queer kinship. Vitalistic yet anti-vitalistic markings of Brown dispossession,[51] Mendieta's human and posthuman silhouettes "demonstrate the emergence of the earth in conjunction with the retraction of the body."[52] They also auto-thanato-graphically write and unwrite her own death, uncannily anticipating her suicidal or homicidal fall from an apartment window in Greenwich Village, the event that seems to anarchivally inscribe itself, as a *fort/da* oscillation, on the material surfaces of her installations as a

Figure 1 Ana Mendieta, *Untitled* (Silueta Series, Iowa), 1979. Digital image © Whitney Museum of American Art / Licensed by Scala / Art Resource, NY. Whitney Museum of American Art/New York, NY/USA.

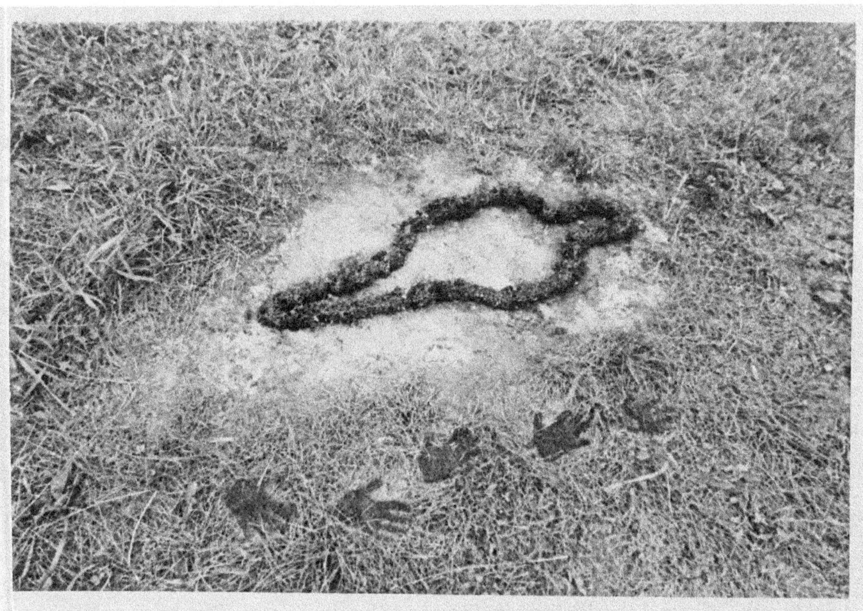

Figure 2 Ana Mendieta, *Untitled* (Silueta Series). August 1978. Gelatin silver print. The Solomon R. Guggenheim Museum/New York, NY/USA.

rearward prophecy or proleptic recollection. Even though we have been conditioned to read Antigone's death as a straightforward suicide, its precise dynamics, as reflected in Sophocles' account, are ambiguous too, as Matthew Hiscock has argued,[53] involving complex or confused layers of agency between Antigone and Haemon, her betrothed who is found dead in the cave with her.

Mendieta's installations help us understand "*this strange place of being between life and death, of speaking precisely from that vacillating boundary*,"[54] to cite a line from Sara Uribe's *Antígona González* (2016), which rereads Sophocles' and Butler's *Antigone* in response to the discovery of the mass graves of the victims of the 2011 San Fernando massacre, committed by a drug cartel in Mexico. The silhouette filled with, or marked by, blood-like matter recalls the distinction that Butler draws, in discussing Hegel and Irigaray, between, on the one hand, "blood" and bloodlines, an image of untouchable, conventional, zero-degree kinship, and, on the other, the encrusted blood sedimented after "bloodshed," an "echoing trace of kinship," alternative kinship, like the "remainder" that Antigone is herself.[55] For Butler, Antigone is the unruly contour that puts the "regimes of representation into crisis," a phrase anticipating Jacques Rancière's identification of the collapse of representation, its surrender to the "aesthetic unconscious," with the effects of *pathos*, which, for him, is a force expressing the Freudian death drive.[56] Antigone jeopardizes representation because, like Mendieta's visual auto-thanato-graphies, she operates in the thin space of appearance in disappearance, possession and dispossession. "Facing what disappears: what does not disappear," says Uribe in *Antígona González*, which Butler calls an "act of poetic testimony and fierce interpretation, making emphatic graphic marks precisely where there is no trace of loss"—a statement reverberating with the words of *Antigone's Claim*: "the feminine ... becomes [the] remainder, and 'blood' becomes the graphic figure for this echoing trace of kinship."[57] Uribe recounts that on the day of the discovery of the San Fernando mass graves she was attending an awards ceremony at a theater, which remained entirely indifferent to the breaking news:[58]

> From my seat and then later after leaving the premises, I could not shake a feeling of frustration that was overwhelming to me: how was it possible for us to act as if nothing was happening? How could we have the speeches ... without anyone having mentioned the bodies? The bodies buried below ground, silenced, invisible. All of us at some point succumb to fear and silence, because the barbarity surpasses us. But afterwards came the need to say something, the urgency of speech: something is happening here. In this land, bodies disappear, bodies are taken away, tortured, hidden.... Fear and silence have left us isolated, and it is the word, language, which re-positions us in the public sphere, thus the need to name the voices of the bereaved, to gather them together, to accompany them and to allow others to accompany them, the need for community.[59]

Like Mendieta's auto-thanato-biographical self-inscriptions, and like the survivors from whose viewpoint Uribe speaks, her lyrical "graphic marks" shatter the void space of silence and complacency with, in Uribe's words, "a lengthy line that moves neither forward nor backward," leaving "something that remains, lurking, latent," vestiges of "that stabbing pain that settles firmly in the belly, that shelters in the muscles, in every pulse of blood, in the heart and temples."[60]

The space of appearance in disappearance, possession and dispossession in which Antigone places herself is opened by the formal intricacy, the double negativity, surrounding her refusal to deny the act—a fundamental turning point in the theorization of *Antigone's Claim*. In Butler's rendition of and commentary on line 443—a response to Creon's question "Do you admit it, or do you deny having done it?" (442)—Antigone proclaims:

> I will not be forced into a denial, I will refuse to be forced into a denial by the other's language, and what I will not deny is my deed—a deed that becomes possessive, a grammatical possession that makes sense only within the context of the scene in which a forced confession is refused by her.[61]

With an overstretching of abstract grammatical logic, the Greek idiom corresponds more literally to "I will not deny not to have done it" (*kouk ap-arnoumai to mê* [*dedrakenai*] 443), where the second negative, *mê*, almost homophonically conjures an objectified "I" (*me* "me"), the subject manifesting itself only as negativity, as in Mendieta's *siluetas*. Antigone's "denial" (*arnoumai* in *ap-arnoumai*) punningly coincides with the perverse possession of the verb *arnumai* ("I obtain" 903), which she uses when she is about to be dragged away to her subterranean tomb (her imprisonment is, in fact, what she "obtains," her perverse gain).[62] While, through a double crasis, Antigone's individual agency in tending to her brother Polynices' corpse disappears in the products of her caring tasks (washing and adorning the corpse) and an enjambment almost dispossesses him from his body,[63] the apparently affirmative "I" of this *arnumai*—emphasized by *auto-cheir* ("with my own hands" 900)—ironically signposts her becoming Polynices. By acting on his behalf, she brings upon herself the same condition of defiant outcast, the same exclusion from the community, from the sense of belonging delineated by the state interpellation. Here *auto-thanato-graphy*, the inscription of self-denial through the ambivalence of *mê/me*, slides into what we can call *bio-thanato-heterology*, the lifedeath of becoming other. As Butler says: "In defying the state, [Antigone] repeats as well the defiant act of her brother, thus offering a repetition of defiance that, in affirming her loyalty to her brother, situates her as the one who may substitute for him and, hence, replaces and territorializes him. She assumes manhood through vanquishing manhood, but she vanquishes it only by idealizing it."[64]

Becoming Polynices, continuing his defiant legacy, is wed, for Butler, to Antigone's incestuous desire, which we can read as a violation of the singularity or the non-contradictoriness of kin relations and roles. Incest here is overdetermined: it is not just a para-erotic attachment to a brother, but it emerges precisely from the violation of the principle of kin non-contradiction that lies behind Antigone's becoming (her) brother, her being sister as well as brother. Heteronormative kinship is subjected here to a process of "aberration," which engenders a "proliferation" of apparently incompatible positions and relations or "a slide of identifications"[65]—not just Oedipus as both father and brother of his children, but, more radically, Antigone as both sister and brother:[66]

> Considering how many are dead in her family, is it possible that mother and father and repudiated sister and other brother are condensed there at the site of the irreproducible brother? . . . This equivocation at the site of the kinship term signals a decidedly postoedipal drama, one in which *kin positions tend to slide into one another*, in which Antigone is the brother, the brother is the father, and in which psychically, linguistically, this is true regardless of whether they are dead or alive; for anyone living in *this slide of identifications*, their fate will be an uncertain one, living within death, dying within life.

This proliferation of kinship—a "k-incoherence" that manifests itself only as a trace, as a displacement of the prohibited incest[67]—causes Antigone's "living within death, dying within life." When Butler maintains that, in saying "mother," the child "might expect more than one individual to respond to the call," or that, in saying father, the child "might mean both [an] absent phantasm she never knew" and "the one who assumes that place in living memory,"[68] we think of a crucial scene in the history of psychoanalysis, Freud's memory of his grandson Ernst's *fort/da* game in *Beyond the Pleasure Principle*. We might, then, want to re-read Butler's Antigone alongside the before and after of Ernst's mother's death in the Great Influenza Pandemic of 1918.

Antigone's and Freud's Auto-bio-thanatography

At the end of "Freud's Leg(acies)," Derrida coins the terms *auto-thanatography* and *auto-bio-thanato-heterography* in his commentary on Freud's death-driven archiving (or an-archiving) of Ernst's amusements. Here, Derrida is interested in the vicissitudes of writing *Beyond the Pleasure Principle*, in the fraught, continuous back and forth, *fort* and *da*, between theoretically surrendering to self-loss and reasserting mastery and reparation.[69] This psychic alternation, which, for Derrida, is tied to Freud's own ambivalences in the writing of the book, instantiates the workings of the death drive (Freudian as well as Lacanian) and their implications for the interpretation of the aesthetic experience of tragedy.[70] In this passage, Derrida draws attention to the identification of Sigmund with Ernst, which borrowing Butler's notion of the "proliferation" or "slide" of identifications, I prefer to characterize as a disidentificatory spiral:

> In a trivial sense . . . he recalls, he remembers . . . a memory that he recounts: a scene that happened to *another, to two others, but others who are his daughter and grandson*. . . . Ernst recalls . . . his mother; he reminds one of his mother. Who happens to be Freud's daughter, Sophie. Already at the time Ernst was doing this, Freud could identify with him, could recall his daughter to himself . . . through an identification with the grandson . . . recall Sophie as his mother.[71]

If Sigmund "becomes" Ernst, Sophie, Ernst's mother, becomes Sigmund's mother; but if Sigmund sees himself simply as similar to Ernst, in the same position as Ernst (rather than as Ernst himself), he becomes a brother, while Sophie, Sigmund's favorite daughter, synchronically viewed as the child of his memory, is, at the same time, a sister. Ernst, Sigmund, and Sophie form a trio of siblings. In this k-incoherent micro-community, which prompts a *fort* and *da* between apparently incompatible positions, Sigmund is the one who has to bury his "sibling" Sophie, as it were, just as Antigone buries Polynices. We can, thus, also imagine that, just as Antigone becomes Polynices in the defiant act of burying him, Sigmund, through the sibling horizontality fostered by the figure of the child, twists or queers parentality into sisterhood in the very moment that he recollects the burial of his daughter. Sigmund becomes Antigone as the character who, in becoming Polynices, is unwilling to accept "the cost of articulating a coherent identity position by producing, excluding, and repudiating a domain of abjected specters that threatens the arbitrarily closed domain of subject positions." This is a formulation from *The Psychic Life of Power* (1997),[72] which resumes the idea, elaborated in *Gender Trouble* (1990), of a gender identity produced by the melancholic introjection of discarded cathexes, attractions, and identifications.[73] The ego, as Butler movingly reveals, is the product of melancholy, for "only by turning back on itself does the ego acquire the status of a perceptual object."[74] The consequence of this death-driven dynamic is that the ego operates through "the psychic compulsion to substitute for objects lost"; it is "the sedimentation of relations of substitution over time, the resolution of a tropological function into the ontological effect of the self."[75] The Antigonean "slide of identifications" continues this substitutive process that makes the ego by unmaking it, undoing the apparent solidity or insurmountable self-referentiality of indexicality.[76] "Suspending the demand for self-identity or, more particularly, for complete coherence" and "counter[ing] a certain ethical violence which demands that we manifest self-identity and require that others do the same"[77]—what William Connolly, in an interview with Butler, calls "an ethos of plurality"[78]—can perhaps be revisited as Antigone's plural disindividuation or even self abolition, as we will see.

Many times, in his oeuvre, Freud explicitly likens himself to Oedipus (while his daughter Anna, destined to leave with him for London, is assimilated to Antigone accompanying her old father to Athens)[79]—but I want to make a case for Freud-as-Antigone to suggest that, in light of *Antigone's Claim*, we reconceptualize the death drive as a continuing, radical heterology, a form of Antigonean plural deindividuation. In one of his homoerotic letters to Wilhelm Fliess (July 15, 1896), Freud previews the Oedipus complex that he will enunciate explicitly in a letter to Fliess fifteen months later, after the death of his father:

> Dear Wilhelm, For the situation is this: the old fellow has paralysis of the bladder and rectum, is failing nutritionally, and at the same time is mentally overalert and euphoric. I truly believe that these are his last days but do not know how long he has and do not dare to leave, least of all for two days and for a pleasure I would like to indulge in fully. To meet you in Berlin, to hear about the new magic from you for a few hours, and then suddenly to have to rush back during the day or night . . . that is something I really want to avoid, and to this fear I sacrifice the burning desire once again to live fully, with head and heart simultaneously, to be a *zoon politikon* . . . and, moreover, to see you.[80]

Here the triangle (father, mother, and son) that structures Freud's future vision of Oedipal attachments has a patently queer inflection. Clinging to life, the moribund father prevents the son, Sigmund, from accessing an eroticized intimacy with a male friend, the freedom to "indulge fully" in a forbidden pleasure, to fulfill an anti-normative—even anti-social—desire, which is, however, presented as the sine qua non for becoming a *zôon politikon*, a social being. Blocking the *jouissance* not of incestuous heterosexuality, but of homosexuality, the castrating father of Freud's familial drama seems to lead the "complex" astray even before it is officially formulated. A queer reading of Jacob Freud's "paralysis of the . . . rectum" is irresistible[81]—as though his disease sanctioned the principle that the rectum is *indeed* a grave,[82] thus enforcing a hierarchy (and reduction) of sexual pleasures, ensuring that certain anatomical routes remain unexplored. The image of a father whose flesh is waning even as his internalized surveillance waxes seems to transition from the embodied Freudian father to the Lacanian law, the interpellating Symbolic, the invisible eye of the Big Other. This father is the main obstacle to enjoyment, while the mother seems to be absent. Yet maternity still has a way of emerging through disidentification. Oedipus/Sigmund is conscripted as a female, or maternal, caretaker, becoming a version of his unmarried sister Adolphine (cited in the letter) and of the future Anna, that is, an Antigone. In the undone familial plot, the failure of the complex is not homosexuality as such. It arises from a self-annihilating care for the other (or Other), Antigone's complex, but, more broadly, the feminine as a condition of domestic segregation—the condition of the *étrangère* (as Derrida calls Antigone), who is denied (but continues demanding) a *bios politikos*.[83]

But Freud's Antigonean plot thickens—implicating his own interests in cellular biology and the pandemic of 1918—if we return to Derrida's discussion, where he mentions the death of Ernst's brother, Heinerle, three years after the publication of *Beyond the Pleasure Principle*. At that time, Derrida recalls, Freud asked his colleague psychoanalyst Helene Deutsch to help him "disappear from the world with decency" and confessed to his friends Ernst Jones and Marie Bonaparte that this loss "killed something inside him," "had struck him more than his own cancer," causing him to suffer "from depression for the first time in his life."[84] As a brother of Ernst, Heinerle is another sibling whom Sigmund, his brother or sister, like Antigone, had to bury: "this was the only time Freud was seen to cry," Derrida adds, before concluding that Freud "died in his grandson."[85] In a discussion of this Derridean passage, Mark Featherstone maintains that *Beyond the Pleasure Principle* is "marked by . . . the logic of . . .

'unmourning'"—a term that evokes the characterization of Antigone in Derrida's *Of Hospitality* as the *étrangère*, the foreigner condemned to infinite mourning because of the prohibition of mourning, her forced separation, in Sophocles' *Oedipus at Colonus*, from her father's tomb.[86] For Featherstone, this "unmourning" is tightly bound up with the biological and metabiological concerns of *Beyond the Pleasure Principle*, where Freud's adherence to August Weismann's theory of the eternal life of the germ cell, of "the sexless protozoan that divides endlessly without passing through the horror of death," discloses his attempt to "immunize himself against the atmosphere of death circulating from 1914 through 1920,"[87] an atmosphere of war and pandemic. Freud's immunitarian "unicellular utopia," as Featherstone puts it, implies that "the most basic form of life is irrepressible, unstoppable, and immortal and that it is only when we move towards more complex, multicellular organisms that the dystopia of death and the death drive enters the picture."[88] While Freud seems to yield to the consoling fantasy of a viral sameness, a viral law of immortal life in opposition to his viral law of endless death, Derrida connects virality with the death-driven movement of *différance*, with the force of *auto-bio-thanato-heterology*, "an autobiothanatoheterographical *fort/da*,"[89] an auto-immunitarian dystopia.

Butler's "proliferation," or "slide of identifications"—the anti-foundational foundation of her theorization of Antigone's claim—configures a viral heterology, which is reflected in the dissemination and interchangeability of kin positions in the auto-thanato-biographical framing of Freud's *fort/da* discussion. The "slide of identifications," which is epitomized by Antigone's becoming a brother after touching Polynices' body to perform the rituals denied to him, seems even to look ahead to Butler's theorization of pandemic phenomenology in *What World Is This?* (2022), an intervention centered around the perception of the radical relationality brought about by the haptic diffusion of the Covid-19 virus, an all-too-tangible reminder of the disintegration of the notional self that is inherent to touch. The awareness that one "cannot come into being without being touched"[90] runs into the discovery that, therefore, one cannot exist without a death of the self. The "slide of identifications" that we have observed in the metaphorical mutual touching of Sigmund, Ernst, Sophie, and Heinerle proceeds with the same cadence as the chain of haptic intertwinements explored in *What World Is This?*: touching you, I become you, you become me, etc.[91] Situating elements of a "deconstitution of singularity," a proto-death drive, in Spinoza, in a 2006 article Butler observes: "the 'I' is . . . responsive to alterity in ways that it cannot always control. . . . It absorbs external forms, even contracts them, as one might contract a disease."[92]

In interpreting the Freudian death drive as an Antigonean heterological drive that shapes *Antigone's Claim*—an ungovernable, ever-shifting impulse to deny the self and become other—I am proposing comparisons and connections with Maurice Blanchot's idea of heterology, but also with theorizations of "self abolition" such as that of Marquis Bey. This passage from Blanchot's *The Unavowable Community* powerfully illustrates the convergence between Butler's political ethics of interdependence and the Freudian death drive:

> A being does not want to be recognized, it wants to be contested: in order to exist it goes towards the other, which contests and at times negates it, so as to start being only in that privation that makes it conscious . . . of the impossibility of being itself, of subsisting as its *ipse* or . . . as itself as a separate individual: this way it will perhaps ex-ist, experiencing itself as an always prior exteriority, or as an existence shattered through and through, composing itself as it decomposes itself constantly, violently and in silence.[93]

In this lyrical explanation of the self-exit that inheres in ex-istence, the process of ongoing self-shattering and decomposition constitutive of life's negative vitalism seems to be simultaneously informed by a Freudian motion toward material disorganization, the reconnection with a priority or an exteriority (the inorganic) that undoes self-formation, and a critique of the logic of individuation, of the fantasy of bounded impermeability—in Butler's terms, "the egological and self-interested bases of [traditional] ethics itself."[94] In other words, Blanchot helps us realize that the Freudian subordination of the life instinct to the death drive—or the idea that, as Derrida would put it, life is death[95]—is germane to the "cross-weaving of intersubjectivity itself,"[96] to Butler's foundational observation that "life is the place where I lose my self-centeredness and discover the porous character of my embodiment,"[97] and to the ethical imperative that we "understand ourselves less as separate entities . . . than as complexly bound together in a living world that requires our collective resolve to struggle against its destruction."[98] Touching upon Butler's (perhaps anti-Foucauldian) critique of the "regime of the self" in *The Force of Nonviolence*—a regime "including as part of its extended self all those who bear similitude to one's color, class, and privilege, thus expelling from the ... subject/self all those marked by difference within that economy"[99]—Bey proposes that we dispose of the "self" as an instrument of "regulative violence." The resistance to self-otherization—to what I would call death-driven self-annihilation—instantiates, for Bey, "the a priori exclusion of that which might have been or how something might have been otherwise."[100] Arguing for the abolition of the self, Bey visualizes this operation as "an unsettling of ground that is, too, an unsettling ... of that which uses the ground to remain standing"[101]—an image suggestive of Antigone's cathexis to the corpse's horizontality and the ground beneath it, her refusal to instrumentalize the ground by standing, but also of the earth's quasi-seismic opening to maternally receive back Oedipus at the end of *Oedipus at Colonus*. When Bey says, "I have been perversely and perhaps unintentionally enabled by Butler to *want*—to demand—the *execution* of the *self*,"[102] I recognize all the conceptual elements of Freud's death drive, of Freud's idea of a volitional rush toward the disintegration of the organism, recrafted, reorganized, put to the service of an abolitionist ethics and to Butler's ethics of interdependence.[103] Butler's anti-Lacanian Antigone, an Antigone rejecting seclusion in the Real of death, seems, thus, one who brings out and embodies the heterological politics of the Freudian death drive, the disindividuation and paradoxical "anti-social thesis" behind the projection toward self-denial, self-dissolution, self-shattering.[104]

The Underworld, Blackness, and Antigonean Self Abolition

At this point, I wish to elaborate on the relation between the Butlerian Antigone's spiral of disidentifications and the ontology of the Underworld by placing her in the imaginary of the Black "underlife," in Sylvia Wynter's phrase. To do so, I closely read Saidiya Hartman's 2022 "Litany for Grieving Sisters," a poetic prose engagement with Sophocles' and Butler's *Antigone*, and W. E. B. Du Bois's novella "The Comet," Hartman's primary subtext.[105] In Hartman's Antigonean experiment, published in *Proximities: Reading with Judith Butler*, an "Antigone of the ... Black mourning ... roams through a city in ruins, clutching a child she could not save from death, in search of a brother who might no longer be alive."[106] Walking in a deserted Harlem, Hartman's Antigone resurrects Jim, the protagonist of "The Comet," published in the same year as Freud's *Beyond the Pleasure Principle*, in the wake of the Great Influenza Pandemic, which killed his daughter Sophie. In this short story, Jim's return to above-ground New York City, after a descent underground at the bank where he works, leads to the discovery that the world has come to an end, that he might be the only surviving man. Writing on "The Comet" in 2020, in the early days of the Covid-19 pandemic, Hartman draws attention to the epiphany, at the end of the story, of a surviving female figure—perhaps Jim's lover, partner, wife, or sister—who, as I speculated elsewhere, is none other than the Antigone in Hartman's "Litany for Grieving Sisters."[107] At the end of the (white) world, in solitude the Black man feels liberated from the world and, thus, alive for the first time.

Mirroring itself in Antigone's walk along the desolated streets of Harlem, Hartman's "Litany," like Du Bois's "The Comet," construes post-disaster life as a relocation of notional (Black, underground) non-life to the ruins of conventional life, to the devastation of the (white) upper world. "Care," as we read in Hartman's "Litany," "will swallow [Antigone] whole, steal her last breath, crush and destroy her"[108]: even though she is above ground, her unconditional investment in care implies a gravitational pull not just *toward*, but *below* the earth. The selflessness of care, the self-mutilation or self-killing it entails, is a plunge into an underground Real or, we could say, a subterranean undercommons, coinciding with what Lara Langer Cohen has recently called "the subterranization of Blackness."[109] Cohen uses this phrase to explore the underground as a racist and racialized space, the symbolic (as well as physical) relegation of Black people to the depths of the earth, in a dark abyss that engulfs them as both an extracting and extracted instrument of colonialist capitalisms. The words of David Walker in "Appeal to the Colored Citizens of the World" (1829) come to mind, his reference to "the very dark and almost impenetrable abyss in which our fathers for many centuries have been plunged."[110] Yet "the subterranization of Blackness" also implicates an ever-present, ever-imminent, underground threat to extractivist racialization, evoking Sylvia Wynter's idea of "underlife," Hartman's assimilation of slavery to "the underground" catapulted "to the surface of discourse," Fred Moten's Fanonian characterization of Blackness as "ontology's underground," Stefano

Harney and Moten's "undercommons," and Fanon's own notion of insurrectionary non-being as a "descent into a real hell" where "an authentic upheaval can be born."[111] Hartman's Butlerian Antigone, like the protagonist of Du Bois's story, embodies a seismic underontology that she brings upward, her post-disaster wandering marking a spiraling upward of an insurrectionary non-being, the anarchic, looping ascent of the underground.

In Du Bois's "The Comet," in which Jim approaches the underground as at once a place of exile and a regained home, this ascent manifests itself as persistent phonesthetic harshness, as the formal upheaval of a tragic subterranean texture. The contracted passages of air produced in descriptive turns mimicking arduous bodily motions in the underground labyrinth conflate pandemic, slavery, mining, and the self-suffocations of the Middle Passage, multiple "-cides," "aero-," "eco-," and "geno-." As though bringing a wounding power outward or upward, the insurrectionary, interruptive force of Black underlife is diffused in the stumbling of the reader's voice, the breaking up of breath in the midst of contorted velar, rhotic, and fricative accretions, crashing consonants, insistent hissing. The verbal roughening of the descriptive surface enjoins mental exertion, a thickening of articulatory air, like the broken breathing brought on by the comet that brings the world to an end, spreading a "sickening stench," filling the nostrils with exhalations that, though delivered by an extraterrestrial object, figure the self-destructive consequences of colonization:[112]

> He groped forward, a great rat leapt past him and cobwebs crepts across his face; with a choking cry of utter fright he lunged, leaned giddily. . . . He met a business man, silk-hatted and frock-coated, who had crept, too, along that smooth wall and stood now stone dead with wonder. . . . On a store step sat a little, sweet-faced girl looking toward the skies; the terror burst in his veins, and with one great, gasping cry he sprang . . . and ran—ran as only the frightened run, shrieking and fighting the air.[113]

Coiling and recoiling sound effects here materialize the "great, dark coils of wire" that, as Du Bois puts it, "came up from the earth," making the descent into the Underworld and the Underworld's ascent to the surface unfold as a break, or in the break. Like the whirlwind rising upward in the aftermath of the removal of dust from Polynices' corpse in *Antigone*—an atmospheric rage shaking up textual form as well as the Law[114]—underground insurrection bursts out and the ground's solidity breaks, withdrawing its support. The rebellious impetus of depleted geopower[115] is inseparable from the irruption of Blackness through the subliminal intensity of surging form, notwithstanding the protagonist's persistent guilt, an internalized Law that survives in his consciousness even after the white world has been decimated (or has decimated itself).

The return of Hartman's Antigone to the world is marked by the impression of her continuing residence in an underground labyrinth, a spatial confusion that carries with itself a collapse of time, an achrony reproducing ontological horizontality, the removal of generational barriers, of kin distinctions and roles:

> Grief and despair, not reason, drive her, push her forward. Time has fallen away, and the only reliable measure left is one step forward, then the next, as she cuts a blind path through the labyrinth of the city. She will search for him. . . . She remains trapped in the *graveyard* of the world.[116]

It is not clear where Hartman's Antigone is walking, but there are signals that she may be in a space that blends lower and upper realms. The labyrinth of the Underworld has broken through the earth's surface, while the world resembles a graveyard, a landscape of extinction. The apparent linearity of her gait ("one step forward, then the next") runs up against the closed circularity of time, which can no longer be measured. In this disappearance of a temporal distribution of the sensible, the step itself, which takes the ground for granted as a measurable surface, as the support that gets "ground" down in the act of counting, turns uncounted or uncountable.[117] The step is trapped in the loop of pastftuture and futurepast, an underground achrony, the interruptive achrony of the pan-endemic. This is the underground temporality (or lack thereof) that, in the removal of the biological hierarchies of priority and lateness, parentality and filiality, makes room for synchronic siblinghood, whether imagined for Freud in his *auto-bio-thanato-heterography* or posited by Butler as a slide of proliferating identifications, an ever-shifting k-incoherence, which I argue is the product of a horizontal death drive.

The Freudian death drive could be seen as a desire for this Antigonean emergence of the Underworld, for an irruption of the underground into what only some of us can call "our" world. Mendieta's silhouettes can be interpreted not simply as the graphic traces of refuge sought in the underground but as a coming into sight (or relief) of geopower out of an ecological undercommons. In Du Bois's story, the "death of the world"—the extinction provoked by the poisonous effluvia released by the comet from New York's underground—"creates an opening," as Hartman says, "that might allow [Jim] to breathe inside his skin and be released from the enclosure of nothing"[118]; similarly, it might rescue beneath-the-earth darkness from the position of abused support, instrumentalized non-being. In Sophocles' *Antigone*, the sense of almost apocalyptic solitude that crushes Creon feels like telluric requital: holding the body of his son, a horizontal burden, he becomes human ground, an encumbered or broken base, like the earthly support that opens itself into the cave where Antigone died.[119] Participating in the proliferating "slide of identifications," Creon becomes Antigone because the underground non-being is occupying his own familial and bodily space, is filling his arms, is mixing with him. His own death drive, symptomatic of the auto-immunitarian impulse of the state, enables underlife, a subterranean undercommons, to burst into his world.

Read alongside Hartman and Du Bois, the radical heterology in Butler's *Antigone*—which I construe as an ethico-political take on the Freudian death drive—enters into a productive dialogue with theorizations of disindividation and critiques of the subject, especially in Black studies. In Du Bois's fantasia of pandemic destruction, the final image of a dead baby in the arms of the woman who will become Hartman's own Butlerian Antigone curtails "hope about the future," as Hartman says, the idea of a lineage, the pleasure principle's genealogical line; the image denies "closure or resolution," even while "offer[ing] a glimmer of relation in the wake of devastation."[120] What sort of response is possible to the curtailing of a lineage, which the Symbolic in its interpellation coerces us to identify with life as such, enforcing it as a racializing requisite of a proprietary, familial subjectivity?[121] David Marriott, the author, in 2021, of *Lacan Noir: Lacan and Afropessimism*, published in the same year an article on Huey Newton's 1973 book *Revolutionary Suicide*, an autobiographical account of his experience in the Black Panther movement, which takes as a starting point the assumption that subjecting oneself to the danger of self-annihilation in revolutionary action is preferable to living in the status quo.[122] In Marriott's words, the underlying assumption of self-sacrifice for the radical cause of Black liberation is that "Black life is already decapitated, so to speak, and only by killing itself (rather than being endlessly killed) can it more abundantly live as resistant."[123] Such risk-taking can perform Black life-affirmation "not by willing life or negating it, nor by preserving life as life, but by an act of creative willing,"[124] though he clarifies that "it is not life that must be resisted, but the world that expels black life from the human."[125] Equally responding to a world that deceptively and cruelly identifies itself with life as such, Hartman proposes the following portrait of her Antigone: "The no-longer mother, the not-wife, the kinless sister, the lost daughter, the not-woman, the not-man, the nobody, the cipher.... she is still here."[126] From a different perspective, when Marquis Bey says, "I settle nowhere other than within the desire to not be, to not have to be," he enables us to see the death drive not as a refusal of existential being as such, a longing (resigned or heroic) for non-life, with the consequent looping spiral of desire, but as a refusal of categorial being, a demand for the removal of predicates.[127] Such a position is similar to John Paul Ricco's incongruity and unbecoming, which he, in fact, defines as "being free of predication, identification, reification, or any other definitive form or conclusive state of completion" and "nothing but the infinite abandonment of being and becoming to the existential force of finitude."[128] Hartman's non-definition of Antigone through an asyndetic proliferation of negations— "The no-longer mother, the not-wife, the kinless sister, the lost daughter, the not-woman, the not-man, the nobody, the cipher ... she is still here"— is the flipside of the excess we saw in Freud's own Antigonean becoming other. This proliferation also has affinities with Fred Moten's theoretical project of "detach[ing] difference from individuation," where "individuation" is intended as a "regulative concept, a concept of law enforcement, that is meant to control and create a certain kind of separability that then becomes associated with difference."[129] When Moten, rejecting "that sense of ... propriety, or property, or properness ... so easily ... attached ... to a proper noun," observes that "there's an interesting *numerical glitch* or rupture that takes place when one consents not to be a single being, indicating that one can, at some point, be no one,"[130] we perceive the affinities between his investment in "an abolition of sovereignty"—or "an abolition of a certain horrible and brutal individuate notion of freedom"— and the Antigonean/Butlerian slide of identifications.[131]

In an interview with Moten, the dispossessive energy of the glitchy intertwinements, of the Antigonean slide of identifications—I become you, you become me, I am (your) brother, I am (your) son—vividly comes through, merging familial and intellectual kinship:

> There are all these traces and rivers of work, all these particularly beautiful sets of differences that we associate with proper names, like Baraka or Nate Mackey or Gayl Jones or Angela Davis, my mom, my grandma. That was their project. That's Cedric Robinson's project. When I read Dionne Brand or when I read Cecily Nicholson, I feel like yeah, that's their project. That's my project. I wanna be with them.[132]

The same aesthetic effect of disindividuation permeates the lyrical interweavings of *Antígona González*, where the possessive violence of pronominal denomination—the primary means of individuation, a traumatic repetition of the murderous separation of the dead from life and their loved ones—is pre-emptively countered by the command "not to forget that all the bodies without names are our lost bodies" and forcefully ironized by this litany:

> I came to San Fernando to search for my brother.
> I came to San Fernando to search for my father.
> I came to San Fernando to search for my husband.
> I came to San Fernando to search for my son.[133]

Kinship divisions fall apart and the normative imperative to be "a single being" collapses, as the same individuals (dead or still alive) are at the same time brothers, fathers, husbands, sons, in relation to each other, to the "I," and to us—pronominal determinations, markers of notional self-possession that simultaneously get depersonalized and deindividuated.[134] The San Fernando mass grave, like the auto-bio-thanatographical installations of An(tigon)a Mendieta, projects upward and outward the relational excess, the glitchy deindividuation of Butler's queer kinship, a death-driven k-incoherence that, in its heterological rupture, brings to the world's surface the looping simultaneity, the achronic time of the underground, an ever-shifting horizontality.

In the next section I will connect this horizontality with Antigonean neuroqueerness as intimated in Toni Morrison's Cornell M.A. thesis on Woolf and Faulkner;[135] as an entry point into this new phase of the argument, I want to close with a brief consideration of the reference to *Antigone* in a 2010 conversation between Angela Davis and Morrison at the New York Public Library. Invoking the testimony of Edwidge Danticat in *Create Dangerously: The Immigrant Artist at Work* (2010), Morrison reports that at the time of the installment by Haitian dictator François Duvalier of the Tonton Macoute—murderous secret police tasked with spreading terror and cruelly eliminating any form of dissent—"in [Danticat's] neighborhood . . . somebody organized a little theater in her garage, and the local people came to participate in this play, some to be in it and some to watch it, and they did it every night, and the Tonton Macoute would come by and check . . . to see what they were doing and walk on by . . . [and] the play was *Antigone*."[136] Danticat observes that, as a result of this production, "Sophocles too became a Haitian writer."[137] An asyndetic excess in Morrison's language configures the same exchangeability that corrodes the law of individuation in Uribe's *Antígona*:

> In Haiti when the Tonton Macoute was running around chopping everybody up, they established a rule if somebody died— *your son, your neighbor, a stranger,* on the street, if, you know, they killed him, you couldn't pick him up, you could not go out and get the body, even if it was yours, I mean, a relative. At some point a few days later, a garbage truck would come along and pick it up and put it in the garbage, do whatever they did. So if you went out to pick up a body to bury it or whatever, you would get shot. *So everybody was afraid.*[138]

This Polynices' pronoun ("him") becomes the referent not of distinct individualities, but of a singular plurality—just as Antigone is both "sister" and "brother," the Haitian Polynices, who is at once "son" and "neighbor" for loved ones both distinct and the same, precipitates their notional individualities into an overdetermined compulsive dispossession—the condition of being "anybody," being a stranger, becoming or rather unbecoming "everybody." Morrison's verbal re-creation of Antigone/*Antigone* in Haiti seems to dispel the fantasy of "single being," to contest the identification of separability with difference.

Morrison's (and Butler's) Autigone

There is a strong homology between the Butlerian Antigone's demand for queer kinship and the neurodiverse contestation of current configurations of the social, of the conventional equivalence of *asociality* and *anti-sociality*. I want to zero in on this homology—and conclude this chapter's discussion of Antigone's infinite heterology—by staging an encounter between the first play in Butler's trilogy and Toni Morrison's unpublished 1955 Cornell M.A. thesis, "Virginia Woolf's and William Faulkner's Treatment of the Alienated." Interpreted as tragic structures, in an Aristotelian sense, the novels that Morrison writes about here—*Mrs. Dalloway*; *Absalom, Absalom*; and *The Sound and the Fury*—build "a community of the isolated," dramatizing, as she puts it, "a stage of tragic disorganization and breakdown within the structure of modern civilization."[139] This breakdown is centered around a conflict between mortal finitude and fate or, differently put, individual volition and the Real of a deterministic force received as divine malignance. As we will see, this conventional interpretive schema can be defamiliarized by reading Morrison's approach to Oedipus and Antigone—the tragic figures with whom she compares Woolf's and Faulkner's characters—against the grain, by construing it as the articulation of a proto-neuroqueer discourse.

Running across Morrison's comment that Faulkner is interested in the "tragic flaw" or "tragic failure" and that "he uses isolation as the theme in some of his attempts to write tragedy," one is reminded of the emphasis on alienation and isolation as expressions of the larger-than-life yet abject subjectivity of Sophoclean characters in a highly influential literary-critical approach exemplified by Bernard Knox's 1964 book, *The Heroic Temper: Studies in Sophoclean Tragedy*.[140] The zeitgeist of new-critical, liberal humanism, which seems to be an unconscious endorsement of as well as a warning against white American post-war individualism, resonates in Morrison's commentary on Quentin Compson, a character whom we find in both *Absalom, Absalom* (1936) and *The Sound and the Fury* (1929): "Though he suffers he does not learn humility. His pride is the pride of isolation and he is unable to survive suffering."[141] Because of his isolation, which Morrison calls "self-imposed, contrary to nature and morally destructive," Quentin is, in her view, similar to Oedipus: just as the tragic hero "is too proud to accept the warnings of the blind seer" Tiresias, so Quentin "is unable to understand the lesson of *Absalom, Absalom*."[142] If Quentin is Oedipus, Clarissa in Woolf's *Mrs. Dalloway* (1925) is easy to assimilate to, or simply link up with, Antigone in Sophocles' play, which is pivotal to Woolf's feminist and queer classicism and which, in fact, Clarissa is familiar with (a passage of the tragedy is cited not in *Mrs. Dalloway* but in *The Voyage Out*, its prequel).[143]

Without regarding Morrison's thesis or Greek tragedy as an origin, the *archê* of her novelistic inspiration, I will suggest that reading the mortalist humanistic orientation of this archived text *together with,* or *beside* the subversive cognitive aesthetics of her novels can help us conceive of a new interpretive paradigm for understanding Antigone that dovetails with Butlerian radical heterology. "Intransigence," "stubbornness," "unyieldingness," the terms that Knox employs to characterize the Sophoclean hero, are part of an ableist frame, which marginalizes and pathologizes what neuroqueer theorists have called autistic "perseveration" (including "rigidity," "obsession," "routinization").[144] If we filter out the moralistic and ableist language, the "heroic temper" can be perceived as an expression of neurodiversity or neuroqueerness, which, as we will see, Moten has discussed in relation to Blackness.

The isolation and alienation discussed by Morrison and Knox as almost willful conditions are germane to *arelationality* and *asociality,* the ableist terms that, as Melanie Yergeau puts it, "position the autistic as deadly or death-wishing, collapsing [her] into all that is alarmingly inhuman."[145] Reversing this perspective, Yergeau has claimed that autistic—or neuroqueer—asociality is "inherently relational" in that it "defies" and "reclaims," "embrac[ing] the expansiveness that countersocialities can potentially embody."[146] It is not a refusal of relationality as such, but of the sociality that the normative world construes as the only possible horizon for *being with*—a conceptual revision parallel to the transition from the Lacanian notion of an anti-social Antigone to the Butlerian Antigone, who makes a claim for queer kinship or queer sociality. Yergeau says that autistic bodies "not only defy social order, but fail to acknowledge social order's very existence"; in other words, "autism . . . poses a kind of neuroqueer threat to normalcy, to society's very essence."[147] For Moten, "all black life is neurodiverse" inasmuch as, "in its irreducible and impossible sociality and precisely in what might be understood as its refusal of the status of social life that is refused [to] it," it "constitute[s] a fundamental danger—an excluded but immanent disruption—to social life."[148] Erin Manning observes that "a more-than defies the concept of the human" in the case of neuroqueerness and "a more-than that deeply unsettles the human as . . . defined by the (white) discourses of neurotypicality," which she characterizes as "akin to structural racism—as the infusion of white supremacy in the governing definition of what counts as human."[149] The phrase "more-than" recalls "larger-than-life," the adjectival expression customarily applied to the Sophoclean hero by scholars sympathetic with Knox's paradigm. When Moten observes that "*all black life is neurodiverse life*," he is making a claim for the undercommons, which, as we have seen, is integral to the imaginary of the underground in the Black radical tradition and the underlife that Antigone transfers upward, seizing hold of the (heteronormative) law, reshaping it, becoming *auto-nomos*.

While ableist discourse positions the alleged "other-directness" of neurotypicals—which neuroqueer discourse slyly calls *allism*—against autistic, anti-social self-absorption,[150] Antigone's "*auto*-nomy," cast as her solitude and embrace of the Real of death, appears to stake out a space of neuroqueer countersociality. In the same speech in which Creon laments the becoming-woman foisted upon him by Antigone—"And now I am not a man, but she is a man (*ê nun egô men ouk anêr, hautê d' anêr* 484)—he warns Antigone, calling out her "intransigence," "stubbornness," and "unyieldingness" (473–76):

> Know that *too-hard temperaments* (*ta* ***sklêr'*** *agan phronêmata*)
> are the ones that mostly fall, and that *the strongest* (*ton en-kratestaton*)
> iron, baked by fire so as to become *hard* (*peri-**skelê***),
> is the one that you would see is most frequently *broken* (***thrausth****enta*) and
> *shattered* (***rhag****enta*).

Comparable to the phonesthetic emergence of the menacing underground in Du Bois's "The Comet," the harsh sonic surface of these lines displays—and releases—the very threat that the speaker is seeking to ward off or crush. Defiantly inhabiting, in the texture of their writing, the stereotypical image of neuroqueer stuckness, Yergeau maintains, "The autistic symbolic is always a reduction. . . . It is mechanistic, *r*igid, *r*outinized, *r*educible."[151] A "reduction" in its own right—of the phonetic possibilities and variations of language—the rhotic alliteration in the last three words enacts the same *rig*idity, or (temperamental) "difficulty," spread by the rhotic and velar insistence (epitomized by *rhag*enta) in Creon's dramatically ironic speech.[152] Such insistence—a cacophonic effect of brokenness—embodies the "*bristl[ing]* against the compulsoriness of interaction, of human engagement, on compliance with the neurotypical" that Yergeau ascribes to autistic (a)sociality, with its "cripped kind of betweenity," its "kakokairotic, kakoethical" cadence, that is, "asyncopated motions that defy time, space, and character."[153] The metallic image used by Creon, which configures a kind of "mineralogy of being" (or becoming),[154] might also be placed alongside Yergeau's view of autistic (a)sociality "as that which is ecologically oriented . . . that which extends notions of communion and relationality beyond the human"[155] (Butler's grounding of human sociality in a non-humanness that at the same time enables and undoes it will be a major concern of the next chapter, on *Bacchae*.) The "rigidity" and "unyieldingness" of Antigone, which cannot be bent by diseases or punctured by swords (819–20), also frames one of the climactic moments of Sophocles' play—the choral coinage of the word *auto-nomos* ("autonomous") in a passage (821–22), rendered below by Anne Carson in *Antigonick*, a dramatic production in which Butler played Creon:[156]

> you chose to live *autonomous* (*auto-nomos*)
> and so you die
> the only one (*monê*) of mortals to go down to Death alive.

A perfect anagram of *nomos* ("law"), which is contained a line earlier in *auto-nomos*, *monos*—the adjective expressing Antigone's solitude more than her exceptionality—is the opposite of quietist Lacanian renunciation, or of an isolated singularity. Rather than simply placing itself beyond or *outside* of the law, *monos* in all its semantic implications (not simply solitude, but also the "remaining" of the cognate *menô*) bespeaks an insistence that turns the law upside down, that deterritorializes it, that upsets the system of hierarchical positions it presupposes. In fact, this insistence resembles—to cite Yergeau again—the "asociality . . . often represented by clinicians as a nonsociality," which "is inherently relational in that it . . . embraces the expansiveness that countersocialities can potentially embody."[157] Accompanied by the word *monê* (the feminine of *monos*), Antigonean *auto-nomos* seems to approach *autism* and *autistic*, terms that can be reclaimed as countersocial responses to what neuroqueer activists have called *allism*, wryly casting normative sociality as "an inability to express independent emotions, an inability to fruitfully occupy one's own time, and a pathological need for the presence, interaction, and approval of others."[158] Replete with *autos* compounds, Sophocles' play begins with *aut-adelphon*, with which Antigone addresses Ismene as "full sister" (*ô koinon aut-adelphon Ismênes kara* 1), but, as Mark Griffith notes, "the expression lacking feminine endings may suggest also their common brother"[159]—as though the play's first word announced Antigone's sororal dispossession, the "becoming brother" discussed by Butler. In the same scene, Ismene's abbreviated account of Oedipus's self-blinding and the reciprocal murder (or suicide) of Eteocles and Polynices generates a concentration of four *auto* compounds (51–58):

> As a result of *self-discovered* (***auto***-*phôrôn*) crimes, both
> eyes did he *himself* (***autos***) strike with *his own self-working hand*
> (***auto****urgôi cheri*),
> and [his] mother and wife, a double name,
> harms her life with woven nooses;
> . . . *killing each other* (***auto***-*ktonounte*), the wretched (*talaipôrô*) pair
> inflicted common death on each other with their hands.
> And now the two of us alone (*mona*) . . .

Paired once again with the adjective *monos*, the proliferating *autos* here turns into a refusal "to be a single being"[160] not only because the fraternal suicide, a bodily interweaving re-enacting the grip of Jocasta's suicidal ropes, gives rise to a prenatal disindividuation reflected in the hypercontinuity of verbal form (only the dual article *tô* separates the participle *auto-ktonounte* from the adjective *talaipôrô*). More significantly, the description of Oedipus's self-blinding splits his selfhood, making his hand autonomous, socially expanding him, as subliminally indicated by *autourgos*, not just an adjective but also a noun, meaning "farmer."[161] Just as Antigone's suicide seems to involve a multiplicity of agencies, Oedipus's self-blinding, the virtual suicide that makes him while unmaking him, entails a kind of cross-social, inter-class heterology. The formal and conceptual vicissitudes of Antigonean *autos* thus presuppose a kind of autism— "reconfigur[ing] what it means to be self-focused and without self, in all of the paradoxicality of that simultaneity."[162]

Returning now to Morrison, I will expand on Antigonean "autism" by analyzing two of her observations on Woolf's Clarissa and Quentin, and compare them with Knox's take on the relation between time and the "heroic temper." When we read Morrison's interpretation of Quentin's extreme gesture of breaking the watch ("he secretly hopes to stop time"),[163] we might think of the neuroqueer resistance to the division of past, present, and future, but also of the Antigonean underground, a space of radical synchrony and archival (or an-archival) achrony.[164] Similarly, in Clarissa's movement toward what Morrison calls "life itself as caught and lived moment by moment,"[165] we can detect the intensity of repetition, a break in the biopolitical commodification of time, and a neuroqueer shattering of neurotypical relationality, of a sociality informed by or coinciding with the capitalistic (and inevitably racializing) virtues of docility, flexibility, and efficiency—the values implicitly elevated by Creon in Sophocles' play, as we have seen. In breaking the watch, an archive of sorts, which "makes" time by containing or constraining it, Quentin is perhaps seeking to connect with the individual parts of the object, the invisible workers in a mechanical structure constituting a labor chain, a network, a community (or an undercommons) of interrelated, minuscule functionaries at the service of the user. Breaking the watch also resembles an attempt to liberate time from its container, from the engine of normative or productive efficiency, to break it down into its individual moments, to expand it into a dilated infinity of instants. Alternatively, we can say that, in destroying the watch, Quentin mimetically enacts what Morrison calls the perception of time not as "change" but as "destroyer."[166] Knox's view of the heroic temper's rejection of time, an Antigonean being "in love with the impossible,"[167] acquires new, unexpected resonances in light of neuroqueerness, which is indifferent to the distribution of time in the service of productivity, while leaning into an object-oriented psychology.[168] Perhaps, following Morrison's lead, we can propose another juxtaposition between Quentin and Clarissa, between his encounter with the watch and a queer moment in her story. In *The Voyage Out*, just after the citation from an ode of Sophocles' *Antigone*, Clarissa is visited in a dream by the Greek letters, which become people, liberated from their verbal consignation, their aggregation into the chain of the signifier.[169] Removed from the temporal pacing of word division, the letters become Antigonean, showcasing a wayward autonomy, an unlawful *auto*-quality—a challenge to the pre-formed formal sociality of language—that encapsulates the autism of tragedy's heroic temper, another dimension of Butler's queer kinship.

This unlawful *auto*-quality is distinctive of Pecola in Morrison's first, programmatically "tragic" novel, *The Bluest Eye* (1970), a character whom we could perhaps name *Auti*gone, if we heed the ego narrator's description of her:

> Pecola stood a little apart from us. . . . She seemed to fold into herself, like a pleated wing. Her pain antagonized me. I wanted to open her up, crisp her edges, ram a stick down that hunched and curving spine, force her to stand erect and spit the misery out on the streets. But she held it in where it could lap up into her eyes.[170]

Voicing an ableist, neurotypical viewpoint, Claudia—the ego narrator—reads Pecola's defiant, antagonistic *arelationality* as asocial apathy, an intolerable recoiling into inanimate objectality ("a pleated wing"), a privileging of obliquity, the unbalance of inclination, as Adriana Cavarero would put it, over the rectitude, the upright position, the verticality that is conventionally conceived as the sine qua non of relating.[171] But, as Butler has demonstrated on multiple occasions, relationality is precisely the recognition of the support, of the infrastructures that undo the illusory self-sufficiency of "standing."[172] Pecola's earthward pull, the orientation identified by the internal viewer with her ostensible self-enclosure, is autistic asociality, the disavowed horizontality, a reorientation of relationality to the ground, or the underground as it were. The spatiality of Antigone's own refusal—a corpse-like horizontality, her earthward orientation—codes her apparent death drive as a refashioning (or queering) of relationality, as an encounter of horizontalities. To head willingly toward the cave, the space that will allow her to "fold into herself," means for Antigone, as for Pecola, rejecting not the social as such, but the social as currently given; not refusing life, but, as Lauren Berlant might have it, refusing to live in a world that opens us up, that tears some of us apart by pathologizing melancholy[173]—the "blues" filling Pecola's eyes instead of the coveted chromatic blueness. To recraft the queer claim of Butler's Antigone, we could say that this is a world that hystericizes any divergence from neurotypical monoculture, any friction with a contingent configuration of the social that is cast as an insurmountable facticity.

Pecola's disability "makes the consequences of institutional and internalized racism visible, disclosing the struggles that occur at the intersection of race, class, and gender *without being a metaphor for those struggles*."[174] Her desire to become other, to embody the whiteness symbolized by the titular blue eyes, signals the introjection of racism and racializing oppression. But, as Morrison declares in the foreword, what interested her in the writing of *The Bluest Eye*, was "not resistance to the contempt of others, ways to deflect it, but the far more *tragic and disabling consequences of accepting rejection as legitimate, as self-evident*."[175] As Jessica Williams observes, "*The Bluest Eye*'s fragmented narrative structure attempts to provide a shape for what Morrison terms the 'void' of Pecola's self-identity: a void that stems from the intersection of a contemporaneous view of the autistic child's absence or deferral of self with the racism that can destroy positive black identity."[176] Here Williams refers to Morrison's point in the foreword that, as she was writing, Pecola's "passivity made her a narrative void,"[177] following the observation that "some victims of powerful self-loathing turn out to be dangerous, violent," while "others surrender their identity."[178] The assumption is that the introjection of racism depletes Pecola of her "identity," reducing her to a void invasively filled by oppressive ideologies. Williams notes that Pecola's "'schizophrenic' dialogue indicates an absence of self (consistent with both contemporaneous and current medical ideas of the autistic mind), for which ... *The Bluest Eye* provides internalized racism as cause";[179] yet the reduction of what she calls "the deferral of self" to the outcome of racist introjection is in tension with neuroqueer heterology, the autistic "leaky sense of self,"[180] which is powerfully reflected in the formalistic features of the novel: its "multiple voices, shifting perspectives, and dilatory chronologies,"[181] the "elaborate patterning of framing devices" that "deflect attribution, dispers[ing] sympathy and identification," parts "jostl[ing] against one another, sometimes ... blend[ing] with each other,"[182] and in particular the shift from the first person to the impersonal one. In *The Bluest Eye* Morrison withholds punctuation and spacing in chapter titles,[183] a formal counterpart to self abolition, disindividuation, the refusal of single being:

> HEREISTHEFAMILYMOTHERFATHER
> DICKANDJANETHEYLIVEINTHEGREE
> NANDWHITEHOUSETHEYAREVERYH

In *The Bluest Eye*, Pecola's mother, Pauline, inflects an Oedipus-like disability and an Antigonean heterology (her autism), which consists in becoming limping Oedipus, in becoming (Antigone's) father. As we read, a "wound left her with a crooked, archless foot that flopped when she walked, not a limp that would have eventually twisted her spine, but a way of lifting the bad foot as though she were extracting it from little whirlpools that threatened to pull it under."[184] This Antigonean "leaky self" brings us back to Butler, in particular their conversation with Sunaura Taylor, entitled "Interdependence," a philosophical dialogue that took place on a walk in San Francisco's Mission neighborhood in 2010.[185] Butler observes that "feet can be one means of mobilizing the body, but certainly not the only one, and not even a necessary one"—a consideration that leads one to "rethink what a walk is in terms of all the things that power our movement, all the conditions that support our mobility."[186] Taylor recounts her own experience of moving in a wheelchair: "I could go into a coffee shop and actually pick up the cup with my mouth and carry it to my table, but that becomes almost more difficult because of the normalizing standards of our movements and the discomfort that's caused when I do things with body parts that aren't necessarily what we assume they're for."[187] Butler continues:

> There's a norm . . . not even [of] what the body should be like and look like, but what parts should move and what those movements should be like. . . . Sometimes when we say, "I move" or "I'm moving by myself," we imagine completely self-generated movement, as if the body is completely independent of an apparatus, of a machine, of even nutrition, of all kinds of things that one needs to move.[188]

Antigone's (or Autigone's) claim for queer kinship spreads the uncomfortable feeling that what is called the norm is nothing but *one* possible arrangement of parts, that the "I" is a fragile, ever-shifting combination of parts and multiples, which makes it never fully individuated. In the nick of time, at a moment of global crisis, the parts' mutability and exchangeability push us toward *asociality*, a neurodiverse vision of the social that makes room for the coming into partial view, the emergence of countersocialities and underground intimacies. In a 2012 review of *Antigonick*—"more transference than translation . . . a halting and then a rushing of words structured by the syntax of grief and rage, spanning centuries"—Butler says:

> The nick is the time of the line itself, the scan of poetic meter, but not as something that stays regular or predictable. It stops and starts, alters its pace and spatial form, breaks open white space unexpectedly, and registers a loss it can neither forestall nor redeem. We are left with the question, What kind of time is the time of tragedy? It is the time of the metrical and not so metrical line, to be sure, but also some graphic trace left from the time of life,

something nicked away by some brute force, or perhaps the bracket within which life vanishes.[189]

As we read of "some graphic trace left from the time of life," nicked away, we return to An(tigon)a Mendieta—and to her distinct yet broken lines, similar to a tragic line whose metrical resolutions build on the reshuffling of parts, on the appearance, disappearance, or reappearance of deindividuated "feet" that rearticulate the rhythm of time and being-with. When Morrison says that Woolf "suggests . . . that by isolating oneself into the fragmentary experiences and sensations as they come, the dread of time eating at the edges of life can be avoided,"[190] we can perhaps glimpse her own heroines living "at the edges of life," pushing against time, like Butler's Antigone, in order to reinvent sociality, to perform the failure, the dismantling, of the typical.

2

Trans-parentality, Abortion, Social Ecology: *Bacchae*

> *One kind of gender trouble that [*Gender Trouble*] could not have anticipated was, alongside three decades of some of the most significant progress in LGBTQ rights in U.S. history and an explosion in visibility for trans and gender-nonconforming people, a vicious backlash—including, crucially, a targeted assault on our very right to exist. The phrase "gender-affirming care" had not yet entered our lexicon in 1990, but as I write this, more than a dozen states in the U.S. have banned or are actively considering bans on gender-affirming care for trans youth. Some states have even considered extending restrictions to adults. This is to say nothing of the child-abuse cases brought against parents who have supported their trans children, the trans adults who have been fired for coming out, the conversion therapy that has been forced on trans teenagers, and the near-constant violence visited upon our community.*[1]

At this moment when, across the globe, violence against queer and trans lives is condoned or perpetrated by resurgent fascist ideologies and, in the US, abortion rights are under aggressive attack, reading *Bacchae* may induce us to view Euripides' play as a corrosive ironization of a right-wing nightmare of the collapse of the world precipitated by the "liberal nonsense" of trans-parentality and tolerance for the "dismemberment" of fetuses. It is the disturbing currency of the reactionary denial and rejection of "gender trouble" that provides the background of Judith Butler's *Who's Afraid of Gender?* (2024), a book foreshadowed, to an extent, by their specific intervention on *Bacchae*, the second play of the trilogy that is the concern of this book. In Euripides' play, a queer classic,[2] Pentheus denies the reality of Zeus's trans-parentality, insisting that the story of Dionysus's relocation from Semele's womb to his father's thigh is a fabrication. An archetype, like his grandson Creon, of the authoritarian ruler who responds to the "outside" (in its various inflections) with hostile skepticism and mistrust, Pentheus is also inclined to translate his paranoid fantasies into fact: patently projecting his own forbidden desires (adulterous, homosexual, incestuous) onto Dionysian rituals, he seems unshaken in his belief that it is wild sex that binds the mysterious foreigner—Dionysus himself in the guise of a follower—to the Maenads: "They say that a foreigner has arrived [in Thebes], a charlatan, an enchanter from the Lydian land, with blond curls, fragrant in his hair, wine-colored, carrying in his eyes Aphrodite's graces, he who day and night has intercourse with young girls, prolonging joyful rites" (233–38). In a 2021 interview with *The Guardian*, reacting to transphobic feminisms in and outside the UK, Butler observes that "positing cis womanhood ... as under attack by trans people" invokes "older and more paternalistic and protective approaches to womanhood."[3] Even though, as Butler says in their reading of the play, *Bacchae* is not—at least on the surface—a tragedy of feminist liberation under Dionysus (a tyrannical god in his own right),[4] these patriarchal approaches blatantly inform Pentheus's politics of sexual surveillance, as reflected in his reduction of the effeminacy of Dionysus's alleged emissary—a habitus previewing Pentheus's own gender transition—to a sordid instrument of predation. The horrorism of Agave's filicide may be part of a darkly ironical dramaturgy of paranoia and disbelief:[5] what if—in an uncanny confusion of hallucination and reality, interior and external theatrics—the play cruelly and cleverly plays with our own confused cognition (parallel to Agave's) and Agave's act externalizes not just Pentheus's anxieties, but also the reactionary phobias of our days, the perversely thrilling imaginings of a "liberal" dystopia, of a human world brought to a moral and physical end by birthing trans men and by a furiously *jouissant* practice of feminist abortion? This is the overarching interpretive framework that I will pursue in this chapter, playing up the resonances of Euripides' play with the contemporary, in light of Butler's reading of it in the 2017 A. E. Housman lecture, "Breaks in the Bond: Reflections on Kinship Trouble."

With the suppression of queer and trans rights at the top of the political agenda in Russia, Hungary, Italy, India, Turkey, Uganda, and the US, among other countries, the atmosphere of Euripides' *Bacchae* has been eerily transposed into our lives, while Butler, the theorist and activist, demonized as the deviser of so-called "gender ideology," has taken on the role of a foreign interloper, a Dionysus.[6] As I began writing this chapter in May 2023, Uganda had just voted to punish homosexuality with imprisonment (or even death), lending new urgency to Butler's question in *Undoing Gender* (2004): "What threat of death is delivered to those who do not live gender according to its accepted norms?"[7] The script of the play is perilously rehashed every time a new Pentheus-like figure appears on the political scene, displacing the disavowed disaster of a capital-based ecological crisis—emblematized by climate change and the Covid pan-endemic—onto the so-called "woke mind virus." Also in May 2023, the re-elected president of Turkey, Recep Erdoğan, echoing Pentheus's physical threat against Dionysus at the beginning of *Bacchae*, declared: "In our culture family is sacred. No one can interfere. We will strangle anyone who dares to touch it." Two weeks earlier, tech mogul Elon Musk declared, "The disaster that is downtown San Francisco, once beautiful and thriving, now a derelict zombie apocalypse, is due to the woke mind virus." The auto-immunitarian catastrophe of technocapitalism, whose death-driven logic engenders the racialized poverty and abjection disturbing the eyes and noses of white privilege, is the open secret, the truth barely concealed behind the self-exculpatory ascription of all responsibility for the current sense of impending collapse to "San Francisco values"—another favored right-wing phrase.[8] In the 2002 essay "Is Kinship Always Already Heterosexual?," which was then republished in *Undoing Gender*, Butler refers to a *Le Monde* editorial in which their name "figured as a sign of the coming monstrosity" bound to hit France "if lesbian and gay people are permitted to form state-ratified kinship arrangements."[9] Since then the attacks against Butler have continued, including a witch-like effigy-burning in Brazil, before their arrival in November 2017—a few months after the delivery of the Housman lecture on *Bacchae*. Butler's visit to the country provoked, they say, "a petition [that] called for the cancellation of my lecture, and assumed that I would be speaking on gender since the allegation is that I am the founder of 'the ideology of gender' . . . which is called . . . 'diabolical.'"[10] On that visit, Butler and Wendy Brown "were accosted" at the airport "by a group of about 20 people, holding signs with a blown-up picture of me (doctored) with banners telling me to go home or go to hell."[11] The intellectual star who, in the European and South American right-wing imaginary, introduced the epidemic of "gender ideology" with *Gender Trouble*, who is cast as the principal culprit in the global diffusion and normalization of sexual fluidity, who is ostensibly destroying the world—that is, the world of domineering heteronormativity—through the legitimation of the apocalyptic diseases of queerness, transness, and non-essentialist feminism, Judith Butler *is* Dionysus. The Jewish anti-Zionist thinker, inhabiting and embracing a diasporic non-identity, whose spellbinding writing has touched the lives even of those who never directly read their books, enraging or consoling them; the iconoclast whose fan base has enacted the possibility of an alternative kinship (an expanded "queer family"); and the performer who, having theorized the performativity of gender, played Creon in Anne Carson's *Antigonick*, Butler is easy to assimilate to the dangerous, Orientalized foreigner, the glib, gender-bending enchanter who gathers crowds of acolytes, luring them into abandoning their homes, and awakens trans desire in Pentheus. When Serena Bassi and Greta LaFleur, in their analysis of transphobic feminisms, discuss the "distinctively postfascist strategy that, by framing 'gender theory' as suspiciously 'fashionable' imported knowledge, affectively binds it with fears of foreign contagion," they further enable us to associate Butler with Dionysus. In the "safe" of white heteronormativity, the expansion of gender positionalities and embodiments, the expression of unrecognizable kinship and relational potentialities, and the extension of reproductive rights feel like unbearable encounters with an Orientalized *outside*, an invasion of undocumented possibilities,[12] the arrival of a guest indistinguishable from an enemy,[13] a collapse into the void.

In "Kinship Trouble," where the reading of *Bacchae* functions as a choral, pluralized, or depersonalized continuation of *Antigone's Claim*, the queerness of kinship dramatized throughout the play is defined for Butler, first and foremost, by the intrinsic uncertainty, ambiguity, and fragility, or breakability of the kinship bond. Numerous plot elements prompt Butler to postulate that kinship is held together by its breakability: the proliferation of narrative uncertainties surrounding Dionysus's parents (is Zeus his "real" father? Did Semele conceive him with a mortal and then lie about it? And did Zeus carry him in his thigh as a uterine surrogate?); the weird or "wild" circumstances of his birth (a traumatic separation from the maternal womb and, then, a second cut from Zeus's thigh at the end of his male pregnancy);[14] the Theban women's abandonment of their homes, which amounts to "find[ing] oneself outside the contained spatial organization of kinship itself"[15]; Dionysus's reduction of his aunts, his mother's sisters, to a state of madness; and Agave's inability to recognize Pentheus as her child, both at the moment of the murder and in its immediate aftermath. It is the intrinsic possibility of a break that defines the kinship bond; the ontological trouble is, paradoxically, what holds the bond together. As Butler maintains, the desire for the kinship bond—for its discovery, its ultimate verification, its definitive recognition, its epistemic possession—is an expression of the "drive" (or death drive), the disaggregative energy, that undoes the affective structure it strives to (re)construct. As we read at the end of Butler's essay:

> One recurring feature of becoming kin is . . . to ask the question . . . Who are you to me? And who am I to you? Perhaps kinship happens precisely when we are least sure, trying to focus, vacillating, suspended in a state of protracted incredulity. . . . Does the play perhaps open up a wider set of questions about what or who is justifiably killed, and who is not? . . . If kinship delimits who we may kill (and who we most want to kill), then it would seem that if the prohibition on killing is to be as general as possible, so too must be our understanding of kinship. If the very concept of kinship dissolves as it expands, that may be a necessity—or an occasion for new vocabularies through which to grasp our most basic ties and basic passions.[16]

In tragedy, as Butler notes, many kinship bonds can be ascertained only through a breach. In the most emblematic example, Oedipus discovers who his biological father is only by killing him; he discovers who his biological mother is only after the breach of the prohibition of incest and the fallout—visualized by Jocasta's sudden, silent, pre- or proto-suicidal exit offstage. In *Bacchae*, as Butler puts it, "kinship takes form as an accusation, a fantasy, or a guilt-ridden recognition."[17] If "kinship is . . . dependent on the possibility of disruption, understood as relationships that are invariably marked . . . by the possibility of failing or fading,"[18] then, notwithstanding its normative anchoring within the relational yet closural logics of recognition and intelligibility, it opens up a productive space for unintelligibility, for questioning and undoing the existing structures of obligation, mutuality, and care that it circumscribes. While a bond seems, by definition, to aim at creating bounded relational assemblages—plural singularities that draw upon implicit or explicit mechanisms of exclusion ("us" versus "them")—kinship's indissoluble bond with rupture and misrecognition, its coming about through its latent or potential coming apart, problematizes the very boundary it seeks to mark. Kinship thus prompts us to think of "k-incoherence,"[19] of impromptu forms of expansive relationality exceeding its constitutive force of exclusion. The breakability tightening the kinship bond leads us to ask, "How do we distinguish . . . between family, kin, friendship, cross-species cohabitation and community, and even broader modes of belonging that provide some kind of provisional and iterable structure to intimate and social relations?"[20] Additionally, "If kinship is exclusively defined neither by reproductive nor by marital relations, how do we then delimit the field of kinship relations? Or are we of necessity launched into a domain that cannot be delimited?"[21] Butler's interest in the precarious kinships of *Bacchae* partakes of a broader theoretical preoccupation with the heterology discussed in the previous chapter; with the exclusionary implications of any kind of bounded relationality, of any subject-centered temptation to cling to the self-versus-other distinction; and with the negative (that is, self-denying, self-undoing) ethics of being as being-with.[22]

As illustrated by the climactic scene of *Bacchae*—where Agave attacks her son Pentheus, in female attire, mistaking him for a lion cub—the break that brings kinship into view may result in the emergence of an unexpected (or disavowed) kinship, in an intertwinement occasioned as one supersedes the other. Commenting on this scene, Butler wonders, "Is it that there already are affinities, if not forms of kinship, between the one gender and the other, and between human and animal, such that they can become confused with one another?"[23] Butler's interest in kinship is part of a commitment, initiated especially with *Precarious Life* (2004), if not earlier, to "a non-anthropocentric" (and, thus, ecocritical) "philosophical anthropology," which, as they put it in a 2009 interview, "seeks to resituate the human within the non-human, not as a contingent fact of existence, but as a necessary ontology, an ontology that articulates certain constitutive *bonds* and *binds*."[24] In emphasizing the excess of human kinship, its lending itself to recognition through becoming other than itself, through in-humanity, through the ever-repressed kinship with the animal, Butler seems to construe Euripides' play as a tragic instantiation of the posthumanist presupposition of their ethics of precarity—i.e., that "wherever the human is, it is always outside of itself in the non-human, or it is always distributed among beings, among human and non-human beings, chiasmically related through the idea of precarious life."[25] As we will see, chiasmus—a rhetorical figure pivotal to Butler's theorization of interdependence by way of a re-reading of Merleau-Ponty on touch—formally situates kinship, that is, kinship troubles, in the recalcitrant indeterminacy of "father" and "mother" in Zeus's trans-parentality, parallel to the collapse of "human" and "animal" in Agave's fantasies of feral cross-species becoming. In the same interview, Butler adds that "we can neither lodge the human in the self, nor ground the self in the human, but find instead the relations of exposure and responsibility that constitute the 'being' of the human in a sociality outside itself, even outside its humanness."[26] This sociality is also ecological[27] in that it encompasses not just animality, but also "sympneumatic togetherness"[28] in a wider environmental outside, the air that, like the intoxicating Dionysian atmosphere of Thebes and the verdant woods of the Cithaeron, is the life- or death-giving substance of an experiential commons manifesting the world in the inbetweenness of interobjectivity.

The reason that we should "care about kinship"—and, consequently, about *Bacchae*'s dramatization of "kinship trouble"—is, for Butler, "that rights of parenting are highly disputed, and in some states and some countries, sexual orientation and marital status are preconditions for adoption or even access to reproductive technology . . . and sometimes . . . people lose their children when their gender status changes, or when their sexual orientation becomes known." In June 2023, an Italian prosecutor in Padua revoked the birth certificates of thirty-three children of lesbian couples, following the neofascist government's order that city councils stop recognizing non-biological same-sex parents.[29] The rationale behind this measure is, *simply*, in the words of the prosecutor, that a child cannot be born from two mothers. The paranoia surrounding the birth of Dionysus—apparently born from two wombs (Semele's and Zeus's) and thus two mothers, as we will see—spreads, affecting and altering the law in the name of phantasmic "natural law." Kinship bonds breaking conventional notions of kin recognizability—bonds that are, in fact, expressive of kinship's constitutive predication on rupture (that is, on potential expansion, on potential decentering of modes and structures of care)—are liquidated as lies or travesties by the Pentheuses of our day.

The play is bookended by two events that can be equally characterized as enactments of a break in the bond, of a bond in the break, or a bond as break:

the transgender birth of Dionysus and Agave's dismemberment of her son Pentheus. In the first instance, the bond between Dionysus and Semele is broken by her death and by the transfer of the fetus into Zeus's thigh; through the somatic rupture necessitated by this transition of a father (becoming mother) and son, Dionysus's bonds with Semele and Zeus are both tightened and broken, through trauma as well as physical (re)attachments.[30] In the second, the dismemberment—the physical break—is the outcome of an excess, an excessive attachment, which, in breaking, engenders new possibilities of bonding. Both breaks in the bond provoke cognitive disorientation: Pentheus responds with skepticism to the account of Dionysus's birth (effectively denying Zeus's trans-parentality, his trans-mothering), while Agave cannot recognize her (mis)deed or her son. We can read Agave's killing of Pentheus somewhat allegorically, precisely as a dismantling of the inevitable normativity of kinship, of the hierarchical axiology among bonds that it establishes. Staying within the conceptual field of *sparagmos* ("dismemberment"), we can perhaps imagine a kinship dispersed into countless potential, minor, transversal bonds. But this is not simply a question of deterritorializing kinship and stretching relationality into a Deleuzian-Guattarian assemblage of swarming micro-connections.[31] Tyler Bradway and Elizabeth Freeman coined the neologism "k-incoherence" to dethrone the "tyranny" of kinship.[32] The word "coherence" (from the Latin verb *co-haero*) etymologically partakes of the logic of non-contradiction determined by an orderly bond, a harmonious synergy ("a clinging together") of parts;[33] k-incoherence, then, becomes an unbound bond—the bond resulting from unbinding—but also what is left in the breaking of a break, that is, of a distinction (a break in itself), in this case, the distinctions between kin and non-kin, mother and father, parent and child.

In what follows I will start by elaborating on *Bacchae*'s disturbing hyper-topicality, on the uncanny effect of finding right-wing fears about trans-parentality and abortion echoed in a canonical classical text, on the discomforting "recognition" that the text prompts. In the later parts of the analysis, I propose critical-theoretical experiments in close reading inspired by, proceeding alongside, Butler's reading—together with other thinkers' arguments on transness and interspeciesism and Butler's various other theorizations. I will thus track the collapse of formal bonds, or the formation of verbal bonds "in the break,"[34] and the consequent intimations of an aestheticized discourse of trans-parentality, interspecies unbecoming, and elemental trans-corporeality that furthers the gender and kinship troubles dramatized at the plot level.

Reactionary Paranoia

Euripides' *Bacchae* is a foundational text for queer and trans theory and activism as well as sexuality studies broadly conceived, perennially alluring in both academic discourse and the continuous practice of adaptation and performance. A great deal of attention has been duly devoted to the metatheatrical central scene of the play, in which Dionysus induces Pentheus to don a female outfit to spy on and join the Maenads on Mount Cithaeron. In this scene—arguably, a case of Butlerian gender performativity that Froma Zeitlin uses as a programmatic instantiation of Greek tragedy's carnivalesque "drag," of its iterated social investment in "playing the other"[35]—all the ambiguities, contradictions, and queer and trans latencies of the heteronormative Oedipus complex explode,[36] in particular the (thin) line between "desire for" and "identification with" the maternal body activated by the incest fantasy. Replacing what she calls the Freudian "finitude of one-sexedness," of one fixed sex per person, with Deleuze and Guattari's anti-Oedipal view of sexuality as an "emission of particles," an infinity of "chaotic mutations,"[37] the "production of a thousand sexes,"[38] Victoria Wohl, in 2005, produced a paradigm-shifting reading of the play:

> Desiring the god, Pentheus becomes the woman he desires in the god.... Through the feminine desire for that feminine man, Pentheus himself will become woman-shaped.... Male and female blur, as do homosexuality and heterosexuality.... Traditional gender and sex categories ... implode and from the confusion emerge new shapes ... perhaps even new sexualities.[39]

In a 2010 interview with Vikki Bell, Butler explains the stakes of *Gender Trouble* with deliberately Deleuzian language, locating the book's agenda in the attempt to articulate "a certain kind of possibility of becoming otherwise and becoming what is not fully anticipated," to imagine what it would mean "to be neither man nor woman, but be working, living, within or between those categories and yet spawning some new set of categories or some new set of spaces outside or between."[40] This position coincides, to an extent, with views expressed by Susan Stryker, Jack Halberstam, Paul Preciado, and Marquis Bey, among others, who identify the asterisked "trans*" with a radical refusal of recognizable identity, with an anti-teleological or para-ontological unbecoming, rather than becoming.[41] While Anne Carson's interpretation of the robing scene in Euripides' play as a disclosure of "Pentheus' repressed transsexual desire" was cast by Kay Gabriel, in 2018, as an effort to appeal to "a voyeuristic cisgender readership eager to consume a titillating trans narrative with an especially violent conclusion,"[42] Silk Worm, writing about their experience playing Dionysus in Hope Mohr and Maxe Crandall's *Bacchae Before* (2021), observes that Euripides' play offers "an opportunity to remake the show by recentering it around trans people and our needs."[43] In particular, Silk Worm dwells on the entanglement of Dionysus's transness with his non-status as a foreigner, occupying a middle space, torn between inside and outside, caught between recognition and opacity, lingering on the threshold:

> As I inhabit my own body more fully, feeling more embodied and more expressive, I also feel more trapped by expectation; I have to find the woman I am while transforming myself into something publicly legible as woman. "Transition" sounds so decisive, when often the act of changing sex is an endless series of compromises between how I'd like to look and how I have to look in order to pass. And so however two-dimensionally evil Dionysus may be, the insecurity he feels at being misrecognized, cast aside, or laughed at is a soft spot I can relate to.

Writing in 2022, Isabel Ruffell is confident in the possibility of locating "trans-positive elements in the play" even though "Pentheus is not one of them"; for example, the attempt to rationalize Dionysus's worship "in terms of *mythos* (Tiresias) or in terms of its personal benefits (Cadmus) speaks to (some) debates about the status and etiology of trans: . . . as some kind of irreducible supplement to, and production of, the gender system, or as having at least some physical basis . . . or (as seems more likely) a mixture of nature and culture."[44] For Ruffell, *Bacchae* is ultimately a response to, or even an act of resistance against, transphobic violence for it "suggests that one etiology for acts of transphobic speech and action is, as well as unthinking parroting of patriarchal tropes, denial of self and society."[45]

Leaving aside the much-discussed robing scene, I wish to follow Butler's lead, emphasizing the play's nexus of transness and reproduction.[46] For Butler, focusing on the mechanics of Dionysus's birth, "it would seem that Dionysus assumes divine qualities when he is separated from his human mother, beamed up to Zeus, and certainly when he is sprung into the world by the unpinning of the thigh."[47] Butler segues into an analysis of Zeus's parentality, his becoming Dionysus's second mother:

> Since the gestational process is, as it were, sequentially divided between Semele and Zeus, it would seem that Dionysus has two mothers. Confusing, perhaps, but hardly out of the question. These two mothers don't live together, and they don't raise a son in common. . . . The story seems to resolve into the following proposition: "I, Zeus . . . am now the mother. I give birth to my son Dionysus, himself a feminine form, a boy/girl."[48]

Zeus is, in a sense, both a trans-father and a trans-mother: his male body gives birth, like that of a trans man, even while, in creating a womb and an aperture, he is equally becoming a pregnant trans woman, a trans mother. Zeus's elusive, overdetermined role in Dionysus's birth thus resonates with the current debate on reproductive justice, which encompasses "trans and nonbinary people's access to fertility and perinatal health care,"[49] as well as abortion and contraception. The incredulous reaction of Semele's sisters and Pentheus himself to the narrative of Zeus's trans-parentality exposes Dionysus to the prejudice of cisheteronormativity, "the cisgenderist and heterosexist assumptions that only cisgender women become or wish to become pregnant and that all pregnancies take place in the context of a heterosexual relationship."[50] Michael Toze analyzes the persistent primacy of biological gender in UK legislation as a criterion for determining the relational status of a parent. If gender transition is deemed by the law irrelevant in the determination of one's gendered parental position (i.e., father or mother), the possibility of a pregnancy carried by a trans father constitutes by definition an *adynaton*. Transness disrupts the naturalized alignment not only of sex and gender, but also of gender and kinship position. "Since non-binary gender is not recognised in the UK, non-binary parenthood also remains unaddressed," says Toze, who adds: "Trans masculine people in the media often do need to explicitly confront perceptions that pregnancy invalidates expressed identity, and that it is simply impossible to be a pregnant man."[51] Toze analyzes, in particular, the language of the 2004 Gender Recognition Act: "Though a person is regarded as being of the acquired gender, the person will retain their original status as either father or mother of a child. The continuity of parental rights and responsibilities is thus ensured."[52] As Blas Radi observes, "by hiding the ways in which trans subjects are excluded from public policies related to sexual and reproductive health, or by invoking them at a mere rhetorical level," governments operate "in solidarity with passive eugenics."[53] In the onslaught of anti-trans policies across the US—from bans on gender-affirming care to punishment of doctors who provide transition-related services to restrictions on participation in sports and the military—biological sex never stops being assimilated to an ontological and nomological *archê*. By neutralizing the possibility of gender and kinship self-determination, this *archê*, a biological-theological givenness, is seen by its upholders as that which prevents humanity itself from collapsing, though, in fact, it feeds the death-driven illusion of survival without loss, the violent conviction of no future beyond or against cisheteronormativity. Theologically fetishized and thus de-materialized, the biological represents a phantasmic authenticity, a confining given, an abstract being that is self-servingly invoked by the heterosexist Symbolic as an unbreachable hindrance, an inescapable facticity.

I will now consider two episodes, reported by Italian and US media, that illustrate the disorienting effect of reading *Bacchae* at a time when transphobia has converged with reproductive policing. In March 2023, a mural by Italian transgender artist Oliver Vincenzi (aka Kage) depicting a breastfeeding man appeared in Rimini on a street named after martyred preacher Girolamo Savonarola (Figure 3), stirring much scandal at both the local and national level. The bearded, Zeus-like man breastfeeding a baby[54] is wrapped in a rainbow flag, ruptured by the word "Equality," whose middle letter, *A*, is encircled in (socialist) red and thus converted from marker of "origin," "beginning," "birth," or nomological *archê* into a stylized, anarchic symbol of transgenderism. The light blue at the bottom of the mural—the lowest band of the queer rainbow flag—merges into a liquid earth, blending ground and water, a flowing foundation or the anti-foundation of amniotic fluid confused with the marine expanse (Rimini is the most popular non-elite beach town in Italy). This immersion of the individual body in elementality, an aquatic ground, an

Figure 3 Oliver Vincenzi, Kage, *Uomo che allatta*. Rimini.

expansive sphere of being beyond human kinship, is an intimation of what we might call trans* deindividuation, the transformation of birth and gestation into a collective experience, a communist project, into a *mothering* that involves the trans-familial, trans-national LGBTQIA+ community.[55] Trans-deindividuation is also encapsulated here in the two profile heads' minimal details—little more than the thick black contours delimiting the facial surfaces that emerge from the colorful assemblage of the flag. A formal interchangeability of anatomical parts comes into view between the circular faces of parent and child, on the one hand, and the trans-father's breasts and legs on the other. This possibility of redefining, recrafting the terms of biologically sexed corporeality—of re- or un-gendering it—was effaced a few days after the debut of the mural, when it was covered up by a thick layer of chalky paint in an effort to render trans-parentality invisible, to relegate the collective of trans-deindividuation to a sanitized abyss of buried impossibilities, to fold it into a sanctimonious, barely transparent churchy veil. What is remarkable about this unremarkable episode of anti-trans violence in Italy—followed by the not-much-commented-on case of a Brazilian trans woman beaten by the police in Milan—is that the state applauded the vandals' act while drawing on art-historical arguments concerning the dignified conventions of the Christian art of maternity.[56] The undersecretary of culture in the current government—an art critic and TV personality who insistently calls himself "liberal" (in the European sense, referring to economic "freedom")—proclaimed that whitewashing the mural "was the perfect solution." As he put it, "The people do not want to see that garbage." In his view, the anonymous vandals "defended everyone's freedom" against someone (the artist) who "had foisted his personal viewpoint upon others and for this reason was punished by the people." The artist's "blasphemy" was aesthetic as well as ethico-religious. That a lactating (trans-)father is "an image against nature, against the sacred principle of maternity," the undersecretary argued, is demonstrated by the artist's "misguided" attribution to a father of a posture codified by Medieval and Renaissance religious art as distinctly, exclusively maternal. The art-historical convention recalled and endorsed here is the same one that informs Adriana Cavarero's feminist theorization of "inclination." In her analysis of Leonardo da Vinci's iconic *Virgin and Child with Saint Anne* (1510), which she casts as an innovation in the representation of Mary, Cavarero notes that "the oblique line that traverses the painting"—the geometric form of Mary's caring orientation toward the baby Jesus—"is a matrilineal line," the visualization of the Mother as "the *name* for an inclination toward the other" or "for a function that summons the requisite responsibility in the inaugural scene of a human condition in which the absolutely vulnerable . . . becomes an essential figure, first for ontology and politics, and then for ethics."[57] Even though the second part of this quotation encompasses the possibility of a genderless "function," Cavarero seems to defer to the maternal as the privileged direction of the slantwise gaze of the vulnerable. (Looking at the painting alongside the climactic scene of *Bacchae* might lead us to construe Agave's act as one of perverted care.)[58] Responding to Cavarero, Butler brings out the queer dimension of her ethical phenomenology of inclination, gently noting the risk of essentialist generalization implicit in giving the specific name of "motherhood" to the relational ontology of care.[59] The trans-parental "scandal" of the mural, where the trans father, according to Cavarero, would symbolically become (if not biologically remain) the mother, resides not just in the collapse of cisheteronormativity, but, more subtly, in the blurring of the caring and the cared-for figure. As Butler argues, "the inclining figure" and "the upright figure" are "*not* radically distinct and never fully oppositional"[60]; rather, "to be upright" (that is, masculine, paternal) "means to have emerged from an inclination of some kind, a leaning out, a losing of balance, risking potentially disastrous encounter with unwilled gravity that can break a body."[61] The never fully archived temptation of essentialist, rather than queer, feminism—a *pharmakon* against the unbearable of gender and kinship trouble—can align, despite itself, with reproductive injustice. Like the Renaissance pyre that reduced to ashes the unruly body of the excommunicated Savonarola, the stratum of papal whiteness blanking out trans-fatherhood cannot fully obscure evanescent impressions, cindery traces troubling homogenization, whose absent presence subverts the transphobic mutilation of freedom and self-determination, causing the eye to strain itself to perceive the never fully perceptible, an intractable opacity.

In the summer of 2022, during a Senate hearing following the US Supreme Court's decision to overturn Roe v. Wade and thus to allow individual states to make abortion illegal, the Republican senator from Missouri Josh Hawley[62] interrogated Khiara Bridges, a professor at the UC Berkeley School of Law, who had been invited to share her expertise in family law, children's rights, and reproductive rights. It is worth dwelling on an excerpt of their exchange on reproductive justice:

Hawley: You've referred to "people with a capacity for pregnancy." Would that be women?

Bridges: Many women, cis women, have the capacity for pregnancy. Many cis women do not have the capacity for pregnancy. There are also trans men who are capable of pregnancy, as well as non-binary people who are capable of pregnancy.

Hawley: So this isn't really a women's rights issue. It's . . . it's what?

Bridges: We can recognize that this impacts women while also recognizing that it impacts other groups: those things are not mutually exclusive, Senator Hawley. I want to recognize that your line of questioning is transphobic and it opens up trans people to violence by not recognizing them.

Hawley: You're saying that I'm opening up people to violence by asking whether or not women are the folks who can have pregnancies? . . . I'm denying that trans people exist by asking you if you're talking about women having pregnancies?

Bridges: Do you believe that men can get pregnant?

Hawley: No, and that leads to violence?

The discursive violence of commonsensical logic relies here and in *Bacchae* on the instrument of the rhetorical question ("Would that be women?")—a speech act that reinstates what the speaker wants their audience to take as an indisputable fact, nothing but an occasion for uttering a communal, choral "yes" or "no," with no space for dissent. Reporting to the Theban/Athenian community, vicariously enfleshed onstage by the Chorus, the stranger's nonsensical claim "that Dionysus is a god, that he was wrapped in Zeus's thigh" (242–43), Pentheus asks, "Isn't that horrible and worthy of strangling / that this stranger, whoever he is, has this arrogant behavior (*hubreis hubrizein*)?" (246–47). We can locate a similar accusation of hubris in Hawley's questions, which aim to stir outrage in his audience by casting himself as the victim of Bridges's violation of common sense, her "speaking from the place of the unspeakable,"[63] her assault on the (biological) reality principle, an elitist ruination of all that is reasonable and good. With a mix of prejudiced mistrust and phony candor, Hawley as a defender of universal values reverses the directionality of transphobic violence, as though the true violence were against an innocent, infantilized *dêmos* forced to enter the abyss of the impossible. Denying trans reproductive rights is concomitant, in Hawley's speech, with his attempt to sever abortion from the realm of women's rights. If "woman"—so goes Hawley's argument—is no longer an adequate denomination for individuals endowed with the capacity of giving birth, then pregnancy or its interruption can no longer be considered a woman's right. Making a case for trans-parentality, in this frame of mind, cancels out abortion rights, which, caught in the spiral of his own rhetoric, Hawley seems, thus, to be defending. As acts that equally if differently challenge the patriarchal grip on the fetus, the subordination of the child to heteronormative futurity, and the biopolitical surveillance of body, gender, and kinship, trans pregnancy and abortion are easily targeted together, even if opportunistically pitted against each other.

Contrastively intertwined with Dionysus's trans-birth, the *sparagmos* that closes the play, a child murdered by a parent, evokes the imaginary of fetal dismemberment. "Dismemberment abortion" is the phrase customarily employed (instead of "dilation and evacuation") by right-wing voices to describe, with graphic self-indulgence, pregnancies interrupted in the last trimester. Genevieve Marnon, the legislative director of Right to Life of Michigan, defines "dismemberment abortion" as one in which the provider "deliberately and intentionally uses any instrument . . . to dismember a living fetus by disarticulating limbs or decapitating the head from the fetal torso and removing the dismembered fetal body parts from the uterus."[64] According to *The Catholic Voice of Omaha*, a former abortion counselor converted to the anti-abortion cause after witnessing the brutality of the procedure: "She detailed how the little baby pulled its leg away from the abortionist's forceps and curled into a fetal position to further avoid the forceps. She could see the little fetus fighting for its life and realized the baby could feel pain."[65] In one of the most recent legislative efforts to criminalize abortion, US Representative Debbie Lesko, a Republican from Arizona, proposed a ban on "dismemberment abortion," which she described as

> causing the death of an unborn child, knowingly dismembering a living unborn child and extracting such unborn child one piece at a time or intact but crushed from the uterus through the use of clamps, grasping forceps, tongs, scissors or similar instruments that . . . slice, crush, or grasp a portion of the unborn child's body in order to cut or rip it off or crush it.

In all these accounts, the descriptive language is deeply immersed in the affective *jouissance* of horrorism, in the "violence that, not content merely to kill because killing would be too little, aims to destroy the uniqueness of the body, tearing at its constitutive vulnerability."[66] The rhetoric releases a death-driven aesthetics—with a tragic fetishization of the fantasized horror, a cathexis to gory detail—that performs, if only verbally, the crime it condemns. The speech act that launches the law into the world is implicated in the sparagmatic mutilation it purports simply to record.[67] The resonance of these accounts with the climactic moment of Euripides' play— Agave's dismemberment of Pentheus, whose fetal regression is emblematized by his reduction to a bundle of flesh (1125–36)[68]—is chilling. In Anne Carson's rendition:

> Seizing his left arm by the wrist
> she planted her foot against his ribs
> and ripped the arm off at the shoulder—
> not by her own strength, the god made it easy.
> Meanwhile Ino was working away at the other side
> stripping the meat from the bone,
> and Autonoe with the whole mob of Bakkhai
> attacked.

It was one float of hideous sound—
him gasping and groaning,
them shrieking their war cry.
One carried off an arm, another a foot still in its shoe,
his ribs were laid bare of flesh
and every woman
drenched in blood
for they were playing ball with his body parts.[69]

The perverse fascination with dismemberment shaping abortion legislation is a version of a fear of (and repressed desire for) destruction. This feared destruction, like the catastrophic collapse dramatized at the end of *Bacchae*, has driven the anti-trans backlash promoted, as Butler puts it in a talk drawing from *Who's Afraid of Gender?*, by "political formations in which the teaching of gender is understood as 'ideology' or 'indoctrination,' where 'gender' is figured as a destructive force equivalent to a nuclear bomb or the rise of totalitarianism, or where gender is understood as a term and a power that can, or will, strip one of one's sexed sense of self."[70] For Butler, the fear of gender is based on a "psychosocial phantasm," an all-encompassing feeling or an affective overload. In *Bacchae*, the fear felt by Pentheus, and potentially the whole Theban community, is fueled by a viral "phantasm"—Dionysus himself, Dionysian intoxication, and circulating gender trouble, the apocalyptic menace of a transgender pandemic.

Though, later in the chapter, I will discuss some implications of Pentheus's fetal *sparagmos* in light of Butler's own position on abortion rights, especially in *Frames of War* (2009), I want to conclude this section by re-considering an early preview of Pentheus's dismemberment. Overanalysis, a formalistic re-reading spurred by Butler's generative idea of the bond as a break, will occupy the rest of the chapter, helping us position the play's reflection on kinship trouble within a wide web of critical-theoretical relations implicating transness, trans-parentality, and interspecies (un)becoming. This is the threat that Pentheus launches against Dionysus, voicing a naive intention to capture the immaterial, to chain a viral diffusion (239–41):

If I catch him inside this land,
I will make him stop beating his thyrse and shaking
(*pausô ktupounta thurson anaseionta te*)

his hair, cutting his neck off his body
(*komas, trachêlon sômatos chôris temôn*).

As Pentheus utters this threat, he anticipates his own decapitation, a breach of the corporeal bond, of the assemblage of individuated, kin parts that form the assemblage we call body. Pentheus's vow evinces the parallelism between the illusion of bodily unity and the fantasy of political sovereignty. An impression of a Dionysian break in corporeal integrity through wild kinesis—a shaking of the hair, a tossing of the head into space, eerily suggestive of an impetus toward self-decapitation—the enjambed phrase *anaseionta te / komas* ruptures syntactical unity, leaving a coordinating conjunction, "and" (*te*), in suspension. This bond made mobile, left in abeyance, located on the precipice of a void of possibility, is also a figuration of minor kinships, of bonds that can be tightened by their own predisposition toward breakability. A head thrown back, shaking, seems almost the object of a somatechnical operation, the self-rupturing of a body in transition.[71] This gestural agitation also has post-gestational resonances—as though the hair were a baby being delivered into the air in a prolonged labor. The transfer of an internal/external quasi-organ into a new space, the release of such an organ from a bounded container, or the self-unburdening of this container—the bodily transformations encompassed by delivery enable us to look at childbirth as a moment of transness. In the "shaken hair" of Dionysus on the edge of the line, imitated by the Maenads, we discover a breach that joins—a body part separated from the whole that becomes a supplement. I am suggesting that the forbidden movement is a reconfiguration of the body, a breach in a bond or a bond in a breach that recalls Zeus's Dionysian trans pregnancy, the transfer of pregnancy from Semele to Zeus enabled by a double cut. Just as Pentheus's evocation of Dionysian hair shaking portends his death—already enfolding him in the Maenadic pack that he desperately strives to exclude—the chiastic pairing of *anaseionta te / komas* ("shaking the hair") and *trachêlon ... temôn* ("cutting off the neck"), an interobjective juxtaposition and a subject/object dichotomy, insinuates the instability of the latter. Although *komas*, "hair" (accusative), is governed by *anaseionta* (accusative modifying Dionysus), their shared objectality suggests a softening of hierarchical positions. The Maenadic motion cutting the air shakes the grammar, assimilating the anthropomorphic-divine actor, the subject of *anaseionta*, and a fortiori the proximate human, to that which is acted upon—like Pentheus's head, soon to be reduced to a macabre relic. This interobjectivity fills the gap in the parental kinship intimated in the very gesture of shaking the hair; but it also foretells that the body that shakes and bends one of its constitutive parts may be subjected to the same shaking and bending. The bodily assemblage that calls itself subject cannot be entirely distinguished from the part; it is formally sandwiched between two individual parts or objects, a thyrse and hair, which press upon it, impressing on it their rhizomatic character, their liminal status between singularity and plurality, inside and outside. Interobjectivity—not just a placement of the ostensible subject alongside (or among) objects, but a subject's tending toward assimilation to the object—approximates trans-species un-becoming, the quivering of a crossing with no telos.[72] The horizontality of *thurson anaseionta te komas trachêlon*—wherein the thyrse is almost conflated with the figure who brandishes it—flattens the syntax, configuring an "intertwinement," to use a concept dear to Butler, in this case of the human and vegetal, of equal objects.[73] Such an intertwinement bespeaks the notional self's predication on, co-implication with, the outside that exceeds and undoes it. A working *within*, *between*, and *across* realms and categories, this intertwinement—an "interdependency that moves beyond the ontology of isolated individuals encased in discrete bodies"[74]—is a form of transness in its own right.

Trans-parental Troubles

The kinship trouble—always mingled with gender trouble—begins in Dionysus's prologic self-introduction, in the third line, *Semelê locheutheis' astrapêphorôi puri* ("Semele midwived by lightning-carrying fire"). Semele's encounter with Zeus is cast as an intimacy on the edges of human or anthropomorphic embodiment, an intercourse with fire, with the elemental principle rather than with the god within it. A few lines later, this masculine fire, which already appears quasi-pregnant, as it is said to "carry lightning" (*astrapê-phorôi*),[75] morphs into a grammatically transgender entity, "the fire's (*puros*) living flame (*zôsan phloga*)" (8), so that the feminine flame, a remainder of the incinerated Semele, hauntologically constitutes the masculine fire. In the continuation of Dionysus's narrative, gender trouble slips into gestational trouble. The phrase that singles out the women of Thebes—the instruments of Dionysus's revenge—is the uncanny *to thêlu sperma* (35), "the race of women," literally, "female seed" (!), in which the adjective for "female" is itself neuter. The disruptive literality of the phrase, its violation of biological "common sense," cries for critical attention, while the ensuing parenthetical—"those who were women" (*hosai / gunaikes êsan* 35–36)—which has troubled textual critics and commentators,[76] may amount to a retraction of the verbal scandal, a palinodic softening. This phrase, one could say, exemplifies the Deleuzian-Guattarian becoming other that, as Wohl argues,[77] shapes the play's contestation of Oedipal sexuality; but the apparent *adynaton* of "female seed"—almost a symmetrical counterpart to Zeus's "male womb" queerly referenced later on[78]—captures the play's thematics of trans-parentality in the microcosm of tragic form. In a narrative that is all about lineage and descent, Dionysus's contagious transformation of the Theban women also resembles an act of delivery. The frenzied language describing the wives-turned-Maenads seems to reflect Dionysus's own birth as a marginalized god; his ressentiment, released into the world like a baby, has engendered the "rebirth" of Theban wives. Not dissimilar from the lightning borne and unleashed by Zeus, the emotional burden of the god, his anger, sprung out into the world, has provoked multiple exits or deliveries, pushing the women *out of* their houses (*ek domôn* 32; *ex-emêna dômatôn* 36) and *out of* their minds (*para-kopoi phrenôn* 33), or *out of* their head—which, in Zeus's case, served as a uterine container for Athena.

Through Pentheus's vigorous yet traumatized voice—stuttering, broken—the state manifests an anxiety that multiplies the scandal of Dionysus's trans birth while striving to ward it off. Already under the spell of Dionysus, Pentheus inadvertently bears out what he denies in the very moment that he mentions the name of Zeus (***Dios*** 243), which is not just resonant with but is swallowed by the son Dionysus (***Dio****nuson* 242) in a patent re-enactment and inversion of Zeus's cannibalism of Mêtis and, especially, of his pregnancy, the "stitching" (*erraphthai*) of the fetal Dionysus in his thigh (*en mêrôi* 243). While reporting (and shedding doubt on) the circumstances of the birth of Dionysus—swaddled *in, within* the container of Zeus's lower body—Pentheus unwittingly shows Zeus to be fetally wrapped within the receptacle of Dionysus's name. The name, the primary instrument of Symbolic interpellation, in this case, betrays Pentheus, rebels against the state's wish to bind it to its design of normative rectitude. The uncontainable suggestiveness of the preposition *en* intimates another impossible possibility—that while the father gestates the son, the son gestates the father. Interrupting Pentheus's account, the sudden appearance of Tiresias and Cadmus in female attire—a sight ironically presented as a *thauma*, a portent blending into the portents that the seer customarily interprets—reads almost like a hallucination, the materialization of the viral spread (the "trans epidemic") that Pentheus is seeking to extinguish.[79] Just as the Erinyes, at the end of Aeschylus's *Libation Bearers*, occupy a zone between materiality and immateriality, apprehension and self-deception, perception and illusion, the epiphany of Tiresias and Cadmus may well realize Pentheus's fear and, at the same time, simply externalize onstage—in an (im)material space of mimetic lifedeath, of ghostly reality[80]—an obsessive feeling, a "psychosocial phantasm," the outpouring of terror that gender trouble contagiously provokes. While Pentheus chastises Cadmus, his grandfather, the father of his mother, commanding him to cast off the thyrse and the other Dionysian paraphernalia, his words seem to take on a restorative or reparative ring structure through the graphic resonance of the phrases "father of my mother" and "my mother's father," which occur respectively at the beginning and at the end of the line, closing the circle, foreclosing alternative configurations of kinship (250, 254):

patera te mêtros tês emês . . .
. . . emês mêtros pater

Yet in a play in which the father (Zeus) becomes the mother, the syntactical juxtaposition of "father" and "mother" visualizes the possibility of a contact, an exchange, an intertwinement between the maternal and the paternal. In line 254—*eleutheran / thursou methêseis cheir', emês mêtros pater* ("Won't you liberate your hand of the thyrse, you, father of my mother?"), the "liberation" of Cadmus's hand from the contaminating symbol of Dionysian worship coincides with the command to break a human-vegetal intertwinement (*thursou . . . cheira*) that is syntactically parallel to *mêtros pater* (where *mêtros*, like *thursou*, is in the genitive case). It is as though Pentheus is at once seeking to liberate the paternal from a contaminating entanglement with a thyrse-like maternity, from a desire for mothering that, as the genitive suggests, has taken possession of the father. Pentheus wants to break up an intertwinement that is predicated on the breaking of the distinction of father and mother.

The chiastic construction that connects the opposite edges of lines 250–54 (*patera ... mêtros ... mêtros pater*) emblematizes the breaking of the bond or the breach that is the bond. As David Quint writes of Virgil's insistently chiasmic style:

> In a perfect chiasmus the two sides exchange terms and may be themselves interchangeable. The reversal chiasmus effect is ... a kind of *double cross*: it sets up a binary opposition only to break it down; it gives one value to one side of an opposition only to load it with the value to which it had been initially been opposed.... When spread over the course of a narrative, the pattern of chiasmus can partake in or resemble *ring composition*. ... Virgil radicalizes the sense of reversibility of these *concentric* forms in the *Aeneid*, their potential inversion of meaning and collapse of distinction: A and B risk becoming identical.[81]

As a result of chiastic concentricity, *father* is *mother*, and vice versa. Butler discusses chiasmus in *Senses of the Subject* (2015), where, referring to Merleau-Ponty's theorization of haptics, they observe that "the acts of seeing and being seen, of touching and being touched, recoil upon one another ... become chiastically related to one other"; that "touched and touching form a chiasmic and irreducible relation"; and that "it is on the basis of this irreducible and nonconceptualizable figure ... that we apprehend the world."[82] In the essay on *Bacchae*, the relations between Pentheus and Dionysus and between humanity and animality are conceptualized through the formal category of concentricity:

> When both Pentheus and Dionysus assume feminine form, it starts a series of misrecognitions that culminate with the *confusion between* animal and human forms.... Shall we conclude that the *trans*position of gender, one that already took place when Zeus violently usurped the gestational process, continues as Dionysus beguiles with his feminine form, and Pentheus becomes a dancing woman? In the course of those *trans*itions, Agave sees that young mountain lion and moves in for the kill. What makes those *trans*itions possible? Is it that there are already affinities, if not forms of kinship, *between* the one gender and the other, and between human and animal, such that they can become *confused with* one another? It is not that Pentheus is really a man, and not a woman, or really a woman at the moment

> his mother sees him, and not an animal, although that is one way to describe the sequence and even one way to try to make it right. The change from one gender to the other and then the move *into* animality articulate relations that work *transversally across* established kinship ties. Those ties represent forms of affinity that work *through* metonymy and *concentricity*, not following the rules of kinship based on claims of paternity and maternity.[83]

Here, with the intense, nervous prepositionality in Butler's crescendo of theoretical interrogation, kinship and gender troubles, working *transversally* and *concentrically*, through barely visible interstices, in impossible motions *across* and *with(in)* materialized in poetic form, implicate species trouble. Butler's discussion of Euripides' play converges with critiques of species discourse that have fostered a sustained dialogue between trans theory and animal studies. For example, Abraham Weil theorizes trans-animality, or tranimacy, as an experiment in "thinking the animal *transversally,* showing . . . that species shift, and are stirred by agitations in composition with an infinite number of possibilities."[84] Weil's commitment to trans-animality is motivated, like Butler's interest in trans-parentality and transversal kinship, by the goal of "plac[ing] the body in precarious relation to the nonhuman, subhuman, or inhuman" and thus articulating a "*transversal* relation, or alternative politics."[85] Re-reading *Bacchae* together with Butler means, as we will see, building, in Weil's words, a "transversal link between the affective dimensions of the animal and the provocation of the pollinating of trans*."[86]

Somatechnics and Trans-deindividuation

In Tiresias's response to Pentheus's outraged announcement of the foreigner's perilous arrival, the account of Dionysus's birth multiplies the subliminal intimations of parturition. At the same time, it enacts a somatechnical trans-formalism, in which the operations of "breaking" (*rhêgnumi*) and "suturing" (*rhaptô*) release an aspirated intensity, an aerial expressivity that reconfigures the conceptual terms of the Dionysian plague, of the "trans pandemic." While attempting to rationalize the circumstances of Dionysus's birth—playing on the phonic similarity of "thigh" (*mêros*) and "hostage" (*homêros*)—Tiresias makes them, in fact, messier (286–97):

> Are you mocking [Dionysus] for *having been sewn* (*en-errhaphê*) in Zeus's *thigh* (*mêrôi*)? I'll explain to you that this is all right. After Zeus had seized him from the thunderbolt's fire and had brought him as an infant to Olympus, Hera wanted to expel (*ek-balein*) him from the sky. But Zeus, being a god, *engineered a scheme in response to* (*ant-emêchanêsato*) Hera: breaking some part (*rhêxas meros ti*) of the sky that encircles the earth, he gave this as a hostage (*homêron*), delivering (*ek-titheis*) Dionysus from Hera's hatred. With time, mortals said that he was sewn up (*rhaphênai*) in the thigh (*en mêrôi*) of Zeus, changing the word (*onoma*)—because as a god he had served as a hostage (*hômêreuse*) to the goddess—and making up the story.

While, in Tiresias's account, Zeus's deliverance (*ek-titheis*) of his son from his wife's hostility replicates his childbirth only metaphorically, Hera's expulsion of Dionysus from Olympus reads as an interrupted gestation that, in the transmitted story, will necessitate Zeus's somatechnic intervention. The position of the overstretched, monstrous verb *antemêchanêsat(o)* in the middle of a line (291) bookended by two short words (*Zeus . . . theos*) configures a formal dynamic—the opening of solid, bound nominality into the processuality of a verbal compound—that brings to mind what trans theorists have called *transmogrification*.[87] Notwithstanding commentators' desire to reduce the fanciful logic of Tiresias's retelling to a clear series of events—a desire parallel to Tiresias's intention to set the record straight—what seems to demand attention is the onomastic transition, the morphing of the name *homêros* ("hostage") into *(ho) mêros* ("the thigh"), by which a human is surrendered to a bodily part. *Onoma* ("name") becomes *sôma* ("body"); the whole, a part; captivity, the nomadic condition of an unstructured organ, of an organ without body; the continuous making of Dionysus (through divine maneuvers and their echoes among humans), a question of *trans-form*.[88] There are, in fact, multiple levels of *trans-form* layering the phonic and graphic design (or the somatechnics) of these lines. With their aspirated excess, a concentration of somatic vibrations and roughened air, the apparently oppositional operations of "breaking" and "stitching"—*rhêxas* (from *rhêgnumi*) and *rhaphênai* (from *rhaptô*), respectively—issue forth a transformative intensity perceptible in the striking phonetic triangulation of the words *meros* ("part"), *homêron* ("hostage"), *mêrôi* ("thigh"), each the product of minimal variations and reciprocal influencing, the outcome of a slight intervention on, or working through, the other. The play of removal and supplementation tying these three words together—by which a phonetic sequence is altered through the addition of an individual syllable or the lengthening of a vowel—brings trans somatechnics into Tiresias's speech, in spite of his effort to erase Zeus's trans-parenting. This revisionism conjures a collapse of linguistic and human matter, on the one hand, and the flesh of the world (of the *kosmos*, implicated here by *aithêr*), on the other. In a context where *meros*—"the part" of the human body and of the sky—self-reflexively signposts the transing brought about by the somatechnics of supplementation and subtraction, by the plasticity of formal flesh, the reconceived birth of Dionysus articulates an expansion of the anthropomorphic nature of divine ontology into the atmosphere—almost an atmospheric conception and gestation.[89] The synergic rhoticity of trans-parental "break" (*rhêxas*) and "suture" (*rhaphênai*) determines a surplus of aspiration, an aerial roughness and thickness that reflect back or directly act on Tiresias's "correction" of *mêros* into *homêros* (a word that aspirates *mêros* besides supplementing it with an extra syllable).[90] Operating through aspiration, through a surplus of aerial matter[91]—both in Zeus's trans-parental gestation and in Tiresias's feeble attempt to cancel it, to turn it *merely* into linguistic play—transness amounts not to a pandemic (the spread of a disease in the atmosphere), but to the possibility of a radical environmental bonding, an escape from the captivity of biological sexedness—a regendering implicated with ungendering—that engenders a fugitive movement toward (un)becoming transcorporeal flesh, what we call air.[92] Peter Szendy has conceptualized air as "the ontological structure of general exchangeability," a definition in agreement with Butler's view of "breathability" as "the social character of air" in *What World Is This?*[93]

At the end of the dialogue with Tiresias, when Pentheus cries, "Don't touch me! . . . Don't you dare put your hand on me, but go to enjoy your Bacchanalia, and don't you wipe your folly on me (*mêd' ex-o<u>mor</u>xêi <u>môr</u>ian tên sên emoi* 344)!," his barely disguised terror of (and desire for) contagion[94] enacts contagion through the stuttering of language.[95] The echoing effect between *ex-omorxêi* ("[don't] you wipe") and *môrian* ("folly"), haunted by the "part" (*meros/morion*)—and the "doom" (*moros*) attached to it—that marks Dionysus's trans-birth, manifests the assimilative potency of breath, of air's transcorporeality.[96] The juxtaposition of the possessive pronouns and adjectives *tên sên* ("your") and *emoi* ("me") in the line materializes the leaky proximity between discrete identities—the grammatical femininity of Tiresias's ostensible *madness* touching, syntactically intermingling with, a notionally solid "I." The gender contagion of Dionysus—a god manifesting himself as smoke, incense, and a seductive, Orientalized aroma—expresses the elementality of air, the material transness that is the substance of life.[97] Gender "purity" or gender unmixedness—or the notion of gender as such, which always presupposes discreteness even when it contests it[98]—encodes an illusory boundedness and sovereignty that can suffocate life, make it unlivable and unbreathable, that strips away the air, the matter of trans-deindividuation.[99]

In the second part of the play, the Maenads' butchering of animal flesh, which stretches poetic form to the breaking point through representational horrorism, congeals into phonic emanations of a mortal wound with a force of assimilation that spreads an excessive bond. The residual mooing of the innocent victim of Maenadic fury strives to break out of the homogenizing container of the Messenger's account: "You would have seen one of the Maenads (*tên men*) holding (*echousan*) apart in her hands a well-uddered heifer (*euthêlon porin*), mooing (*mukômenên*)" (737–38). Even as *mukômenên* ("mooing") modifies the heifer, the juxtaposition of the victim with the victimizer (another feminine accusative singular) in the same line forges a confusing syntactical bond, as though the killer were mooing, were being dismembered at the same time as she dismembers. The additional, crypto-masculine identity ascribed to the heifer by the two-ending adjective *eu-thêlon* ("well-uddered")—an infiltration of lactating gender trouble—connects the animal's protesting cries with the mural of the Italian trans-father, but also with the tale of Zeus's trans-maternity, at risk of being erased or normalized by Tiresias's hegemonic narrative. Bending syntax, spreading undifferentiation, the heifer's mooing—the prolonged aural diffusion of a broken body—manifests Dionysian virology, the aerial rupture that cuts across and expands boundaries, bonds, and relationalities, an ongoing transcorporeality.[100] In the choral ode that precedes Dionysus's orchestration of Pentheus's cross-dressing, repeated phonetic mutations constitute an anti-representational representation of an atmospheric bonding that encompasses and shatters all other bonds, an aerial unbecoming (862–76):

Shall I ever, in nocturnal dances,
move my white
foot in bacchic frenzy, throwing
my neck to the *dewy* (*droseron*) aether
like a *fawn* (*nebros*) playing
in the midst of the meadow's green pleasures
after escaping hunters' fearsome
pursuit, liberated from surveillance,
over well-woven nets,
and the houndsman, shouting,
constrains his dogs' *running pace* (*dramêma*),
and the fawn, with *swift-running* (*ôkudromois*) labors,
rushes (*thrôskêi*), a whirlwind, to the plain
by the river, enjoying
liberation, freedom from men (*brotôn*), and the shoots
of the shadowy woods?

Dro-, *bro-*, *dra-*, *dro-*, *thrô-*, *bro*: these fragments of individual words—the verbal containers that they belong to—craft novel bonds, unbound ties, within the corpus of the lyric section. The deterritorialization from becoming animal to becoming imperceptible that, following a typical Deleuzian schema,[101] we can read into the choral voice's self-assimilation first to a fawn and then to a whirlwind is marked by the transition from simile to metaphor, by the fading out of "as." A human neck becoming dew, dew becoming a fawn, a fawn transmuted into canine kinesis, animal movement stretched into stormy motion: in the unbecoming resulting from these transitions, individualized bonds are subsumed within the intoxicated elementality of Dionysian, theatrical air, which manifests itself as it makes and breaks verbal and phonic aggregations in the infectious substance of inbetweenness.

Enjambment and Watery Trans-corporeality

In the choral retelling of Zeus's trans-parentality, trans-corporeality is watery, as Dionysus is revealed to be the product of plural *mothering*, a *reproductive communism*, that involves a Theban river goddess, Dirce (519–36):[102]

Daughter of Acheloos,
queen Dirce, beautiful virgin,
for you, in your streams,
took Zeus's baby,
when, with his thigh (*mêrôi*), from the immortal fire, Zeus,
who had begotten him, snatched him away, shouting this:
"Come, Dithyrambos, enter
this male womb of mine
(*Ithi, Dithuramb', eman ar-*
sena tande bathi nêdun)."
. . . But you, o blessed Dirce,
you are pushing me away, as I hold
wreath-carrying feasts in you.
Why are you rejecting (*an-ainêi*) me? Why are you escaping from me?
In the future, I swear by the (*nai tan*) cluster-shaped
grace of Dionysus's vine, Bromius will be a concern of yours.

The amniotic liquid of maternity is deterritorialized, transferred outside of the human body and located in non-human waters, whose welcoming currents blend mothering agencies in a way that makes the category of the biological barely tenable.[103] The upshot is a Dionysus who, after losing Semele, undergoes a second gestation through the collaborative efforts of two trans mothers: one embodying the un-becoming of liquidity and the other, Zeus, breaking his masculinity in refashioning a thigh into a womb, as emphasized by the enjambment (*ar-sena*). The enjambment is the formal break that suspends masculinity on the edge of the line, a fleeting interruption of a trans-feminine anatomy.[104] The idea of a masculine womb that comes into view or into being in these lines draws attention to the ambiguity of an adjective, *arsên* ("masculine, male"), which, in its morphological duality—a "two-ending" adjective, whose masculine form can also modify feminine nouns, as it does here—shifts "masculinity" to a kind of gender neutrality, an absenting or co-existence of anatomical markers. Grammatically feminine, Zeus's womb is both "masculine"—a possibility raised yet destabilized by the metrical/syntactical suspension—and non-masculine: it is an un-gendered or over-gendered organ that is both trans-masculine and trans-feminine. A space of cross-ontological communion, Zeus's trans-mothering enacts elemental ungendering, mimetically absorbing water's resistance to partitioning and regimentation, the political constrictions that gendering and regendering impose.[105] While lamenting Dirce's—that is, Thebes'—current hostility to Dionysus, the Chorus performs the liquid fugitivity of trans-form, the unbecoming of watery elementality, from which the king of the gods requested and received surrogate care for his reproductive ends. In the formal recursivity of *an-ainêi . . . nai tan,* the liquid play of composition, decomposition, recomposition, and decomposition again—a watery trans-corporeality—casts "fugitivity" (*ti me pheugeis;*) as an escape from the poles of "yes" (*nai*) and "no," affirmation and negation, visibility and invisibility—some of the deeply divisive poles in the debate on trans and queer theory.[106] A counterforce to the inscriptive capacity of the river—its ability to "spatialis[e] memory" and make it resonate with the impressions of tragic form[107]—this fugitivity mimics the fluvial kinesis of "underflows that well up into the surface, then seep back down the hyporheic," riverine motions surrounding Dionysus, enveloping him in unbound currents of trans-species kinship.[108] The abundance of *an* sounds encrypted in the cited sequence—and in the compound verbs *ana-boasas* and *ana-phainô* (525 and 528)—generates an ongoing flowing of the particle conveying potential, *an* ("may, might"), a marker of what Kevin Quashie calls "subjunctivity," the aliveness of aesthetic potentiality.[109]

Thinking in a theoretical framework influenced by Merleau-Ponty, Butler, and critical phenomenology, Joseph Pugliese observes that "life . . . is, as such, always already intercorporeal—an intextuation of water and flesh bound by permeable and breathing membranes, an autopoietic morphology that is always already bound in an aqueous topology."[110] The surrogate of the amniotic environment that Zeus's divine anatomy cannot reproduce, the riverine water welcoming the fetal Dionysus disrupts the hierarchical positionalities of "mother," "father," and parentality as such by presenting life as "intercorporeal"—an "intextuation"—and the forming of human flesh as an elemental "intertwinement," a word that Butler borrows from Merleau-Ponty to theorize a social ecology of vulnerability, precarity, and interdependence. We can say that Zeus's trans-parentality dramatizes a "topological blurring and enfolding of thresholds between water and living matter," whereby the privileged status of reproductive kinship is decentered as merely one expression of an elemental "kincentric vision in which all entities are inscribed in an affective and ethical ecology."[111] The god of liquidity, gestated in two distinct aqueous environments, Dionysus re-etymologizes "origin" as the very opposite of a fixed point or the punctual coming into being of being.[112] Cognate with *orior* "to rise" but also with *rivus* "river," *origin* nods at a merely notional place where life an-archically springs into the world, into a flowing motion that resists the Symbolic pressure to establish a before and after, to partition rhythm into discrete cadences. Dionysus's trans-parental and trans-elemental birth instantiates what Sophie Lewis, commenting on her own *Full Surrogacy Now: Feminism against Family*, regards as one of the most generative contributions of Paul Preciado's *Testo Junkie* (2008)—that is, the invitation to imagine "more-than-human, genderless (or many-gendered) valences of uterine creativity that point beyond the propertarian dispositif of biogenetic transmission, heredity, parenthood, and the family."[113]

Involved in the gestation of Dionysus, Dirce acquires a quasi-personhood that connects with recent development in environmental law. While writing this chapter in June 2023, I read that the town of Guajara-Mirim in Brazil passed a law, proposed by an Indigenous representative, that extends personhood rights to the endangered Komi Memem river and its tributaries, protecting them and the forests around them.[114] When, in *The Force of Nonviolence* (2020) Butler maintains that "Human creatures living somewhere, requiring soil and water for the continuation of life, are also living in a world where non-human creatures' claim to life clearly overlaps with the human claim,"[115] they are implicitly advocating for similar measures; as environmentalist activists have pointed out, "If the injuries to [a] river are not recognized in court, then they cannot be compensated for, which means that the true costs of environmental impacts may be underestimated."[116]

In the Messenger's report on the Maenads, becoming animal entails a form of interspecies ungendering that reconfigures parentality and reproduction as unmarked bonds—difficult to distinguish from the thick, intricate relationality of being—filling the constitutional gap, the hierarchical breach, between nourisher and nourished, those who parent and those who are parented. In the Messenger's words, the Maenads blend into the herd of cattle—in the neuter gender (*agelaia* 677)—enacting the privileged relation between dramatic chorality and becoming animal that Page duBois, in particular, has illustrated (680–82).[117] The peaceful slumber that the Maenads enjoy in the woods, relaxing *alongside* (*par-eimenai*) the cattle, places them in a liminal condition, a parenthesis of mere life or just living. Before their sparagmatic frenzy, this liminality causes a gentler rupture (of their bodily ties and joints) conducive to ontological rebonding, as signposted by *sômasin* in this line (683): "[The Maenads] were sleeping, all relaxed (*par-eimenai*) in their bodies (*sômasin*)." What is called an intrasubjective "dative of relation"[118] ("*they* ... in *their* bodies") conveys the glimpse of an outward-directed comitative valence ("*they* ... with [*other*] bodies"), for the outcome of the corporeal disjuncture brought about by sleep is a bonding, an intermingling, with, alongside *other* animal bodies. An instrument of corporeal and social reindividuation, sleep here sets off a bodily loosening that translates into intertwinement with plants.[119] While configuring a repose similar to vegetal being, this intertwinement also outlines a deeper communing with leaves, an infiltration into the domain of phyto-somatics, a participation of explicit, marked femininity in the genderlessness (the grammatical "neutrality") of *phulloisi* (684–88):

> *Some* of the women (*hai*) rested (*ereisasai*) their backs on (*pros*) the leaves of fir trees, while *others* (*hai d'*) among oak leaves (*phulloisi*) cast (*balousai*) their heads on (*pros*) the ground, randomly, modestly (*sôphronôs*), not the way you say, inebriated by the mixing bowl and the noise of the pipe, hunting for Aphrodite, abandoned alone in the woods.

The trans-species ungendering, the intermingling intimated here through a surplus of *towardness* (*pros*), deindividuates bonds, achieving an expansive relationality through the counterintuitive eroticism of asexual attachments. Paired with the (para)ontological intermingling—the radical bonding that stems from the breaking of the cage of "gender"[120]—"modest, proper" asexuality becomes the zoo- and phyto-philic "improper" or "wild,"[121] unsettling the limits of relationality, pushing beyond anatomical or para-anatomical exploration.

In the most astonishing moment of the Messenger's account—in which Maenads breastfeed deer and wolves—the trans-speciesism that comes into view undergoes a further twist through Butlerian chiastic intertwinement (700–703):

> Others, having in *their arms* (*an**kala**isi*) a deer or the wild cubs of *wolves* (***lukôn***),
> had given them *white milk* (***leukon gala***),

> those who, *having just given birth* (*neo-tokois*), still had a swollen *breast*, and their babies they *had left behind* (*lipousais*); they placed on their heads crowns of ivy (*kissinous*), and of oak and of flowering yew.

As a result of a formal and somatic intertwinement (***ankalaisi*** *... lukôn / ... leukon ...* ***gala*** 699–700), the maternal arms dissolve into milk. At the same time, an effect of anatomic reshuffling—what Preciado might call "a mutating somatheque"[122]—makes arms barely distinguishable from breasts, a supplement or a replacement of breasts. Another consequence of the chiasmus is the transformation of milk's "whiteness" into a space for trans-animality, the substance of a human-lupine intertwinement. We can imagine the Maenads breastfeeding wolf cubs with their arms; but we can also view their milk as a lupine substance, a kind of "wild" liquidity—the whiteness (*leukon*) of milk nearly indistinguishable from the word for "wolf" (*lukôn*). Not just feeding the cubs, the Maenads' milk is "of the wolves"; it *belongs* to them. In that sense, their lactation is an act of reparation for the dispossessed cubs, a restoration of dispossessed liquid substance to its ostensible "origin." This reworking of what belongs to whom and even of what "belonging" means contests the very notion of origin, demonstrating the potentialities of Dionysian trans-form, of the new bonds that are formed in the break of verbal, somatic, and familial structures.[123] The Maenadic mothers are not only the nourishers, but also the nourished—their bodied filled with a lupine liquidity that they, in turn, release into animal bodies.[124] As arms supplement or replace breasts, and human milk turns into the liquid "lupine being"—the substance of wildness in an apparent act of domestication—we discover the subjunctive force of the adjacencies (and overlaps) of breaking and bonding that, in the play, inform the various manifestations of trans-parenting and trans-speciesism. In the final lines of the passage, the appearance of a single, swollen breast in the masculine gender (*mastos ... spargôn*) activates phallic resonances, exemplifying the Freudian correspondence between the two anatomic protrusions.[125] More importantly, the breast casts a shadow on the mismatched phrase (*neotokois ... lipousais*) that opens the line—the masculine ending (*-ois*) of the two-ending adjective *neotokois* juxtaposed with a feminine one (*-ais*)—another marker of transgender reproduction, of parenting beyond the apparent limits of anatomical sexedness that language, in its interpellation, conventionally enforces.[126] In line 702, the syntactical interleaving of male vegetality (*kissinous*) and female humanity (*lipousais*) that punctuation, a Greek colon, both suggests and disavows while the Maenads crown themselves with varied foliage is another intimation of the trans-corporeality brought about by the break as a bond, by a rupture that connects, unraveling the exclusionary constraints of kinship, subjecting it to minoritarian possibilities of dispossessive intertwinement.[127]

A defamiliarization of the mechanics of reproduction also informs the ecological wonders recounted in the first Messenger speech. Quivering fountains spring from the soil trodden upon by the tread of the Maenads. In the hands of a Maenad (*tis*), the thrusting of a phallic thyrse (*thurson*) against a rock (*petra*) reads as an interobjective clash of two feminine masculinities (Maenadic penetrator and hard feminine rock), while the verb indicating the "blow" (*epaisen*), in the middle of the line—which is itself bookended by the two agents (*thurson* . . . *epaisen* . . . *petran* 704)—delivers the specter of a child (*pai*).[128] Even though the interobjective encounter is orchestrated by the hand of a Maenad, the indefinite pronoun *tis* depersonalizes this procreative act, in which the objectal projections of queer genitals seem to be subsumed into decentered parental roles. The dewy spring produced by this erotic friction "jumps out" (*ek-pêdai* 705) of the *petra*—a masculine womb or a lesbian phallus[129]—like an infant. The subsequent lines stage another scene of queer/trans procreation, as a second Maenad (*allê* 706) drives another Dionysian phallic prosthesis—a "giant fennel" (706)—into the earth, giving birth to a stream of wine, which Dionysus himself delivers (*ex-anêke* 707) as both a mother and a midwife. Dionysus—the unnamed, unnameable god closing the loop of the verse structure (*allê* . . . / . . . *theos* 706–7)—is both the maternal god, and the (liquid) son delivered by this mother. The bond between a Maenad and Dionysus—trans-father and trans-mother, respectively—reproduces by breaking the very logic of reproduction, by stretching it into a kind of parthenogenesis, which reproduces the broken bond of Semele with her son. Impressions of Dionysus's fetal movements are overlaid onto the Messenger's account, when, reconstructing his "leaping out" (*ex-epêdês'*) from the secret spot (***loch**mên* 730) where he lies in wait for Agave, he re-creates Dionysus's unconventional gestation (***loch**os*), the god's sudden, traumatic exit from his mother's womb before finding his second womb. An overdetermined break—the breach of the secrecy, the interruption of the crouching body's quiescence, the violence of the attack—emerges from a disavowed desire for a bond. In the Messenger's reaching out for Agave, in the violent verb *sun-arpasai* ("to seize")—an impulse for relationality to fill the void left by his "emptying out" (*kenôsas* 730) the ambush spot—the ambiguity of this sudden physical projection toward a mother is encoded in the prefix *sun*: it is the marker of the bond in the break, or of the break (of time, of "natural" gestation) as a bond that scars Dionysus while prompting the proliferation of alternative procreative scenarios. The filial-parental bond proves to be *trauma*, a tearing of the empty space, of the notional zone of solitude or self-absorption that, in our fantasies, precedes the encounter with the other.[130] Here the Butlerian notion of the break as the bond, which I am reading into this scene, may intersect with the position of Lauren Berlant, whose *On the Inconvenience of Other People*, their last book, theorizes the sense of initial discomfort, the feeling of psychological and aesthetic rupture occurring at the moment of the bond, in the awareness that forms of the inescapability of being-with.[131]

Uncanny Births

Dionysus's torturous play with Pentheus—as detailed in the second Messenger's account of the horrific wonders he witnessed on Cithaeron—is another perverted scene of birth. Tricked by Dionysus into sitting on the branches of a fir tree that the god has pulled down to the ground, Pentheus is like the "shoot" (*blastêma*) he sits on, sent "upright" (*orthon*) into the aether (1070–71). Initially maneuvered by Dionysus, the sadistic game is then autonomously carried out by the tree itself: "upright (*orthê*), the tree was towering into the upright (*orthon*) sky, having my master sitting on its back." As "upright" as the fir tree (*orthê* 1073) and the sky itself (*orthon* 1073), Pentheus (*orthon* 1071) is cast as the child of these parents, one feminine and vegetal, the other masculine and elemental, both identified with phallic rigidity. Of these two phallic agents, the feminine one penetrates the "masc" one, performing child care at the moment of conception, further ironizing this miraculous act of non-human generation of a human child. Madly energized by the "breaths" of Dionysus (*theou pnoaisin emmaneis* 1094)—by the viral dissemination of divinity as aerial matter—the Maenads turn this intimation of trans-human reproduction into a joint effort, a collective *mothering* (or *fathering*?). Hurling their javelin-like thyrses at Pentheus through the sky, they pursue their own collective penetration, whose issue is enjambed at the beginning of the line in the syntactically loose appearance of his name (1099–1100).[132] This is a delivery, a formal coming into being, which defies the temporality of reproduction and temporality as such—no sooner does Pentheus appear than we are told that the Maenads missed their target, conception undone.

In a perverse delivery, the Maenads attempt to shake off the tree where Pentheus is ensconced—to eradicate the vegetal support of his precarious life—in a preview of the impending *sparagmos*, of the dismemberment that they will carry out with their own bare hands (1103–4): "At the end, they tore up the roots with ironless crowbars, thunderbolting them with oak branches" (*telos de druinois sun-keraunousai kladois / rhizas anesparasson asidêrois mochlois*). In the second line of this redoing and undoing of Semele's conflagration, hissing and rhoticity are the inscriptional traces of Dionysian air, of the material trans-corporeality that binds (vegetal and human parts) while sundering. The collapse of branches into hands—an intimate, anti-foundational bond effecting human-vegetal undifferentiation—arises through dismemberment, through the displacement of roots, through the dismantling of a support that (un)grounds the subject/object and parent/child opposition.[133] The delivery does not bring out an individuated subject—rather, it births trans-species bonds, which resist the reproductive desire to build a bounded figure. (Like the individuating name, "the name that abbreviates kin relations," says Butler, "bears a story of binding connection . . . even as it marks the limit of our telling of any story we might carry."[134]) Rather than cutting an umbilical cord, this delivery, a separation from the vegetal, trans-parental parent, continues to bind. When, urged by Agave, the Maenads put their hands to the tree, uprooting it from mother earth, the maieutic exertion engenders a singular-plural hapticity, a single hand out of a multitude (1109–10): "They applied myriad hands (*murian chera*) to the fir tree and drew it out of the earth (*kaxanespasan chthonos*)." While grammatically singular (*chera*), the prehensile prosthesis lacks bounded physiognomy; partaking of a disarrayed kinship, it is a collective of parts sliding into each other, like Pentheus's "myriad laments" (*muriois oimôgmasin* 1112) maenadically cutting the air at the moment of his fall. In this affective echo of the overdetermined maieutic cut, human and non-human pain resonates as a shared (non-)property of the Dionysian atmosphere, a singular-plural hapticity.

I will now shift my focus to the exhortation that launches the Maenadic attack and to the final horroristic turn in the Messenger's account, two moments in which a dissolution of rhythmic and thus poetic recognizability binds Dionysus's (unrecognized) trans-birth with the trans-animality and trans-vegetality of his female acolytes. In her analysis of the gender trouble activated by Agave's call to the Maenads, Isabel Ruffell comments: "The consequence of the cis male attack is a different mode of gender transgression, violent not peaceful.... For the messenger, the women are displaying super*human* strength, but also invert gender norms, putting the men to flight, despite being armed only with the thyrsus (731–5 and 759–65)."[135] In the formal arrangement of Agave's command, trans-masculinity is intimated by the thyrse, a prosthesis anatomopolitically conspiring with imagery and meter toward transition (731–33): "Agave shouted: 'O running she-dogs of mine (*hê d'aneboêsen; Ô dromades emai kunes*), / we are hunted down (*thêrômeth'*) by these men; but follow (*hepesthe*) me (*moi*), / follow (*hepesthe*) armed with thyrses (*thursois*) in your hands.'" Trans-masculinity is accompanied by the trans-animality announced (or imposed?) by Agave's apostrophe, *Ô* ... *kunes* ("O ... she dogs"). The human-animal, master-slave dichotomy ostensibly enforced by this address is undermined by the following "we are hunted down," which folds Agave herself (the notional huntress) into the animal pack. The text invites us to linger on its syntactical weave and bring out, once again, the interpretive (im)possibilities that dispossessively ensue from what Butler calls a "messing with grammar"[136]—as well as meter. Agave's metaphor disrupts the pronominal possessiveness of the "I" (or the "me") that hierarchically mediates the relation between Agave as the Chorus leader and the Chorus itself; this disruptive effect continues in the syntactical illusion orchestrated by the (instrumental) dative *thursois*, which, coming after the repeated imperative *hepesthe* ("follow"), deceptively parallel with the dative *moi*, subsumes the "I" into the vegetal realm. The consequence of this assimilation of Agave to the thyrse, of Agave's becoming thyrse, is a preview of the play's final scene—with a filial Agave held in the Maenads' hands, just as the head of Pentheus, the quasi-lion cub, will be fixed atop the thyrse held in Agave's hands. Both Pentheus and Agave seem to be embedded in a trans-animate continuity of humanity-animality-vegetality, a shared k-incoherence, a stretching of kinship, a triple slippage. There is a similar stretching, a k-incoherence, in the metrical texture of Agave's address (731), centered around the brachytrisyllabic word *dromades* ("running"), followed by another short syllable—a semantic and rhythmical marker of trans fugitivity. E. R. Dodds notes that "the tribrach composed of a single word coinciding with the fourth foot" is an "exceptional rhythm . . . used for emotional effect,"[137] which occurs again at the very end of the Messenger speech (1147), at the moment he announces Agave's impending arrival (1144–47): [138]

> Relishing her ill-fated hunting she goes,
> within these walls, invoking Dionysus,
> her co-hunter (*xun-kunagon*), her collaborator (*xun-ergatên*) in the catching of the prey,
> the beautiful victor (*ton kallinikon*) for [or by] whom she carries tears as a victory prize (*hôi dakrua nikêphorei*).

In Agave's apostrophe to the Maenads, the sequence of four consecutive short syllables, which compromises the "recognition" of the iambic trimeter's distinctive structure, fracturing the bounded rhythmical corpus, transes the line by pluralizing syllabic value (replacing a long syllable with two short ones), opening it to an unbecoming that reflects Agave's own choral flight from egological individuality, her joining the animal or the vegetal "pack" (dogs or thyrses). What is perceived as an anomaly or an "abnormal" rhythm is a disruption comparable to the unbearable violation of "the normalizing standards of movement" with respect to disability, as Sunaura Taylor says in her 2010 conversation with Butler, who adds: "Right, well, there's a norm of what—not even what the body should be like and look like, but what parts should move and what those movements should be like."[139] The philological aversion to a (metrical) foot with an unconventional number of syllables—a disruptive, unheard-of, inconceivable rhythm— resonates with a "broader kind of morphological politics," one whose hostile purview includes "gender, people with intersex conditions, disability, race."[140] In the second instance of the metrical anomaly, the rhythmical fragmentation brought into the line by Agave's tears (*dakrua*) configures a dissolution, an aqueous expansion, which, as suggested by the chiastic figura etymologica of the compound formations *kalli-**nikon** . . . **nikê**-phorei* ("beautiful victor . . . she carries as a victory prize"), establishes a special kinship between Dionysus and his aunt, making one pregnant with the other. Her maternal tears—provoked by the marginalized god and dedicated to him as an offering—reproduce the back and forth of Dirce's fluvial mothering, her elemental trans-parentality, and Dionysus's trans-elemental gestation.

Gestational Melancholy and "Dismemberment Abortion"

The trans-parental embodiment that sets Dionysus's life in motion, refracted, as we have seen, through tragic form's viral motions of (pro)creative unbecoming, of gestational polymorphism, is at odds with the obligation imposed on Agave by hetero-reproductive kinship, that is, *Be a mother!* As the Messenger reports, just before being killed, Pentheus supplicated Agave to spare him, addressing her twice as "mother" (1118–21):

> "Mother, it is me. I am your son,
> Pentheus, whom you gave birth to in the house of Echion;
> pity *me, mother, and don't* (*mêter me mêde*) kill your son because of my mistakes!"

Pentheus is voicing the constraint of biological, parental/filial interpellation and seeking to re-enter the maternal body through the form of his stuttering plea, in which an objectified "I" (*me*) is enfolded between *mêter* and the prohibition, *mêde*, that prolongs the sound of maternity. Kinship, like gender, is, for Butler, always a condition of melancholic disavowal, which, as they famously argued, is exposed by drag:

> Drag ... allegorizes *heterosexual melancholy*, the melancholy by which a masculine gender is formed from the refusal to grieve the masculine as a possibility of love; a feminine gender is formed (taken on, assumed) through the incorporative fantasy by which the feminine is excluded as a possible object of love, an exclusion never grieved, but "preserved" through the heightening of feminine identification itself.... What drag exposes is the "normal" constitution of gender presentation in which the gender performed is in many ways constituted by a set of disavowed attachments or identifications that constitute ... the "unperformable." [In a culture of heterosexual melancholy], the straight man becomes (mimes, cites,

> appropriates, assumes the status of) the man he "never" loved and "never grieved"; the straight woman becomes the woman she "never" loved and "never" grieved. It is in this sense, then, that what is most apparently performed as gender is the sign and symptom of a pervasive disavowal.[141]

The "drag" practice central to the production of ancient theater—and metatheatrically exhibited in *Bacchae*[142]—lays bare the "pervasive disavowal" that kinship symptomatizes. The unmarked cis-maleness of the actor playing Agave signals the female character's introjection of a voided trans-parental possibility, of a denied paternity, of a loss of fatherhood. Pentheus's filial interpellation, his appropriation of the voice of the Law of the Father, even while addressing his biological mother, renews the traumatic loss inflicted by kinship. Rejecting this normative plea, she "spits out" (*ex-ieisa* 1122) foam, violently expelling the melancholic object, just as she will break into pieces the virtual paternity represented by the body of Pentheus—the father of Menoeceus and the grandfather of Jocasta and Creon. In the aftermath of the *sparagmos*, a disintegrated body, the impossibility of discerning the whole from the part, a head (1139) that becomes the body as such, flesh transformed into a quasi-excremental toy (1136), parts impossible to retrieve—lost under hard rocks or in a forest's "deep-wooded" foliage (1137–38)—all figure the encrypted loss, the melancholic accumulation of disavowed gender and kinship trouble.

At the beginning of the chapter, I underscored the disturbing resemblance between the climactic moment of the Messenger's report (and of the whole play)—Agave's lethal mutilation of Pentheus—and the right-wing's synecdochal usage of "dismemberment abortion." We can appreciate further implications of Agave's act if we consider Butler's own reflections on abortion and, in particular, their use of the "framework of precarious life to sustain a strong feminist position on reproductive freedoms."[143] Pentheus's desperate interpellation of his mother resonates with the precarizing responsibilization[144] of the pregnant woman, assigned "both a sovereignlike and a biopolitically inflected power of decision or impact on the futures . . . her conduct is considered to unfold"—whether they affect the individual or collective, with ramifications for "the social good."[145] The madness of Agave might be linked with the tendency to reprimand the pregnant person for failing to live up to the demands of responsibility, of decisional sovereign—a blame concealing the state's effort to exculpate itself for its inability or unwillingness to repair the precarizing social differentials that deny many pregnant subjects adequate conditions for exercising the right to choose.[146] Alternatively, Agave's act could be regarded as the pregnant subject's seizure of the state's biopolitical prerogatives, its control over life and death, its power to decide who deserves to live (the fetus) and who can afford to die (the mother).[147] To the representatives of the "pro-life" movement—who ground their opposition to abortion rights in "an ontology of personhood that relies on an account of biological individuation" and on "the idea of the 'person' . . . defined ontogenetically" as "the postulated internal development of a certain moral status or capacity of the individual"[148]—Butler responds:

> There is no life without the conditions of life that variably sustain life, and those conditions are pervasively social, establishing not the discrete ontology of the person, but rather the interdependency of persons, involving reproducible and sustaining social relations, and relations to the environment and to non-human forms of life, broadly considered.[149]

A life conceived apart from the social ontology of precarity and interdependency is not life, or, rather, it is life without livability. Observing that "the decision to abort a fetus may well be grounded in the insight that the forms of social and economic support needed to make that life livable are lacking,"[150] Butler suggests that, rather than an interruption or cancellation of life, abortion might be a desperate demand for it. When the concept of the "right to life" is severed from an ethics of precarity—from the recognition of the social conditions that make life livable and grievable—it merely becomes a "pretension" or "the function of an omnipotent fantasy of anthropocentrism (one that seeks to deny the finitude of the *anthropos* as well)."[151] Rejecting Dionysus, the foreigner, Pentheus resembles the "monadic individual" disavowing that "we are . . . social beings . . . dependent on what is outside ourselves." As we infer from the aftermath of the filicide—Agave's inability to recognize Pentheus, her belief that he is a lion cub—this apparent "outside" is first and foremost animality, the fleshy ground of human finitude, which biological kinship marginalizes, enforcing speciesism along with racializing anthropocentrism.[152] The animal is, in fact, a privileged target of "the violence of the foreclosed life, the one that does not get named as 'living'"[153]—a phrase from the preface to the second edition of *Gender Trouble* that captures Butler's continuing theoretical preoccupation with the ontology of "livability" and "livable lives."[154] We can say that, in pulling apart Pentheus, breaking the joints and seams between various bodily parts, Agave aborts biological kinship as such, as the imposition of an intraspecies relationality, an inward-oriented closure more than an opening, a claustrophobic system of predetermined, discrete positions and roles, which seeks to abort the trans-animality of human life itself.

There is, in fact, a somatechnical dimension, a paradoxical "constructive" dimension to Maenadic dismemberment. The grip that deforms and detaches also channels the force of an anti-biological craft, of a trans-making activated by the repetitious reference to hands, to their powerful instrumentality. Seeing her father, Cadmus, Agave proudly displays her human/animal prey, which she captured, "not with the hooked javelins of the Thessalians, not with nets, but with the hands (*cheirôn*), the arms' white spear points." As she continues, "We captured this prey [i.e., Pentheus] *with the hand itself* (*autêi cheiri*) / and *tore* (*die-phorêsamen*) *apart* (*chôris*) the limbs of the beast" (1209–10).[155] In the dative form *autêi cheiri* ("with the hand itself"), the instrumental valence cannot be entirely separated from the comitative one (indicating accompaniment), which is perhaps contrastively activated by the alliterative adverb *chôris* ("apart"). The same contextual co-presence of *cheir* and *chôris* occurs in the Messenger's description of the aftermath of the *sparagmos*: while Pentheus's body (*sôma*) lies "in pieces" (*chôris* 1137), his head is held by his mother in her hands (*cheroin* 1140), as though this contact were a consolation for the solitude of decapitation, the fashioning of a hybrid body, neither Pentheus's nor Agave's, but belonging to both. I am proposing that the loss engendered by sparagmatic violence does not exclude the glimpse of an intertwinement—a somatechnical replacement of the notion of a bounded part of the biological body with a material impression of a haptic connection, with a sense of matter as transing. "The domination," an *ostensible* domination, "that the flesh enacts is achieved through the dehiscence or fission of its own mass," says Butler, "and when one touches a living and sentient being, one never touches a mass, for the moment of touch is the one in which something comes apart, mass splits, and the notion of substance does not—cannot—hold."[156] According to Cynthia Citlallin Delgado Huitrón, "although Derrida seemingly opposes two forms of touch, the blow (striking) or the caress (stroking), we can understand the caress as a stroke that, in its equivocation, strikes."[157] Reversing the argument, we could say that, parallel to the stroke, the dismemberment may entail, if not a caress, at least a latent repositioning of bodily seams, a resuturing, a recomposition. Jeanne Vaccaro has observed:

> The labor of making transgender identity is handmade: collective—made with and across bodies, objects, and forces of power—a process, unfinished yet enough (process, not progress).... The handmade is a haptic, affective theorization of the transgender body, a mode of animating material experience and accumulative felt matter ....[158]

"If touch is always already trans-, then to transgender touch ... may release its performative potential, particularly in relation to its ability to undo gender and sexuality as abided and prescribed by the law," Delgado Huitrón says.[159] This transgender touch may apply to Agave, not just to Pentheus: when the Messenger notes that, having fastened her son's head to the top of the thyrse, Agave carried it through Cithaeron "*as though* (*hôs*) it belonged to a mountain lion," after "leaving behind her sisters among the choruses of Maenads" (1141–43), we may detect another somatechnical operation, her own exit from the oppressive realm of human kinship, her becoming the "part" fleeing the oppressive familial "whole"—the normative Chorus of obligatory bonds—and approaching humananimal k-incoherence.

Furry Fugitivity

> "'No, I am not his father, but his mother' (that might be Zeus' utterance); 'That is not my son, it is a mountain-lion' (Agave's propositional form); 'That cannot be my mother' (Dionysus, looking at Zeus).... The ties of kinship that cross and link the man and the animal are not opposites, not mutually exclusive possibilities, but cousins, even kissing cousins.... Who is more animal in the killing scene, Agave, the huntress, or Pentheus, crossdressed, killed as a lion?"[160]

The monosyllabic conjunction *hos* ("as," "as though") that, in lines 1141–42, encapsulates Agave's folly—her hallucinatory delusion that Pentheus is a lion—marks the thin line of separation between human and animal, but also the cruelty of the anthropocentric Symbolic, which insists on the exclusiveness of intra-human kinship and prohibits trans-animality even in the narrowest linguistic interstices. Agave's tragedy—her horroristic reconnection with

Pentheus through filicide, through her failure to recognize the biological bond—may lie in part in the foreclosed possibility of recognizing a lion cub as kin, fur as (s)kin. The continuity or intimacy between striking and touching informs the lyric dialogue between the Chorus and Agave (1179–84):

> CHORUS Who was the woman who *struck*? (*tis ha balousa*). . . . Who else (beside you)? . . . AGAVE After me, after me, the offspring of Cadmus *touched* (*ethige*) this beast (*genethla / met'eme met'eme toud'ethige thêros*); this hunt was fortunate (*eutuchês*). Participate in the banquet (*meteche . . . thoinas*).

The transition from "struck" to "touched" is usually interpreted as a symptom of Agave's progress toward reintegration and psychic normalization by way of recognizing her "proper" kin. The same teleological motion is located by critics in the apparent perceptive shift (a less hallucinated hallucination?) from lion to bull. As one commentator observes: "The hunt requires a wild animal, the lion, whereas the sacrifice . . . requires one that is closer to humankind. . . . Accordingly it is as a bull that Pentheus also seems to acquire a more human aspect, as a young man with his first beard" (1185–88):[161]

> AGAVE The *bull* (*moschos*) is young; *he has* just
> *sprouted* (*thallei*) hair on his jaw
> under *his delicate-haired crest.*
> (*koruth' hapalotricha / katakomon*)
> CHORUS Yes, in its *hair* (*phobêi*) it looks like a *beast* (*thêr*) of the wild.

Two elements in the formal texture of this climactic moment seem particularly fertile for re-reading: the confusion between an objectified "I" (*me*) and the preposition *meta*, signifying not just "after" but also "beyond" (*met'eme met'eme . . . met-eche*); and the striking concentration of aspirated sounds (in particular *th*), which convert the thematic lingering on hairiness and furriness into the phonosymbolic feeling of Agave's vexed caress.[162] The impression of a subject losing itself in an ongoing beyondness is at odds with any clear-cut transition, a return to the cognitive self-possession associated with conventional subjectivity, with the apparent boundedness of the skin.[163] Unsettling the border between inside and outside, materializing a corporeal beyondness, an "after-oneself-ness," hispidity is the aesthetic manifestation of a relational projection, a fugitivity, an intertwinement breaking species divisions, a trans impetus. The philological controversy around the sudden appearance of a bull instead of a lion—can *moschos*, the word for "bull," mean "lion cub"?[164]—unwittingly pinpoints what could be at stake here, not just an ironical, Dionysian play with hybridity, but, going further, deindividuated animality, species abolition.

Agave's language displays the fantasy of becoming hispid, the persistent desire for the trans-species kinship that her reattachment with her son curtails. A lion has been spared, but the price of this isolated act of (narrative, textual, authorial?) mercy is the interruption of the possibility of any bonds beyond human kinship, beyond the species. In this sense, sparing the animal, excluding it from Agave's too-close, too-tight grip—while exposing Pentheus to the brutal treatment that is the unmarked trait of animalization—paradoxically enforces the violence of anthropocentric biopolitics, which categorically divides kin from non-kin. Still, formal hispidity comes to the fore as the symptom of an irrepressible fetish—the surrogate of the lost object, the disavowed desire. We can give this desired object the name of trans ferality, referring to a condition inhabited by Dionysian satyrs and by contemporary queer performers of animal drag (werewolves, cervids, furries).[165] According to Debra Ferreday: "The cervid queers the human/nonhuman binary through practices of nonhuman cross-dressing and performance. . . . By parodying the notion of either being 'fully human' or becoming/'returning to' the animal, these practices perform the anxiety and melancholia at stake in anthropocentrism."[166] Exhibiting "transgender characteristics as well as . . . the ability to shift species," cervids, as Ferreday continues, express a "subjectivity . . . haunted by the necessity of constructing one's identity through language and through technology."[167] The community of role players in animal drag is referred to as an "endless forest" or "a virtual forest," which Ferreday describes as "a fantasy space which embodies a sense that, in constructing the category of 'human,' something is irrevocably lost."[168] This Butlerian loss is the disavowed humananimality that shapes the melancholic wildness of Dionysian satyrs, that assimilates their zoo-drag to a feral fetish, to a performative rem(a)inder of the encrypted kinship trouble fabricating the human by repression.[169] When the Chorus ironically comments on the "fur" on the face that Agave has not yet recognized as belonging to Pentheus, their use of *phobê* (1188) brings us back to the forest (another *phobê* 1138), the natural abyss where his body—a materialization of Agave's melancholically introjected paternity, as I suggested before—is scattered and concealed. Left behind like the hispidity ostensibly incompatible with a human body, the dismembered body of Pentheus is thus a metaphor of the animal corporeality that anthropocentrism makes the target of masochistic violence, of the self-wounding and self-disposal enacted by Agave's filicide.[170] Does Agave wish to become a satyr or a satyr-like figure? Does her madness conceal this desire, which we can call trans but also meta-trans, since it involves transitioning into figures, the satyrs, who perform trans-species? We can perhaps say that the villose texture of Agave's words delineates a "fursona," which Hazel Ali Zaman defines as "a performance technology for non/human drag, formed out of necessity to survive and resist dominant and hostile public spheres," not "an explicit attempt to pass as, or reject, the 'human' and 'non-human,'" but a practice of "disidentification that makes a mess of . . . the lived experience of continually existing outside of, and within, the politicized state of being 'human.'"[171] In other words, a "fursona" is a medium not just for reclaiming and embracing disavowed animality, but also for defamiliarizing this category. Fully embracing the messiness of texture, it places hispidity's relational ontology in the service not just of species abolition but, further, of a heterogeneous destabilizing of the category of animality, that is, of a pursuit of difference in a non-speciated animal world.[172]

When Agave is joined onstage by her father, Cadmus, the former carrying the head of Pentheus, the latter commanding a group of attendants to bring the re-collected pieces of his body, we can perceive a collective reproductive process involving the whole community in the precarious reconstitution of an adult individual who has regressed to the fetal stage, as suggested by the reference to Pentheus as "a wretched burden" (*athlion baros* 1216). Cadmus and his male attendants "carry" (*pherontes* 1216; *pherô* 1219) and deliver Pentheus, along with Agave. This collective mothering is an exercise in distributed reproduction, which seems, however, to conform to species boundaries. Yet Agave's "fursona" haunts this picture, enabling her to disrupt kinship once again through the suggestion of a feral paternity which, as we will see, the daughter "illogically" gives birth to. When Agave addresses her fellow Thebans, urging them to come admire her trophy, the formal configuration of her words engenders the scandal of further kinship trouble (1203–4):

> Come to see this *booty* (*agran*)
> *of a wild beast, whom we, daughters of Cadmus, have hunted down*
> (*Kadmou thugateres thêros hên êgreusamen*).

The English translation cannot do justice to the intricacy of the word order, to the effects of "subjunctivity" it engenders.[173] "Cadmus" is in the same case, the genitive, as "wild beast" (*thêros*), while the contiguity between *thugateres* ("daughters") and *thêros*, which is heightened by phonic resonance, raises a subliminal alternative genealogy: that Cadmus—whom, at the end of the play, we discover to be destined to metamorphose into a snake, that is a *thêr*[174]—may be nothing less than a furry animal, in the feminine gender. The daughter(s), assonant and syntactically intertwined with the feminine beast (*thugateres thêros*), are kin to this animal, a snake like the future Cadmus. The object of their hunting, their violent extraction, a maieutic drawing out, the father becomes the animal, both child and cub, that Agave purports to deliver. The introjected, repressed paternity that Agave spat out in rejecting Pentheus's interpellation, in turning him into a material figuration of the disavowed lost object, is (re)born here in the form of animality.

* * *

In 2021, Butler employed images of ferality to characterize the rhetoric of so-called gender-critical (that is, trans-exclusionary) feminisms,[175] which has the effect of assimilating trans women to predatory animals:

> Political fearmongering about the threat that gender diversity poses to the political and social order frequently returns to invocations of the putative threat to "women" and children that these politics bear. This is . . . just an effort to pathologize trans people, and especially trans women and feminine people, by representing trans people as wolves in sheep's clothing, foxes in the proverbial henhouses of feminism and women's spaces.[176]

Like the word *queer*, this trans ferality, as the *Bacchae* read alongside Butler seems to show us, can be reclaimed to underscore the shared exclusion of both animals and trans (as well as Black) people from the protections attached to the privileged label of the human and, above all, to expose the disavowal of non-human kinships that is behind transphobia.[177] As we read in the introduction of *Tranimacies*, a collection of essays on transness and animality: "human-animal intimate relations at the heart of tranimacies point to violent de-animations in colonial histories and in Western metaphysical logics in which speciation reduces some creatures to types."[178] These types "reveal the links between queer sexualities, the animal, the racialized other." In "Ego Hippo"—a programmatic declaration of authorial *fursona*—Florentin Félix Morin declares, echoing Butler, that, "if 'to be forcibly ungendered or to become trans-gendered renders one's humanness precarious,'[179] it is because undoing gender is undoing the very process of materialization of our flesh as a 'human' body."[180] Intervening, in 2020, on the relation between animals and human disability—a topic spurred by Sunaura Taylor's *Beasts of Burden: Animal and Disability Liberation*—Butler resumes some of the language of the *Bacchae* lecture: "We do not take the bounded individual life form as the unit of analysis but understand, rather, that the unit is itself only sustained as a unit to the degree that it is supported in life. Thus in the very notion of the individual we find the principle that breaks it up."[181] Butler emphasizes the masochistic, death-driven logic underlying the idea of the human, an insight that we can see dramatized at the end of Euripides' play: "[The] pathway for achieving a 'dignified' human form . . . requires a self-bestialization, that is, subjecting one's own animality to bad treatment—a vain but adamant effort to disavow the animality that humans share with other animals."[182] This self-wounding, bad treatment of a "self" dismissed as "other," is unveiled in the Euripidean recognition scene, through the (re)discovery of the humanness of Agave's prey—the "other" is "self," after all. Yet, as a "burden" (*baros*), this human remnant is still able to incline the human to animal downwardness, which the human constructs just to marginalize and reject it.[183] The transition from madness to reason, the cognitive realization that the flesh of Agave's child is human, with the separation between "before" and "after" it establishes, is a re-enactment of the "original" human/animal self-cutting. The radicality of *Bacchae* is perhaps associated with the following question, which, as Butler suggests, it forces us to confront:

> Why are we more horrified by doing violence to those who are our kin than those who are not, and should it finally matter whether Agave killed a human or an animal? Does the play perhaps open up a wider set of questions about what or who is justifiably killed, and who is not? . . . Should we be concerned only to safeguard the lives of our kin, or do we need, rather badly, to expand that category until it achieves a global dimension? After all, if we claim that some human who was killed was not really a human, but only a human shield, or if we claim that some animal does not deserve the same solicitude

> as a human life, we are deciding a rather arbitrary limit to our prohibition on killing.[184]

Bacchae and Greek tragedy in general provide Butler with imagistic material for reformulating some of the ethico-political questions that, already implicit in *Gender Trouble*, have explicitly occupied them since at least *Precarious Life*. In that later work, we read, for example: "Some lives are grievable and others are not; the differential allocation of grievability that decides what kind of subject is and must be grieved, and which kind of subject must not, operates to produce and maintain certain exclusionary conceptions of what is normatively human: what counts as a livable life and a grievable death?"[185] In the wake of a similar observation by Pope Francis, the Italian Minister of Family, Eugenia Roccella, a fierce enemy of queer and trans parenting, expressed dismay at the perceived spread of affective attachments to pets, construing them as dangerous attempts to dislodge humanity from its position of primacy, as a deviation from "what is normatively human."[186] Queer and non-human kinships are similarly stigmatized because, in challenging the social status quo, which is automatically identified with the "human," they expose the possibility of a different humanity or the human's inescapable predication on—and precarious differentiation from—what is conventionally located outside or beyond itself.[187] As we reread Euripides' play at a time of war, re-creating the contextual circumstances of its original production during the final stretch of the Peloponnesian War, we perceive the affinity between the Italian minister and Putin, with whom her party, before his invasion of Ukraine, had always sympathized. As Butler has remarked, Putin "has identified feminism and LGBTQ and gender issues as national security issues, as if the security of Russia as such were challenged or could potentially be destroyed by these Western influences."[188] The responsibility for the devastations of war, for its apocalyptic threat—now and then—is displaced onto the gender and kinship troubles that expose the human's insurmountable co-implication with the non-human, which we disparagingly and disingenuously call inhuman. In the aftermath of Hamas's massacre on October 7, 2023, the disavowal of humananimality continues to ground the establishment of racialized axiologies of grievability in the rhetoric surrounding Israel's assault on Gaza—which Butler qualifies as an act of "revenge" with genocidal purposes:[189] "If Palestinians are 'animals,' as Israel's defense minister insists, and if Israelis now represent 'the Jewish people' . . ., then the only grievable people in the scene, the only ones who present as eligible for grief, are the Israelis."[190] Reread at a time when the broken bodies of Palestinian children, through bombardment, are implicitly or explicitly cast by Western states and media as less horrifying than those of Israeli ones,[191] *Bacchae* challenges us to wonder whether Agave's decapitation of a lion cub would also have been less horrifying. As Butler says in 2023, "if the dominant frame considers some lives to be more grievable than others, then it follows that one set of losses is more horrifying than another set of losses."[192]

In the work of the Guadeloupean artist Kelly Sinnapah Mary—in which the animality of the human is embraced through radical visual experiments in transanimal hybridization—we witness a refusal "of the politics of respectability that have demanded that colonized people prove their humanity, that we are not animals,"[193] as Andil Gosine says. "What opens up for us, Caribbean people," he adds, "when we are freed from proving ourselves not animal?"[194] In the 2016 photographic series entitled *Hotmilk*, Sinnapah Mary re-imagines the she-wolf who suckled Romulus and Remus as a hispid female human holding a sleeping human baby in her arms (Figure 4).

Expanding from her upper and lower body into the larger empty space behind the caretaker-baby assemblage that is surrounded and delimited by the golden lines of a chair and a ship-like container, her villosity blends into the

Figure 4 Kelly Sinnapah Mary, *Hotmilk*. Reproduced with the permission of the artist.

black backdrop, the point of contact of the notional individual with her environment, the thick marker of the illusion of boundedness. The luminous blackness embodies the finitude of animality, an all-embracing reservoir of (un)becoming, a zone of material possibility, the indispensable (and disavowed) support that infiltrates what seeks to exclude it. This trans-species collapse of (human)animal and animal brings us back to the reactionary phantasm of moral catastrophe and societal collapse. At a time when a different collapse, the end of the world that climate-change-deniers dismiss as a liberal lie or impute to queer or trans rights, has become "a *predicament* that envelops everybody, human and non-human," as Christopher Julien observes, we might handle it not just as a predicament, but also "as a heuristic."[195] Discussing Wayne Shorter and esperanza spalding's 2022 operatic version of Euripides' *Iphigenia in Aulis*, Butler wonders, "How does Greek tragedy ... give us a way to think about collapsing social structure—a social structure that doesn't just collapse once but that is collapsing all the time?"[196] The paternal and patriarchal sacrifice of Iphigenia, which Shorter and spalding multiply through multiple Iphigenias, is, for Butler, the primary "collapsing structure":

> How many Iphigenias are there in the world who have been sacrificed? How many women have been killed? How many women have been raped or abandoned? We can transpose Iphigenia into many different contexts and see, for instance, the horrific character of femicide or sacrifice. And in a way we're dumbfounded and horrified by the repetitive character of all these sacrifices. How often is this happening? Where is this happening? Is this happening in every place in the world? ... That's the social structure that repeats; it also collapses precisely because it repeats.

The language of horror echoes Butler's comment on the ethico-political consequences of the ontological distinction between (human)animal and animal: "Why are we more horrified by doing violence to those who are our kin than those who are not, and should it finally matter whether Agave killed a human or an animal?" This question can also apply to *Iphigenia in Aulis*—a play belonging to the same trilogy as *Bacchae*, wherein a female deer seems to have replaced Iphigenia, who is saved at the last minute thanks to the ordinary, unremarkable sacrifice of the animal.[197] Kinship trouble here converges again with trans-animality. Just as the lion cub of *Bacchae* is another Pentheus, the deer is another Iphigenia, not simply the metaphor of the virgin suddenly spared, but her sister or cousin, one of the many, customarily victimized (human)animal or animal Iphigenias. The structure that collapses in the play is not only human kinship, but also a broader kinship that collapses all the time, still awaiting, as it seems, recognition as a structure. Iphigenia is thus, like Pentheus, a trans-animal who urges us to bind and rebind bonds across, in between, and beyond, by transing kinship, bonding in the break.

3

The Justice of Rage: *Eumenides*

> *Rage will continue to emerge about a legal system that not only fails to do justice but amplifies racial violence. This is not rage as irrational, but rage as an illuminated response to an unacceptable loss—a loss that did not have to happen, a taking of life and a letting die that is repeatedly conducted by legal institutions themselves. This is a life and death issue, and the rage carries with it an argument, a luminosity, that should not be too quickly shut down in the name of civility.*[1]

In the last chapter of *The Force of Nonviolence* (2020),[2] entitled "Political Philosophy in Freud: War, Destruction, Mania, and the Critical Faculty," Judith Butler dwells on a passage from Freud's "Thoughts for the Times on War and Death" (1915), where, in an echo of Thucydides' prologic reference to the unprecedented scope of the thirty year conflict of the Spartans and Athenians, he characterizes the Great War as "more bloody and more destructive than any war of other days" and "at least as cruel, as embittered, as implacable as any that has preceded it" (278). This war, Freud continues, "tramples in blind fury (*in blinder Wut*) on all that comes in its way," with the result that "all the common bonds" will be shattered and "any renewal of those bonds" will prove to be "impossible for a long time to come."[3] *Wut*, which is cognate with Latin *vates*, a word sometimes applied to a Cassandra-like prophet animated by divine ecstasy,[4] captures the "blind fury" endangering "the social basis of politics itself," as Butler says. The notion of such "destructiveness without limit," which "Freud takes from Greek tragedy,"[5] is a prefiguration, for Butler, of the death drive theorized in 1920. Is Butler specifically thinking here of Aeschylus's Erinyes ("the Furies"), who pursue Orestes at the end of *The Libation Bearers* and are silenced, normalized, stripped of their anger in the last play of the

Oresteia? The title of the *Eumenides* essay, "Fury and Justice in the Humanities" (2023), strongly suggests so, and appropriately closes the trilogy discussed in this book. In this essay, the Erinyes stand for what Butler calls "critical fury,"[6] a vision of humanistic education not as dispassionate positivism or apolitical reconstructive specialism, but rather as an affectively charged critical-theoretical engagement, a commitment to social justice and to abolitionism, understood as the eventual dismantling of the carceral system, in the face of systemic racism. In this intervention, we might say, the punning resonance between *humanities* and *Eumenides* defamiliarizes the normalizing prefix *eu*—the marker of the conciliatory harmony that silences the Erinyes—while troubling liberal humanism, casting the substance of the *humanities* as haunted by *mania* and a melancholic core of not-so-humanistic rage (Iliadic *mênis*). Rather than reading the play as a structuralist transition from revenge to legal justice and the domestication of the furious Erinyes—an imprisonment of sorts, the necessary price of their integration into the community—Butler underscores the intrinsic violence of the law, its identification with punishment as such, a punishment often more harmful than the harm it purports to redress, as demonstrated by critiques of the Prison Industrial Complex (PIC). In one of the first deconstructions of conventional teleological readings of the play—followed then by various interventions emphasizing ambiguity and open-endedness[7]—Yopie Prins suggests that, even after the defeat of the Erinyes, "the *logos* of law is necessarily implicated in the *muthos* of the Furies."[8] Butler's distinctive interest is in theorizing the anger of the Erinyes not as the residual ferality made necessary by the "civilizing" intervention of the law, but, on the contrary, as fury, an affective force of critical survivance demanded by the publicly authorized violence that is the law:[9]

> The assumption is that prison checks the violence of individuals rather than tending to put those individuals in violent cultures, cultures reactive to violent institutional practices, especially when understood to be regenerating systemic racism. In turn, this raises the question of whether prisons produce more violence than they check, whether what counts as a form of "checking" violence is itself a further iteration of violence. . . . The proposition that one sort of violence can and should be checked by an arguably greater violence—the violence of the prison system—is itself angering, and justly so. Fury again.

In this perspective, Aeschylus's play undoes the teleological narrative it stages, making a case for the anger it ostensibly represses, for the "critical fury" that, according to Butler, the humanities can circulate, providing an impetus for resisting and rebelling, as we live with and under the law, as we cohabit with—and inhabit—its validated violence:[10]

> One could also well become angry that the very legal institutions that promise to overcome violence actually embody violence.... How do we understand this kind of anger? Is this not also a legitimate fury, one that can be neither contained nor seduced by the law? Shall we call it a critical fury that forms in relation to an institution that says one thing and does the opposite, and that claims that only the vengeful and destructive fail to grasp and honor the legitimacy of this institution?

In this chapter, I approach *Eumenides* in light of Butler's reading in an attempt to situate justice, the abstract principle, in the affective actions of rage itself, not in the law, which, in order to install itself, as we are told, "justly" suppresses or normalizes rage.[11] This hermeneutic endeavor, which I conceive of as an aesthetic practice of "critical fury" in its own right, will involve a re-engagement with the verbal texture of the play, framed by a comparison of the Aeschylean Erinyes with Walter Benjamin's Niobe and Butler's own Kafkaesque (and Benjaminian) Niobe.[12] Butler's reading of *Eumenides* is thematically connected with their discussions of Kafka's *The Trial* and of Benjamin's "Toward a Critique of Violence" in two complementary essays,[13] which I want to use to read (Aeschylus's) Niobe into (Aeschylus's) Erinyes—and vice versa—arguing for a link, implicit in "Fury and Justice in the Humanities," between the Erinyes' Niobean affect and the rage that the Black feminist radical tradition, starting with Audre Lorde, has regarded as the only appropriate response to the violence of the law. But before addressing the core concern of this chapter—a reading for "critical fury" as the political affect pressing against the law's intrinsic collusion with and enactment of violence—I wish to return, for a moment, to Butler's discussion of Freud in *The Force of Nonviolence* and consider the "blind fury," or the *mania*, of which the Erinyes are iconic representatives, to explore how tragic feeling feeds into Butler's articulation of the nexus of political theory and psychoanalysis.

The Erinyes, Iphigenia, and the Force of Nonviolence

Butler's engagement with the Erinyes is part of an interest in *mania* as a psychic condition that, in mobilizing a collapse of hierarchical structures, fosters the emergence of novel bonds and relationalities. This scenario is captured by Butler's phrases "insurrectionary solidarity" and "improvisational solidarity"—the latter used in reference to Iphigenia, the notional *archê* of the *Oresteia*, the proto-Erinys whom Euripides places at the center of one of his late plays.[14] In the development of the argument of "Political Philosophy in Freud," Butler pivots from *Beyond the Pleasure Principle* (1920) to *The Ego and the Id* (1923), the essay in which, as we saw in the first chapter, the "culture of the death drive" coincides with the superego, the psychic principle ostensibly safeguarding the ego by curbing its destructive instincts. However, this ostensibly salubrious clash of destructive forces is liable to yield a destructive outcome, an "unrestrained suicidal self-beratement."[15] As Butler observes, "If the super-ego works destruction against the ego in order to inhibit the latter's destructive expression, it still traffics in destruction, but the imperiled object is no longer the other or the world, but the ego itself."[16] A rebellion against the tyranny of the superego, *mania* is thus an eruption of internal disarray, a breach of the bond between synergic psychic functions, which "proves to be the only hope for prevailing against the suicidal and murderous aims of the unbridled super-ego."[17] This disidentification within the individual's psyche implicates social disidentification, a dissolution of the ties that hold together the status quo, perpetuating inveterate systems of oppression and injustice.[18] Disidentification here correlates with what elsewhere Butler calls "desubjugation," the formation of "counternormativities" in a subjective self-undoing that "yields critical agency beyond the normative violence of subjection itself."[19] Manic disidentification, for Butler, "operates under the signifier of 'life' but is not ... reductively vitalist: it stands for another life, future life."[20] At the end of the chapter, Butler concludes that, in unveiling the anti-tyrannical potential of *mania* within the psyche, Freud "offers us a glimpse into those forms of *insurrectionary solidarity* that turn against authoritarian and tyrannical rule, as well as against forms of war that threaten the destruction of life itself."[21] Insofar as *mania* can remedy the destructiveness of war by reconfiguring social structures, that is, by breaking oppressive bonds of (civic, political) cohesion through "insurrectionary solidarity"—through alliances that dismantle, through a dismantling that delineates novel alliances—we can say that this *mania* is, to an extent, a version of the force generative of war itself: the "blind fury" that "cuts all the common bonds."[22] What I am suggesting, in continuity with what I argued in the chapter on *Antigone*, is that, if we heed not just the logic but also the formal aesthetics of Butler's argumentation, Freud's "blind fury"— the cause of the Great War, the conceptual precursor of the death drive—paradoxically resembles its *pharmakon*, *mania*, a death-driven force in its own right, layered with conspicuous tragic resonances. In the interview on ...*(Iphigenia)*—Wayne Shorter and esperanza spalding's 2022 operatic adaptation of Euripides' *Iphigenia in Aulis*—Butler singles out the multiplication of Iphigenia figures that is one of the distinctive features of this version, interpreting this singular plurality in terms of "improvisational solidarity":

> The sacrifice keeps happening and it's never fully successful because the Iphigenias start proliferating.... The very fact that the Iphigenias multiply suggests that there's power in numbers and that a kind of multitude of Iphigenias emerge who are struggling with this scene, reworking this scene.... Maybe those Iphigenias are the same, but they are different. They are a kind of feminist multitude. They keep proliferating, as much as the killings happen, the femicides throughout the world. There is a feminist response to violence that plays out in new political strategies for undermining and countering the force of that violence.... I don't know if I would call it kinship. I might be more prone to call it a kind of improvisational solidarity.[23]

Echoing the "insurrectionary solidarity" theorized in *The Force of Nonviolence*, this "improvisational solidarity"—a bond exceeding the restrictions of kinship—seems to originate from the manic force of proliferation, from the bewildering violation of the principle of non-contradiction, from the frenzied disidentification conjured by a character split into a plurality of enfleshed self-alienations, multiple versions of herself. On a smaller, "dual" scale, this proliferation unfolds in Euripides' play, in which Iphigenia's sudden change of heart— opposition to her own sacrifice, then a sudden, heroic embrace of it—prompts an effect of disidentification, exemplified by literary-critical disorientation, by the hypothesis, entertained by some critics, that Iphigenia has gone "mad."[24] The language of madness is constantly shifting in this play: first, upon learning about Agamemnon's plan to sacrifice their daughter, Clytemnestra cries out, "Has my husband gone *mad* (*memênôs*)?" (876) and "Which one of the *demons* (*alastorôn*) is driving him?" (878)—an *alastôr* refers to a category of demonic beings encompassing the Erinyes themselves.[25] Later, when Iphigenia supplicates her father to spare her life, she declares that "whoever prays to die *is mad* (*mainetai*)" (1251–52). In changing her mind, in spontaneously offering herself to immolation, in showing the signs of the fury of madness, Iphigenia becomes, in a sense, the Erinys—the creature who cannot fit in, who will disarray the order of things by preparing the ground for the Greeks' future punishment, who subverts the play's tyrannical *muthos* (which demands the Greeks' departure to Troy) while apparently obeying it, staining it with the portent of her father's murder.[26] Iphigenia's "madness," we can say, defies the super-egoic structure of the play, which steadily polices the interstitial motions that might compromise the law of consistency, the bond of necessity between the parts.[27]

The "insurrectionary" or "improvisational solidarity" brought about by the *mania* of Euripides' Iphigenia, by her becoming Erinys, by her joining the Furies, implies a different arrangement of parts, an alternative aesthetico-political connectivity, a relational and social undercommons—which as such does not follow a conventional logic, which, in fact, defies the tyranny of logic, rejecting integration into the super-egoic structure of the law (psychic, aesthetic, political). Not simply a self-destructive instinct or a plot constraint disguised as the conversion of a collectively imposed decision into a notional act of self-determination, Iphigenia's Erinys-like *mania* is in the eyes of the beholder—it is reflected in the suspended or interrupted critical judgment prompted by her change of heart, in the impossibility of a definitive psychological verdict, in her preventing critics from interpretively "doing justice" to her (an enterprise not altogether different from "bringing her to justice"). In what follows, re-reading *Eumenides* with or alongside Butler will mean tightening the bond between justice and *mania*, construing justice as fury breaking the violence of the law with the unscripted potential, affective and relational, of insurrection and improvisation.

Law and Violence

We can perceive the chief insight of Butler's reading refracted in the microtexture of the prologue of *Eumenides*, where the Pythia's rosy picture of the various power transfers at the temple of Apollo at Delphi thematizes, if only negatively, the relation between coercion and law. The Pythia recalls that Phoebe inherited the rulership over the Delphic shrine from Themis, with no conflict, but "with her wanting it and no violence against anyone" (*thelousês oude pros bian tinos* 5). The introduction of the masculine law of Phoebus Apollo, which Phoebe onomastically previews, is also cast as a peaceful, spontaneous, natural act of succession—even though, as we know, this new regime is founded through the shedding of animal blood (that of the Pythian snake). The claim of "no violence" is a Freudian negation, an *excusatio non petita*, or a deliberate act of suppression. By installing itself with the consent of all the parties, (Apollinean) law sets itself up as the antithesis of violence or of coercion. It is the culture that becomes nature, or the culture that was always nature, that was always predestined as the "just" telos. Yet the untenability of this subterfuge is exposed by the reduction of justice to a matter of aesthetics or mere decorum. When the Pythia says that the "attire" (*kosmos*) of the Erinyes is "incompatible" (*oute . . . dikaios* 55–56) with the gods' temples and the houses of men, this impossible relationality is couched in the language of justice—as though Apollinean law, setting the terms of *dikê*, makes allowance neither for loss, displayed by the blackness of the Erinyes' robes, nor anger, the unbearable matter, aerial or liquid, exuding from their noses and eyes. Both their heavy breath made audible by their snoring (53) and the spilled dense blood (54)—a coagulated and symbolically overdetermined liquid—convey an accretion of time and feeling, which cannot be sustained (*pherein*) by the Apollinean body, for they would deform, stain, or overburden the monumental law, the beauty of justice, or justice as an abstract beauty. These lines thus raise the question of whether law can make space for anger—the "ugly feeling" that this play seems too quick to pit against justice and erase by tendentiously equating it with mere revenge. The unsustainability of the idea of non-coercive law comes to the fore in the same place, in the Pythia's praise of Apollo, who is imaginatively summoned, made vicariously "present," through the abundance of epithets (61–63): "healing priest" (*iatromantis*), "diviner" (*teraskopos*), and "purifying" (*katharsios*), but also "very forceful" (*megasthenei*). Combined with the futural perspective of divination, purification enforces the removal of the grime, the accumulated rage—it coincides with the (un)lawful coercion in the compound *megasthenei*. Later in the play, just before his famously misogynistic speech—which absurdly purports to demonstrate that there are no mothers, or that mothers are useless for reproduction[28]—Apollo implicitly equates *justice* with the *coercion* associated with him, with the epithet *megasthenês* (619): "Learn *how much force* (*sthenei*) *justice* (*to . . . dikaion*) has."[29]

"Justice" in the play seems hard to distinguish from the pleasure of disciplining and punishing. The place of the Erinyes, Apollo declares (186–90), is not in his temple but

> where there are *head-chopping* (*karanistêres*), *eye-gouging* (*ophthalmôruchoi*) *judgments* (*dikai*), and *slaughters* (*sphagai*), and children's masculinity is ruined by the corruption of the seed, and there are *cuttings of extremities* (*akrôniai*) and *stonings* (*leusmoi*) and, impaled beneath the spine, they wail and moan constantly.

The juxtaposition of "head-chopping" and "eye-gouging" with "judgments" is jarring[30]—for the law allegedly embodied by *dikê* is identified here with torture, with the practices of vengeful mutilation carried out in the previous plays of the trilogy. Michel Foucault's description of the Attica penitentiary in upstate New York comes to mind: "Society eliminates by sending to prison people whom prison breaks up, crushes, physically eliminates. . . . Attica is a machine for elimination, a form of prodigious stomach, a kidney that consumes, destroys, breaks up, and then rejects, and that consumes in order to eliminate what it has already eliminated."[31] Regardless of whether we accept the syntactical interpretation that posits four distinct items in the list ("head-choppings, eye-gougings, condemnations, and slaughters"), *dikai* is reduced to a small word pressured, oppressed, almost annihilated by two monstrous compounds, which subordinate the cognitive and ethical domain of "justice" to the perverted aesthetics of torture, the voyeuristic art of physical abuse, the castrating fantasies of an Apollinean Marquis de Sade. Court judgments (*dikai*)—the concrete enactments of *dikê*—are folded into the domain of slaughters, the coordinated and rhyming term *sphagai*. Just before the oneiric appearance of Clytemnestra, one of the most memorable moments in the play, Orestes presents himself as victimized, the underdog, a suppliant appealing to the mercy of Zeus, who "reveres the respect-worthiness of strangers" (*sebei toi Zeus tod' eknomôn sebas* 92). Here I reproduce the translation of the most authoritative commentator on the play, who, in rendering *ek-nomôn* as "strangers," confidently notes that the substantive adjective "is *best* connected with νομός [*nomós*] 'dwelling' . . . and taken to mean 'person away from home, stranger, wanderer'; cf. ἔννομος 'inhabitant.'"[32] The most obvious resonance with the word *nómos* (νόμος "law"), which only an accent separates from *nomós*, is excluded here, perhaps to maintain a stable alignment of the matricide Orestes, the future winner, with the "law," to protect Zeus from a dangerous contact with what is positioned outside conventional legitimacy. Being a "stranger" means being "undocumented," unrecognized by the law, inhabiting a condition that precedes (or contests) the social interpellation that defines the law. Orestes is in the same position—the "outcast"—as the Erinyes, while the hint of a rift between Zeus, the patron of suppliants, and the principle of legal authority subliminally seems to come into view, as though caring for strangers on the border means violating the law, partaking in their non-status, their non-belonging, their undefined, unbound political contours.[33]

Butler's Aeschylus with Kafka, Benjamin, and Diop

For Butler, the claustrophobic atmosphere of Kafka's *The Trial*—where guilt turns out to be a metaphysical condition, an ontological given, the inescapable consequence of subjectivization—looks ahead to "indefinite detention," to the necropolitical practices at the border of "imprisoning someone without a trial for an unstated or unknown period of time," and to the incarceration of Brown and Black people in prison facilities that perpetrate institutional, legalized violence.[34] Like the immigrant of our day, Joseph K. is held in a condition of ostensibly lawful suspension: he does not know why he is detained, what he is accused of, or when the trial will take place, futilely waiting for justice until he is killed by state officials for no apparent reason. In Kafka's novella, Butler says, "the allegation becomes the evidence, and its repetition and endless duration become the trial, the judgment, and finally the lethal punishment."[35] In a story in which (unstated) allegation coincides with conviction and execution, and punishment cannot be distinguished from murder, "what is exposed is not the unfurling of justice *through* law but the criminal dealings *of* law."[36] In *Eumenides*, the anti-Apollinean appearance of the Erinyes makes them into the culprits—even though they are officially the prosecutors. As we gather from the initial report of the Pythia, their abjection is a stigma impossible to distinguish from the miasma of guilt, the mark of criminality, the proof of culpability. In Kafka's narrative, Butler suggests, "law is where justice never arrives," for justice is precisely "the unfulfilled promise of the law, the one that, through indefinite detention, is systematically negated."[37] Butler's approach to Kafka resonates with the 2006 discussion of Benjamin's "Toward a Critique of Violence."[38] For Benjamin, "in the moment of instating [*Einsetzung*] as law ... law-positing does not simply relinquish violence; rather ... it turns this violence into the law-positing kind by establishing not an end that would be free of, and independent from, violence, but, on the contrary, an end that ... is necessarily and intimately bound up with it."[39] Thus, justice amounts to opposing the coercion that is constitutive of the law: in other words, as Butler puts it, "*doing the right thing according to established law is precisely what must be suspended in order to dissolve a body of established law that is unjust*."[40] There is a relation between the foundation of the law, with its coercive power, and the world of myth, represented by fate and the gods. As Butler observes, commenting on Benjamin[41]:

> Violence brings a system of law into being, and this law-founding violence is precisely one that operates without justification. Fate produces law, but it does so first through manifesting the anger of the gods. This anger takes form as law, but one that does not serve any particular end. It constitutes a pure means; its end, as it were, is the manifesting itself.

Benjamin famously employed the myth of Niobe—punished by Apollo and Artemis—to exemplify this idea. As Butler notes, "When Artemis and Apollo arrive on the scene to punish Niobe for her outrageous claim by taking away her children, these gods can be understood ... to be establishing a law."[42] In fact, as Butler continues, paraphrasing Benjamin, "Niobe's arrogance does not ... offend against the law; if it did, we would have to assume that the law was already in place prior to the offense." Rather, "Artemis and Apollo ... become the means by which fate is instituted" and "the triumph of fate is the establishment of law itself."

Similarly, in *Eumenides*, we could say, in light of Butler's commentary on Benjamin's Niobe, the establishment of the law—a legitimate, lawful system of retribution—"is not to be understood first and foremost as punishment or retribution for a crime committed against an existing law,"[43] because there is no law (yet). In the last play of the *Oresteia*, the law is installed and invented as a form of punishment—not of the defendant, but, paradoxically, of the accusers, who will be deprived of their punitive power. From the beginning of the play, the establishment of the law is presented as a punishment (imprisonment and reduction to silence) of the Erinyes, whose hubris and guilt are encapsulated by their lack of aesthetic decorum, by their performance of inhumanity. The semantic co-existence of "justice" and "judgment" (or "trial" and "verdict") in the word *dikê* is the clearest demonstration of the problematic identification of law with punishment, of the fact that the latter is perceived as constitutive of the former. Parallel to the relation between the Erinyes and *dikê* as it unfolds in *Eumenides*, "the story of Niobe illustrates law-instating violence"[44] because the gods establish a law to respond to a perceived offense—her boasting assimilated to a violation of decorum, to a transgression of the divine distribution of the sensible, that which, according to the gods, is allowed to be seen or heard. In Benjamin's reading, Niobe's petrification figures the law's petrifying power, its coercive capacity for freezing the subject in a perennial sense of guilt. As Butler comments:

> The anger works performatively to mark and transform Niobe, establishing her as the guilty subject, who takes on the form of petrified rock. Law thus petrifies the subject, arresting life in the moment of guilt. And though Niobe herself lives . . . she becomes permanently guilty, and guilt turns into rock the subject who bears it. . . . In a way, she represents the economy of infinite retribution and atonement that Benjamin elsewhere claims belongs to the sphere of myth. She is partially rigidified, hardened in and by guilt, yet full of sorrow, weeping endlessly from that petrified well-spring. The punishment produces the subject bound by law—accountable, punishable, and punished. She would be fully deadened by guilt if it were not for that sorrow, those tears.[45]

The subject comes into being through guilt. The institution of the law creates the subject by subjecting it to a perennial, almost incomprehensible sense of guilt: "to be a subject . . . is to take responsibility for a violence that precedes the subject."[46] As a result, "the formation of the subject who occludes the operation of violence by establishing herself as the sole cause of what she suffers is . . . a further operation of that violence."[47] While they do not feel guilt but anger—a feeling that shapes Niobe too—the Erinyes become the convicted accusers, destined for a golden prison and reduced to silence. Orestes' acquittal is the triumph of Apollo's misogyny, the marginalization of the maternal, which is made guilty for affirming itself, for rendering its claims terrifyingly visible and audible. Differently from Niobe, the Erinyes are interpellated as citizens through assuming the role of the vanquished in a trial—not just the accusers who lost the case, but the defendants, a priori guilty like Niobe, of offending Apollinean hierarchy with their very presence, with their voice as well as their appearance. The civic monumentalization of the Erinyes is an attempted petrification of their anger, an entombment of their manic potential. In Benjamin's words, Niobe's life is left behind "as an *eternal, mute bearer of guilt* and as a stone marking the border [*Grenze*] between human beings and gods."[48] Although the end of the play heralds the metamorphosis of the Erinyes into solemn goddesses, guarantors of civic stability, they still embody the border that cannot be violated (between Olympian gods and lesser beings), while their latent self remains the outside that needs to be coerced in order for the law to posit itself, to exercise the punitive impetus that is its raison d'être. We can suggest that the last play of the *Oresteia*, like Niobe's story dramatized in Aeschylus's eponymous play, stages how fate—appropriately incarnated by the god of oracles and predictions—"establishes the coercive conditions of law by manifesting the subject of guilt."[49] For Benjamin the deities who eternally incriminate Niobe while pretending to install an abstract principle of dispassionate equity (or justice) "purif[y] the guilty, not of guilt," but of the possibility of justice, "dissolv[ing] the bonds of accountability that follow from the rule of law itself."[50] The monumentalization of the Erinyes may instantiate this "purifying" power, that is, the self-condoning gesture of a biopolitical force that exempts itself from subjection to the law while entombing the possibility of disagreement and contestation in a golden prison, in the shiny stasis of internalized, naturalized guilt.

Butler's 2023 take on the Erinyes, their Niobean metamorphosis, as I see it, finds an illuminating comparandum in a contemporary tragic representation of the tribunal, presented as complicitous in the PIC's legalized violence, Alice Diop's *Saint Omer* (2022). When Butler notes that "for those who argue that justice is served by abolition . . . justice is defined against legal violence, which includes the violence of the prison system,"[51] I think of a similar critique of the identification of law and justice in Diop's rendition of Medea on trial. *Saint Omer* is based on the case of Fabienne Kabou, a Senegalese-French woman who, in 2016, was convicted of infanticide in the northern French town of the title. As in other cases, the infanticide, the misdeed of Medea (ancient and modern), provides a cognitive alibi for the coercive force of the law—for the biopolitical violence that makes the institution of the trial intrinsically incompatible with justice. The law uses such cases to renew itself, to impose itself once again by diffusing the oppressive feeling of guilt as a fact divorced from individuals' actual responsibility, as with Benjamin's Niobe or the Niobean Erinyes. In Diop's film, the trial of Laurence, Kabou's alter ego, reproduces the victim's sense of introjected guilt for not being coopted into the realm of subjecthood, for being brought into existence in order not to be; it displaces onto Medea—the foreigner, the otherized sorceress, the woman who cannot (and refuses to) fully be—the law's own practices of legitimized violence, its own murder, literal as well as figurative, of Black children. As Beth Richie observes, "Black women who do not fit into the traditional image of an innocent victim because they are an adolescent defendant charged with neonaticide, a lesbian who resists a sexually aggressive stranger, or a resident of public housing who is a victim of police brutality rather than interpersonal violence, will not receive the protection of a prison nation."[52] In the film, Medea is the easy, pre-packaged scapegoat for the legalized infanticide continuously committed by the lawful state—from Alan Kurdi, the Syrian refugee cast ashore on the coast of Turkey in 2015, to the children recently allowed to die in the Mediterranean by the Italian government in February 2023.[53] In *Saint Omer*, the border between lawful and unlawful is ultimately left unmarked, for the film prevents the law from rendering its verdict, from having the last word. The infanticidal Medea is the dramaturgical substitute for a murderous state violating the ethico-political obligations of hospitality.[54] Exposing this substitution, the refugee crisis undermines the criminalizing obsession with individual responsibility and objective judicial truth. The trial of the new Medea, if she is understood as a projection of the state's own infanticidal disciplinary power, becomes a (disavowed) moment of self-interrogation and self-incrimination—just as in *Eumenides*, the matricide for which Orestes is acquitted unwittingly puts on trial the Athenian state's misogynistic necrocitizenship, the denial of rights to and condoned abuse (within the home) of mothering women, the makers of its own citizens.[55]

The Furies and Niobe

The subterranean idea of enraged justice lends the Aeschylean Erinyes a "rocky" quality that cements a kinship with Niobe. Set in motion by Clytemnestra's goad, renewing their pursuit of the matricide Orestes, the Erinyes introduce themselves in the play's first choral ode (381–88):

> We are resourceful; we bring things to fruition and are mindful of bad things; we the solemn ones, *impossible to speak to* (*dusparêgoroi*) for mortals, practice (*diomenai*) tasks that are dishonored (*a-tima*), despised (*a-tieta*), separated (*dichostatount'*) from the gods by sunless slime, *inaccessible, rocky* (*dusodopaipala*) *for those who see* (*derkomenoisi*) and for *the sightless* (*dusommatois*) alike.

The abundant *d* sounds that dam up this passage intimate the contours of an affective and ethical alternative to the idea of *dikê*, to a justice that excludes the force of rage. *Dus-parêgoroi* ("impossible to speak to") conveys a refusal of the relationality of address, rejecting the normative affect of consoling speech, the urge to move on, the interpellation within a soothing invitation. In laying claim to tasks, activities "separated" (*dicho-statount'*) from the world of the gods, they activate the quasi-homophony between *dik-(ê)* ("justice") and *dich-*, from the adverb *dicha* ("apart"). The rejection of "honor" encapsulated in *a-tima* is accompanied by an aversion to a certain logic of "retribution" (in *a-tieta* from the verb *tiô*) that points to a mode of abolition, the rough, aspirated version of *dikê*, a *dikê* exceeding itself through refusal. What the Erinyes reject is not just "honor," but also the kind of punishment constrained within the borders of the "honorable," decorous law, a punishment that purifies and sublimates resentment over an irreparable loss.[56] Later, when Athena recuses herself from "adjudicating claims of justice for a slaying that arouses sharp wrath" (*phonou di-airein oxu-mênitou dikas* 472),[57] the proximity and mutual infiltration between *dikas* and *oxumênitou*—with the para-grammatical effect of *oxu-mênitou dikas* ("justice that arouses sharp wrath") instead of *phonou . . . oxu-mênitou* ("slaying that arouses sharp wrath")[58]—contours a different, quasi-utopian political configuration, in which justice juxtaposed with the rage against structural injustice bespeaks a justice that does not purify, normalize, or suppress that rage, but heeds it or operates alongside it. In the

Chorus's first ode, the "marker," the division or distinction from Apollo that the Erinyes will be forced to stand in for, à la Niobe, is converted into a principle of voluntary, willful self-extrication from the violence of (conventional) *dikê*. The tasks and the dishonored prerogatives allotted to the Erinyes are also called *dus-odopaipala* ("rough and rocky"), which "evokes the picture of a traveller painfully struggling along a difficult . . . and rocky . . . mountain road" and the scenario of "a . . . god-forsaken region in which [the Erinyes] exercise [their] functions."[59] How shall we interpret the harsh rockiness of the Erinyes? Is their grief—their melancholic anger—turning them into rocky figures like Niobe, the mother who, after having been deprived of all of her children, was turned into an ever-weeping stone?[60]

To expand on this suggestion, we should address the link between Niobe's grief—materialized in the solid yet liquid ontology of her post-human life—and her rage, a fundamental nexus in Butler's theorization of tragic precarity, as we saw in the Introduction. Noting that the Ovidian Niobe's immediate reaction to the death of her children "is *not* grief" but "astonishment and anger," Ellen Oliensis suggests that, in *Metamorphoses*, her "signature emotion is not softening grief but the hardening force of anger (*ira* 6.167; *irascentem* 6.269)."[61] In her first appearance in the Ovidian narrative, which supplies the most extensive account of Niobe's story, her looks and elegant deportment are compromised by her *ira*, which translators often render as "insolence" or "pride," supposing that Niobe will be held up as an exemplum of punished hubris, of appropriately condemned impiety. Yet, instead of an unproblematic, not-so-Ovidian alignment with moral didacticism, we may see, following Victoria Rimell, an "enraged, sarcastic Niobe," who (perhaps like Ovid himself?) "dares to speak to power by mocking those who worship gods in some desperate act of self-abasement in order to avoid the violence of tyrannical divine whim."[62] Niobe's resentment is the same as the Erinyes': partaking of a minor level of divinity (her grandfather is Jupiter himself), she is deprived of the honors owed to her, of what is permanently granted to Latona's children—Artemis/Diana and *Apollo*. From a Benjaminian and Butlerian perspective, Niobe's *ira* before the tragedy is the affective response to—and the refutation of—a pre-existing inequality, inseparable from life itself, that the murder of her offspring will formalize in law. This expansive *ira* ("anger") circulated by her boastful words rushes into the gap internalized as ontological guilt, contesting the distribution of the sensible troped by the human/divine boundary and the metaphysical alignment of law with violence that will be sanctioned by the gods' punitive intervention. After the slaughter, when we read that Niobe "became angry (*irascentem*) that the gods above had dared such a deed, that they had such a right (*iuris*)" (269–70)—a reaction that further isolates her from our approval[63]—the question of the (im)possible, subjunctive relation between *ira* and *iuris* (from *ius*) arises. How can *ius, iuris* heed the demands of *ira*—a demand for equality, for a law purified of violence? The non-agentic agency of Niobe's petrified silence at the beginning of Aeschylus's play—a preview of her metamorphosis into stone[64]—visualizes a "grief" (*luctu*) that we could characterize, with Statius, as "swollen" (*tumido*), always about to burst out (*Thebaid* 4.576).[65] This swelling evokes a reservoir, a repository not just of tears but liquid rage. The continuing flow of tears liquefies her enraged words, the acoustic insistence, the roughness of the protest, which Ovid and Statius are said to cast as mere insolence, the vocalization of a haughty nature. As Rebecca Comay notes:

> In Seneca's *Oedipus*, summoned from the dead by Tiresias, [Niobe] will appear in the company of the Theban ancestors, voiceless but unrepentent, insolently gesticulating as she continues to tally up the shades of her children (*numerat umbras*). In a related scene in Statius's *Thebaid*, this fury of enumeration will erupt into a *jouissance* of "insane," unbridled lamentation (4.575–78): *percenset . . . insanae plus iam permittere linguae.*[66]

While regarding Niobe's "insane tongue" (*insanae . . . linguae*) as the organ of her ceaseless mourning, the vocal counterpart of her weeping, Comay points us to the bond between Niobe's tears and her rage, or her "dar[ing] to speak to power"—the sarcastic, angry speech that provided a casus belli for the law-installing intervention of Apollo. I have lingered on this passage because the liquid implications of the angry swelling conveyed by *tumido* may enable us to view Niobe's infinite weeping—the vital percolation of somber water through the material sameness of her stoniness—as something comparable to the spitting of the Erinyes, the manifestation of their "insane tongue," of the incendiary orality (or, better, "buccality") that contests the law even before it is officially instated. Weeping is equivalent to spitting, just as the eyes are orifices interchangeable with the mouth.[67]

Buccal Exscriptions

Let us turn to Aeschylus's *Agamemnon*, where we find an emblematic image of the Erinyes' enraged, Niobean orality. In Cassandra's description, three details leap out: their bold gulping down (*pepôkôs*) of wine-like blood (1188–89); their macabre singing (*humnousi*) on the origins of the curse in the house of Agamemnon (1191–92); and their spitting (*ap-eptusan*) on the bed of Thyestes (1192–93).[68] Acts of buccal ejection, singing and spitting spread a bloody contagion and disseminate revenge, keeping the loop of anger always spinning. In the last play of the trilogy, when the ghost of Clytemnestra calls on the sleepy Erinyes to "dry up" their victims by blowing "bloody breath" (*haimatêron pneuma* 137) on them, the breath becomes liquid, respiration a spitting out of accumulated blood.[69] The arduous phonetics of *kat-ischnainousa* ("drying up" 138) generates a concentration of saliva ready to burst out. The Erinyes' pursuit of their victim is the looping movement of a fountain, a "buccal exscription"[70] that vitiates the imposition of the law's signifying breath. ("Buccal exscription" is the phrase coined by Jean-Luc Nancy to capture the inscriptional ejections, primarily saliva, emitted by the mouth as *bucca*, as the organ of non-linguistic orality.)[71] Similarly, Niobe's endless flow of tears is melancholically re-enacted bloodshed, a regurgitation of the vital liquid shed by her offspring, an aggrieved ejection of tear-shaped *cruor* ("shed blood"), which is also a reproduction of *sanguis* ("blood in the veins").[72] Niobe's fountain is the angry conation of deindividuated life in the face of violence[73]—for life, as Nancy puts it, "draws in and presses out always and again, like a pump whose handle one moves."[74] Niobe's weeping rock is life that "pushes itself to live" or life that "receives its own push and undergoes its own drive"—life "flowing away spasmodically pushed and driven toward itself."[75] Every breath of the Erinyes is an ex-pression of anger, imagistically tied to the ejection of blood spurting from an abdomen that, with every breath, feels hit by the haptic remainder of a murderous blow, the pain of a ghostly stab.[76] In the words of Athena (478–79), the "poison" (rotten blood?) springing forth "from their pride" (*ek phronêmatôn* 478)—released by their rage, materializing their rage as an unerasable trace—is a "chronic" (*aianês* 479) disease, a liquid virus endlessly soaking the ground. Certain of his victory, Apollo announces that, if the Erinyes cannot win *tês dikês telos*, "the outcome of the trial," but also "justice" (729), the poison (*ton ion*) that they will "vomit out" (730) will no longer be hurtful. Once again, "justice" is the antidote to the poison of anger, the triumph of an affect-less, aseptic righteousness whose violence resides precisely in the privative prefix, in the suppression of outrage, in the consensual normalization of resentment. The interpretation of Niobe's tears as infinite mourning—without infinite rage—is an effect of this normalization, which from the level of the law seeps into the discursive domain of literary reading.

In *Frames of War* (2009), published after Butler's essay on Benjamin's Niobe, a Niobean mode seems to affect their analysis of one of the poems of Ustad Badruzzaman Badr, detained and tortured at Guantanamo:

> The whirlpool of our tears
> Is moving fast toward him
> No one can endure the power of this flood

The pool of tears is anagrammatically a loop of tears, both human and elemental matter, which, in Butler's words, acts as "a poetic tool of insurgency, even a challenge to individual sovereignty."[77] The insurgency is reflected in the modality of the inscriptional gesture: "The words are carved in cups, written on paper, recorded onto a surface, in an effort to leave a mark, a trace, of a living being," a mark that, like the silhouettes of An(tigon)a Mendieta discussed in the first chapter, is an act of appearance in disappearance, a manifestation of being as mediation. An *élan vital* is impressed upon the surface, which presses back while receiving it, giving hospitality to it; at once made and unmade, inscriber and inscribed, *élan* and medium, are dispossessed by indexicality's production of precarious presence. "The body breathes, breathes itself into words," Butler continues, but "once the breath is made into words, the body is given over to another, in the form of an appeal."[78] When we read that "the body is . . . what lives on, breathes, tries to carve its breath into stone,"[79] we stumble upon Niobe, as breath becomes liquid, bursts into an enraged flood, a menacing whirlpool[80] that the stone does not impede or imprison but precariously enables through its elemental hospitality, its infrastructural support of the impetus it bears.

I want to broaden my perspective on the Erinyes' Niobean liquidity by considering the rebellious phenomenology of spitting. In a 2021 article, J. T. Roane discusses the case of Donnetta Hill, a Black sex worker who acquired notoriety in the early 1990s not for having been the victim of repeated abuse by police, but for having spat on two of the jurors during her trial. As Roane comments, "What the court and journalists described as erratic, violent behavior further evidencing Hill's incorrigibility and her capacity for murder, and justifying her execution" amounts, in fact, to "a claim to rage and its possibilities as the elementary basis of poor Black women's rogue articulations of freedom."[81] For Roane, Hill's gesture—staining the Apollinean violence, the monumental detachment of coercive law—is "part of a lineage of spitting rage, which constitutes a distinctive political-affective structure attributable to the unique social positioning of 'Black captive maternals.'"[82] Spitting, in Roane's words, belongs to "a repertoire of ... disruptions that furtively interrupt the processes of enclosure, violent deprivation, deadly austerity, and the state's ultimate reinforcement of these relations through its arbitration of gendered racial capitalism as executioner."[83] By spitting on the jurors and cursing at them, Hill sought "in a fleeting effort at physical volatility to expose and reverse the state's investments in racialized sexual coercion." When we read Roane's account of the trial, we are reminded of the Pythia's and Apollo's depiction of the Erinyes, their aesthetic condemnation, which closes the play (and the imminent trial) before it has even begun:[84]

> Social workers described Donnetta as unkempt, poorly dressed, defiant, violent, and mismatched between her size and her age in a grammar that drew on enduring sedimented archives of bodily and psychic abjection. In court these profiles helped the prosecution create a picture of Hill as a predestined murderer, corroborating her broader "unfitness" for life and justifying their seeking of the death penalty.

As Roane continues, "Before the state regained control of her and bailiffs subdued her and removed her from court," Hill's spitting at two jurors and thus at the state represented "a small index of her rage, her fierce if ephemeral defense against the state's investments and further entrenchment of sexual coercion in the production of her signed confession."[85]

To understand the implications of this enraged exscription, it is worth elaborating on Nancy's notion of buccality, a theorization of the mouth as a space of pre- or post-subjectivity.[86] Buccality is a contestation of the *os* (Latin for mouth, reflected in English "oral" and "orality"), the channel of signifying sound, discourse, the quintessential expression of the human subject apparently individuated by the semiotic, physiognomic system of the face, which, in fact, as Butler has written in their re-reading of Levinas, "is neither reducible to the mouth nor, indeed, to anything the mouth has to utter."[87] In this frame, the face takes on an (in)human, buccal function, becoming "that for which no words really work," a vehicle for "the wordless vocalization of suffering" and the Levinasian imperative *Thou shalt not kill*.[88] For Nancy, as Sara Guyer observes, the "buccal mouth speaks but its speech is not separate from other actions of the mouth": the *bucca*, that is, "signifies an underdeveloped or faceless cavity in which eating-speaking-breathing-spitting, incorporation and introjection, contraction and distension are undifferentiated."[89] The Erinyes' and Hill's bodily protests channel an enraged contestation of the Apollinean, logocentric sublimation of the *bucca* as *os*, bringing forth the visceral impersonality of an opening, a bodily abyss that manifests, with eruptive force, the ordinariness of pure being, that is, subjectless being.[90] The buccal ordinariness of spitting (as well as eating and breathing) defies the "extraordinariness" of the linguistic act of law-instating, the exceptional situation or the state of emergency that every trial declares and promises to resolve. Language, in particular forensic rhetoric, fashions itself as "extraordinary," as an act of authoritative orality, while disavowing its own buccality, its reliance on breath, the evanescent matter, the nonhuman support that, in Butler's terms, is the "ground" of every speech act and of life itself.[91] (There is a strong connection between Nancy's buccality and Butler's "breathability.")[92] If, from the perspective of buccality, the distinction between speaking and spitting is blurred, Niobe's weeping—a lachrymose exscription—becomes a watery outburst of angry speech. The rage poured out in Hill's trial brings to Niobe's own *torrential* fury:[93]

> Rage, like that expressed in spitting on jurors, is generally understood as an incomprehensible *torrent* of emotion, a fiery and uncontained affective structure, volatile, unproductive, and driven by madness, the sensual and impassioned inverse of reason further evidencing the incapacity for self-control and thus also culpability for a crime of passion.

The Erinyes' and Niobe's spitting—buccal or optic—brings their demand for justice close to the defacement of works of art carried out by protesters, especially climate activists. According to Andrea Gyenge, buccality articulates a version of what Deleuze and Guattari call "a politics without a face," a politics of imperceptibility that would "make faciality traits themselves finally elude the organization of the face," whether that of the protesters themselves or their targets.[94] Yet, as I have just mentioned, Butler has demonstrated that the Levinasian face operates analogously to the (in)human *bucca*, that is, through an expressivity that Deleuze and Guattari might ascribe to the domain of defacement. The "facial bucca" or "buccal face" can thus be aligned with other expressions of public rage, which I would characterize as acts of anti-monumental or counter-monumental spitting. Discussing incidents including a German environmental group throwing mashed potatoes at a Claude Monet painting in a Potsdam museum and activists from Just Stop Oil hurling tomato soup over Vincent van Gogh's *Sunflowers* at the National Gallery in London, Butler, while not condoning these actions, points out that the protesters "are trying to deliver a jolt that interrupts our denial and makes us confront the loss that we are bringing about all the time."[95] I am also thinking of the Columbus Fountain at Union Station in Washington, D.C., defaced with red paint in 1991 and then again in 2002 ("510 years resistance"). The Israeli separation wall, turned into a billboard of European and American art and commercials, was targeted in 2017, as reconstructed by Connie Gagliardi, with an enraged palimpsestic defacing:[96]

> Armed with a can of red spray paint, the defacer quickly scrawled, "Falast in mish lawh rasim" in Arabic text across the centerfold face of Mark Zuckerberg. "Palestine is not a drawing board." Red paint bled down the Wall in places where the calligraphy of the letters looped back on themselves, where the defacer had sprayed too much paint. The defacer was no spray-paint expert. The message, written in haphazard, loopy penmanship, even revealed an untrained hand, lacking in ease with writing in Arabic.

Defacement here is a way to speak truth to power, reveal "facticity's hidden dependence on illusion,"[97] and cry out, as Butler might put it, that "there is no separating wall that can nullify the ethical demand for responsiveness to the suffering of the other."[98] Covering representation or, in Rancierean terms, the representational regime that re-enacts or heightens the violence of the wall, the veil of opacity overlaid by monochromatic painting challenges the aspiration to turn bare matter, the pigment, into a signifying system that seeks to exceed it.[99] Such covering rebinds the self-styled artwork, which occupies a public space and foists itself upon the public eye, to its "abject" origin, a mere expanse of color. Just as the material facticity of the pigment lays bare the illusion of representation, the Erinyes' and Niobe's visceral exscriptions convert the illusion of the law—which imposes itself as an authoritative orality, something beyond air—into the bleak facticity of breath. In their barren immanence, blood, saliva, and tears symbolically splattered onto the edifices of the law—the temples that Niobe disdained and the Areopagus, the courthouse founded by Athena—defile the facade of normativity.[100] Hierarchy's solid power of representational closure is ephemerally undone by an eruption of liquid thickness, by the assaultive force of semiotic and affective loss, which mimetically generates a tear, a radical opening. A material excess brings out the violence that conceals itself behind the ostensible transparency of verbal representation, the wall of the law's punctilious clarity. Gagliardi observes that the defacement "illuminated the brutal face of the Wall . . . as the unmasked face of the Israeli state and its colonial project," as a persistent effort, in Butler's phrase, "to render faceless an entire population."[101] Juxtaposed with the image of Erinyes spitting blood or contaminated saliva, the monumental facade of the Apollinean law loses its aura of untouchability; it reveals its exposure to what Susan Hansen, referring to Derrida, calls the "aesthetics of the outside": "Graffiti breaks the 'law of untouchability' in that it invites viewers to touch and even to leave one's own trace on the wall" and thus to violate law's untouchability.[102]

The analogy between red paint, saliva, and blood leads us back to a detail of Roane's commentary on Donnetta Hill, to his observation that "[her] verbal and physical rebellions register a form of working-class Black women's abolition emerging from self-protection and coalescing as a *sticky* and wet assault on majoritarian publics and the state."[103] The Erinyes' spitting invites us to consider the sticky politics of rage or the very politics of stickiness. In his theoretical treatment of viscosity, Freddie Mason discusses Everett Dean Martin's notorious contempt for what he called "oozing democracy,"[104] a democracy, that is, dominated by the crowd, a conglomerate of people "not working together" but "only sticking together."[105] Martin's fetishization of the individualistic humanism of liberal democracy leads him to reject the contagious cognitive and affective transmission, circulation, blending, and mixing in the space of the crowd—the "unctuousness of mind by which ideas are fastened upon others without their assent."[106] Martin's rhetoric, as Mason puts it, regards "mere adhesion," "blind solidarity," and the "wildnesses of vehement togetherness"—phrases resonant with Butler's distinctive emphasis on the political power of assembly, intertwinement, interdependency, inbetweenness, and porosity in light of the Covid pandemic—as the most destructive threats to liberal democracy.[107] In *Notes toward a Performative Theory of Assembly* (2015), Butler explains the materiality of assembling, the phenomenology of coming or gathering together on the street:

> If the people are constituted through a complex interplay of performance, image, acoustics, and all the various technologies engaged in those productions, then "media" is not just reporting who the people claim to be, but media has entered into the very definition of the people. It does not simply assist that definition, or make it possible; it is the *stuff* of self-constitution.[108]

In this account, *stuff* almost regains its etymological meaning of "what is drawn together," what is "contracted" or "condensed,"[109] as though the assembly manifested and enacted the social ecology of co-being, the political ethics of co-dependence—which we would expect democracy to realize through equality[110]—as a thick substance, something that we do not only see or hear but also touch as it touches back.[111] Mason's critique of "thinking [that is] paranoid about a world longing to clump up" recalls the radical power of social deindividuation attached to Hill's rebellious expectoration, which reflects back on the Erinyes' spitting. The stickiness of saliva and blood brings out rage's demand for "insurrectionary solidarity," to use Butler's phrase—"a wild associative force"[112] that refuses the logic of completion, the call to move on. Stickiness confuses temporality: "it holds things in a liminal state between life and death," troubling the dividing line between the beginning and the end.[113] Oozing rage keeps the trial, or even the prison, open; it challenges institutionalized justice with the slipperiness of a persistent doubt, an adhesive impulse to clump together in the undercommons. It drips with a subjunctive affect, a lingering power to imagine sociality not beyond the law, but beyond the violence of distinguishing who is innocent and who is a priori always guilty.

Countermonumental *Dikê*

In *Eumenides*, the somatics of rage, like Hill's spitting and Niobe's liquid puncturing of her stony self-encasement, pierce through monumentalized law, as we notice in these lines, in which the Erinyes' fury perforate the intricacies of poetic form (155–61):

> Blame that came to me from dreams
> struck like a charioteer
> with a goad that seized me in the middle,
> under the heart,
> under the guts.
> From a destructive, public torturer one can
> feel some heavy, very heavy coldness.
> *emoi d' oneidos ex oneiratôn molon*
> *etupsen dikan diphrêlatou*
> *mesolabei kentrôi*
> *hupo phrenas*
> *hupo lobon*
> *paresti mastiktoros daiou damiou*
> *baru ti peribaru kruos echein*

Urged by Clytemnestra's ghost to renew their pursuit, the Erinyes detail the physical effects of her reproach: a sharp, insistent spasm in the depths of the body. Wounded corporeality cannot be sublimated through the abstract impersonality of the law, through its marmoreal injunction to let rage dissipate. The phonetic conflation of "blame" (*onei-dos*) and "dream" (*onei-ratôn*), and the return of the former as the latter, prefigure the failure of the final reconciliation, by which the Erinyes are figuratively put to sleep, as we found them at the beginning of the play. The blame, the recrudescence of reproach that comes "from the dream," is an affective stab like that of the wildly comparative logic of the oneiric experience itself. Through the adverbial use of the accusative *dikan* ("like, in the guise of"),[114] an accusative of *dika/dikê*, justice coincides with the shock, or the stab, of likeness. As Paul North observes, "Likeness strikes and wakes you, if only for a moment from your ontological slumber."[115] The goad of the charioteer is a meta-simile: it illustrates the very force of likeness, its capacity for conjuring "a huge, if not infinite set of unexpected juxtapositions." While the law tends to impose the "ontological slumber" of common sense, conventional thinking, and conceptual individuation, rage's enfleshed drive for justice—"the very press and push that opens a body,"[116] a resistant exertion that re-enacts the "beating pulse" of shed blood[117]—engenders the same agitation, the same infinite extension as likeness itself. Such an extension is visualized by the seriality of the pairings *oneidos . . . oneiratôn; dikan diphrêlatou*; and *daiou damiou.*[118] Only one letter separates *daiou* ("destructive") from *damiou* ("public")—an indication not only of the impossibility of preventing "destructiveness" from penetrating the sphere of public harmony, but also of the political need for the "destructive" *mania* valorized by Butler in *The Force of Nonviolence* to exercise its divisive power, to pierce the conscience of the community and of the individual. This puncture is intimated by the diaeresis (a phonetic split between the vowels of a diphthong) in *daiou* ("destructive," δαΐου), and by *di-phre-latou* ("charioteer"), which looks ahead to *hupo phre-nas* ("into the heart") in the subsequent lines, visualizing a "piercing" (*di-*) movement through the *phre-nas.*[119] The puncture delineates a justice (*di-kê*) that (un)realizes itself as a throughness (*di-* from *dia*, "through"), a suspension in a pre-made, recognizable, apparently solid structure (in this case the word *di-phrê-latou*). Later in the play, when the Chorus declares, "If I don't obtain *justice* (*tês dikês*), I will again visit this land, being *burdensome* (*bareia*) to it" (719–20), rage appears as the weight of repetition that the community fears will cause it to collapse. The proximity between *dikê* and *bareia* generates a bond, casting justice not as a resolution relieving the community of its burdens by burying the afflictions and traumas of some and thus of all in its recesses, but rather as a deictic gesture, a burdensome presence, pointing to such afflictions, making rage fully visible and audible. In other words, the communication between *dikê* and *bareia*, with its buccal *b* sound, raises the question of how *dikê* can reconnect with its etymological kin *deiknumi* ("to show, to point to"), how it can amount to a form of indexicality, a countermonumental affective deixis, something exemplified by statements such as these from *Notes toward a Performative Theory of Assembly*:[120]

> It is *this* body, and *these* bodies, that require employment, shelter, health care, and food. . . . It is *this* body, or *these* bodies, or bodies *like* this body or these bodies, that live the condition of an imperiled livelihood, decimated infrastructure, accelerating precarity.[121]

This countermonumental deixis of *dikê* reinforces the affinity of the Erinyes with Niobe at the moment that their defeat in the trial is proclaimed. The long lyric refrain, a mourning song (780–93) marking this ending, has an inscriptional quality. Writing yet unwriting the Erinyes' visceral resentment, it gives voice to the burdensome remainder that anger is:

> *I* (*egô*) am dishonored, wretched, and *oppressively angry* (*barukotos*) in *this* land, oh, emitting my heart's poison, a poison in payment for grief, dripping to the ground, unbearable, and from it an ulcer, with no plants, with no children, *O Justice, O Justice* (*ô Dika Dika*), assaulting the plain, will throw mortal-killing stains on the land. *I* wail. . . . How afflicted are we, the ill-fated maiden daughters of Night, dishonored and full of grief!

The initial presence of deictic markers—"I" and "in this land"—engraves a lamentation. The Erinyes mourn in the key of Benjamin's and Butler's Niobe—for they are marginalized by, excluded from, the *dikê* of the law, which assigns them the weight of an a priori, almost metaphysical culpability, while asking them to accept the ascription of this culpability as a transformative moment, the conclusion of a linear narrative or the outcome of a "process," a word that, in some modern languages, means "trial" (see Kafka's *Der Prozess*). The "burden" in *baru-kotos* casts the affective pressure of Erinyes's rage, oriented inward and outward, as the mimetic consequence of stalled, "stony" time, of the unbearability of time reduced to oppressive sameness by imposed marginality, by the encumbrance of timeless guilt. The trial purports to lay down a law whose original installment is, however, lost in the abyss of melancholic, Niobean time, even though, in the play, its establishment is staged as a twofold event, the foundation of the Areopagus and the verdict of the trial. About to be interred in the tombal crevices (*keuthmônas*)[122] of the land, Athens, which Athena calls "just," or "living in justice" (*endikou* 805), the Erinyes face a subterranean petrification coinciding with biopolitical *dikê*. Anger from being deprived of what was owed to them blends, à la Niobe, into the physiology of mourning; poison dripping from their mouths, the pestilential drops are confused with tears, materializations of loss.

This mourning bears on Butler's reading of the play, specifically the most famous lines of the *Oresteia*, when the Chorus in *Agamemnon*, which will metamorphose in the last play of the trilogy into the Erinyes, enunciates the ethical lesson of *pathei mathos* (176–83):

> Zeus is the one who puts mortals on the path to *wisdom* (*phronein*), *the one who has imposed* (*ton. . . thenta*) the principle "learning through suffering" (*pathei mathos*), for it is authoritatively laid down. Instead of sleep, in front of the heart, *a grief-remembering labor* (*mnêsipêmôn ponos*) is dripping; and *wisdom* (*sôphronein*) comes even to those who are not willing to receive it. This is a *grace* (*charis*) of the gods, who sit on a *solemn bench* (*selma semnon*), *imposed by force* (*biaios*).

Building on Anne Carson's literal rendition of *mnêsipêmôn* as "griefremembering,"[123] Butler reads *ponos* as "the painful work of mourning," as the labor resulting from the "the obsessional repetitions of the Furies," from their "struggle to accept the reality of a violent loss when that loss remains unacceptable." The Chorus of old men in *Agamemnon* is already a latent Chorus of Erinyes.[124] The clinging to pain that is figured by the formal extension of the compound *mnêsipêmôn* approximates a melancholic condition, which encompasses an impossibility of forgetting, an enraged unwillingness to move on. This willful unwillingness "oozes," just like the abject, rotten liquid (blood or poison) dripping from the mouths of the Erinyes. Conversely, the inexorable, inescapable "arrival" of "wisdom" (*phronein/sôphronein*) resembles Benjamin's installation of mythical law, which, in *Eumenides*, is exemplified by Athena's foundation of the Areopagus, a law court that constitutively criminalizes the Erinyes (and, to an extent, the whole citizen body) while ostensibly founding democracy.[125] These lines are strongly intratextual with the trilogy's last play.[126] After the formulation of *pathei mathos*, we may glimpse a Eumenidean coloration in the coercive grace (*charis biaios*), the decorum of Apollo in the solemn seat of the Delphic oracle (*selma semnôn*), where phonic remainders of the cruel killing of the Pythian snake are located in the sigmatic reduplication (a persistent hissing). The Delphic oracle, the quintessential monumentalization of Apollinean law, is tainted by a sibilant poison, a snaky fury, the rage of the writhing reptiles wrapped around the Erinyes' arms.

To return to the *Eumenides* passage, we can say that, as the Erinyes are about to become Niobean countermonuments—encased objects oozing liquid rage—their invocation of Justice activates the indexical force of *dikê*, shifting its meaning from the revelation of a verdict to affective deixis, an insistent pointing toward ever-burning trauma, an initiation (rather than a conclusion) of a collective reckoning with injustice. In the Erinyes' mourning song, *Dikê* emerges as the impetus of an apostrophe, an address without response that prolongs rage into an affective *à venir*, a dilated intensity, the mobile immobility of liquid and sonic flow. This intensity infects the law, the self-monumentalizing breath incapable of evading the enraged atmospherics. When the Chorus of the Erinyes performs the lyrical speech act, "I breathe out *forceful impulse* (*menos*) and all my *anger* (*koton* 840)," an excess of rage fills the theatrical air, enveloping Athena, who, in responding, "I will be indulgent (*xun-oisô*) with your anger (*orgas* 848)," admits her own immersion—or participation (as indicated by preposition *xun/sun*)—in the furious cloud, in the aerial *thumos* that has engulfed the stage.

Aeschylus and Audre Lorde

Athena's description of the Erinyes' anger-driven capabilities evinces an aestheticized imagistic cathexis to them, a perversely buoyant dwelling on their formal phenomenology (859–60):

> Don't [throw in my places] incentives to bloodshed, damages to young innards, made crazy by wineless rage.
> *mêth' haimatêras thêganas, splanchnôn blabas*
> *neôn, aoinois emmaneis thumômasin*

It is as though poetic form is thrown into disarray and stalled by a descriptive overload, having introjected the affective swelling of the Erinyes' enraged breath, translated into the thick intertwinement of aspiration and velars. A circulating concentration of heated emotion overcomes diction, the speech act that fabricates the law. We are confronted with an all-too-human ballooning of anger, as we can infer from Athena's ascent to a linguistic no-man's-land in her attempt to characterize the Erinyes' rage as an "excessive excess" (*huper-thumôs agan* 824). In Athena's reference to *haimatêras thêganas*, what I translated as "incentives to bloodshed" is, more literally, "bloody whetstones." I am struck by the epiphany of the same image in Audre Lorde's *A Poem for Women in Rage*:[127]

> The heavy blade spins out toward me
> slow motion
> years of fury surge upward like a wall

and I do not hear it
clatter to the pavement at my feet.

Gears of ancient nightmare churn
swift in familiar dread and silence
but this time I am awake, released
I smile. Now. This time is
my turn.
I bend to the knife my ears blood-drumming
across the street my lover's voice
the only moving sound within white heat
"Don't touch it!"
I straighten, weaken, then start down again
hungry for resolution
simple as anger and so close at hand
my fingers reach for the familiar blade
the known grip of wood against my palm
for I have held it to the whetstone
a thousand nights for this
escorting fury through my sleep
like a cherished friend
to wake in the stink of rage
beside the sleep-white face of love.

The keen steel of a dream knife
sparks honed from the whetted edge with a tortured shriek
between my lover's voice and the grey spinning
a choice of pain or fury
slashing across judgment like a crimson scar
I could open her up to my anger
with a point sharpened upon love.

Functioning as a whetstone itself, poetic language sharpens anger; a concentrated surrogate of the years that build toward an upward surge of fury, it is a constant potentiality, which never exhausts itself, always renewing itself through its projective tension, through a deferral that, even when momentarily interrupted by the semblance of a "resolution," leaves behind a reservoir of blurred past-future intensities. As Lorde declares elsewhere,[128] "I have lived with that anger, on that anger, beneath your anger, on top of that anger, ignoring that anger, feeding upon that anger, learning to use that anger before it laid my vision to waste, for most of my life." This temporal reservoir is the matter solidified into the first line's "heavy blade," an object that makes us look at the "heavy anger" (*barun koton* 800) anxiously mentioned by Athena as a cutting instrument, a weight that, like the poem's phonic and imagistic overload, breaks a surface through accumulated pressure. In the last stanza of Lorde's poem shown here, the sonic sharpening located at the edges of the second line (*sparks* ... *shriek*) climaxes with a similar cuttingly sibilant bookending in the fifth line (*slashing* ... *scar*),[129] which brings us back to the image of "fury" tearing a barrier, slowly rending ("slashing across") the hierarchical individuation that the law calls "judgment" or "justice." Like Athena's warning to the Erinyes not to release anger, the lines of Lorde that present rage as a companion nourished in the calm of sleep ("escorting fury through my sleep ... to wake in the stink of rage") are themselves enactments of anger's internal and external pressure. Buccal exscriptions, the sibilant beginnings of "sleep," "stink," and, in the text of Aeschylus, *spl-anchnôn* ("innards") already amount to performative intimations of infuriated spitting, eruptions from the seething internal pond that Lorde discusses in the following passage from *Sister Outsider*:

> My black woman's anger is a molten pond at the core of me, my most fiercely guarded secret. I know how much of my life as a powerful feeling woman is laced through with this net of rage ... a boiling hot spring likely to erupt at any point, leaping out of my consciousness like a fire on the landscape.[130]

Speaking of Lauryn Hill, whose lyrics (including the song "Black Rage") "encourage enraged black people to politicize their wrath in pursuit of social transformation,"[131] La Marr Jurelle Bruce compares her, in her "early exaltation as prophetess and subsequent derision as madwoman,"[132] to Cassandra in Aeschylus's *Agamemnon*, a character who is another Erinys, or an Erinys-like figure.

Fury Blackness Breath

The formalized persistence of a justice of rage, of an alternative justice located in, inextricably entangled with, intimately attached to rage, which, as I have suggested, we can read into the textured *poiêsis* of Aeschylus's play, connects with Butler's general interest in the Erinyes' "fury" as justice not *against*, but *beyond* the law. Starting from Angela Davis's observation that "once institutions start talking about equity, diversity, and inclusion"—the third point applying directly to the conclusion of *Eumenides*—"those revolutionary ideals have surely been lost,"[133] Butler comments:

> It is only through the turn to the extra-legal that a nonviolent world looks possible. That does not mean getting rid of law, but only not looking to law to address all political issues, all forms of injury and repair. Abolition, on the other hand, asks for a new imagination, asking what other ways of organizing social life are possible in response to violent acts that would not reproduce violence in the proposed solution.[134]

There is a deep homology between political law and the law of literary reading. While the practice of reading ancient literature is still constrained within the hierarchical gates of conventional philology—dominated by the intentionalist and historicist approach to poetic language encapsulated in the commentary's distribution of the sensible, in its division between what can be said and what cannot, what can or cannot be seen or heard in the classical object[135]—in this chapter and the previous ones, I have sought to model a kind of formalistic abolition. This entails an attention to resonances, subliminal suggestions, ostensibly useless or unproductive associations, potential disruptions of syntax (the "law" of formal composition) through the alternative "ways of organizing" offered by juxtapositions, unscripted adjacencies, and, to appropriate some of Butler's own phrases, serendipitous proximities, improvisational intertwinements, insurrectionary solidarities between words, phonetic units, and quasi- or pseudo-syntactical entities.[136] Aeschylus's *poiêsis*—the doing and continuing undoing of form that his tragedy stages—is a performance of rage in its own right. Instead of construing his widely commented-upon "manic" aesthetics as merely a question of aesthetic self-fashioning or poetological judgment, we can translate this poetic, *poiêtic*, and even *poethical* mania—which conventional readings of Aristophanes' *Frogs* have prompted us to link with aristocratic elitism[137]—into a metapolitical discourse, into the "new imagination" fostered by abolition.[138]

Butler's discussion demonstrates the centrality of Aeschylus's Furies to current conversations on Black rage—and its explicit or implicit criminalization, before and after the murder of George Floyd, in Western democracies. "Perhaps one reason *The Eumenides* speaks to us now is that it reckons with a rage over an unacceptable and violent loss, or losses," says Butler, continuing, "If we dismiss the rage as uncivil and applaud its domestication, we may well miss what the rage articulates about how unbearable it is to be asked to live with the radical injustice of certain losses, especially those that are the result of police killing and legal violence," the losses "that not only fai[l] to do justice, but amplif[y] racial violence."[139] I want to juxtapose Butler's words with Deborah Thompson's "exoneration of Black rage" in response to the affective double standard informing the racialized politics of American democracy[140]:

> When expressed by African Americans to combat the injustice of police brutality, both anger and rage are viewed as incompatible, or even dangerous, to the operation of American democracy; meanwhile, the anger expressed by dominant groups (especially heterosexual white men) is easily incorporated into political discourse, normalized as politics as usual. . . . Liberal democracy's failure to understand black rage as a legitimate response to white supremacy reveals the limits of the liberal imagination as a means of challenging America's white democracy.

In underscoring the racist dichotomy between a "good, productive, normal" anger—a welcome infiltration of "popular" authenticity into "elitist" political discourse, a "refreshing" manifestation of "freedom of speech," a libertarian explosion of the constrictions of "political correctness"—and a "bad, dangerous, riotous" one, Thompson invites us to consider the double standard in Apollo's reference to the "just" anger of Orestes (232–34): "I will help and save the suppliant; for the *anger* (*mênis*) of the suppliant is terrible among both mortals and gods." What is the qualitative difference between this anger and that of the Erinyes? The homosocial relationship between Apollo and Orestes is an obvious microcosm of the political status quo that the Apollinean hierarchy seeks to safeguard, manipulating the "outsider" Orestes to legitimize the exclusion of any outside, to ward off the expansive possibilities of hospitality, which inevitably disrupts the state's fetishized self-enclosure, its disavowal of vulnerability.[141] As Thompson continues, "Even as the dynamics of American democracy seek to silence the anger of African Americans by condemning it as inappropriate, misplaced, or dangerous, white Americans 'appropriate for themselves the right to mobilize anger in defense of the political order,' as they seek surreptitiously to maintain their privileged positions while simultaneously denying the existence of racial hierarchies."[142] In conjuring the anger of the suppliant as "terrible" among gods and mortals, Apollo subliminally draws attention to his complicity with Orestes, the mortal. Anger—the hostility toward a contaminating third party masked as the "just" resentment felt by the rejected suppliant—becomes a defensive shield against the disavowed, melancholically introjected erotic cathexis within the Athenian citizen body and similar social configurations of domineering white masculinity, ancient and modern.[143] Thompson points out that "the burden of democratic sacrifice has most often fallen on the shoulders of African Americans, who, though among the most democratically vulnerable, are nevertheless expected to exhibit a kind of acquiescent, nonviolent, and emotionless democratic exemplarity not required of other citizens."[144] Essential to the preservation of the democratic government, that is, to the subduing of the democratic spirit through its enclosure in a governmental structure, the normalization of the Erinyes, their reduction to acquiescence exemplifies contemporary "efforts to promote democratic reconciliation."[145] In one of her many warnings, recommendations, and appeals to the Erinyes, Athena declares the incompatibility between (the Erinyes') anger and justice (887–89): "Please *stay* (*menois*); but if you do not want to *stay* (*menein*), / without justice (*ou … dikaiôs*) you would bring *anger* (*mênin*) and *rage* (*koton*) on this city." Remaining, that is remaining still, acquiescing, immobilizing the motion of anger is, in this perspective, the only possible enactment of justice. Butler says that "to foreclose rage is … to repeat the violence against which it rails."[146] In the words of Athena, "to stay" also means unwittingly "to stay" with the mania that is ostensibly expelled. "Remaining" (*menein*) and "anger" (*mênin*) are almost the same word and the same sound—and a cognate of *mania*, *menos* ("rage"), occurs throughout the play. Athena's command deconstructively turns against itself (and against her), for the permanence, the integration into the community that Athena is offering, inscribes within itself, "infrasonically,"[147] the material traces of the threatening feeling she is seeking to ward off. It is as though the status quo—the permanence—Athena seeks to safeguard cannot be separated from its own manic overturning. If "remaining" within the status quo and, consequently, acting according to justice sounds like "rage," then "rage" and "justice" can no longer be held as opposites—the way democracy can be protected is not by eliminating but by inhabiting the "fury" that appears to hinder or prevent "democratic reconcilation."

Butler draws an apt comparison between the Erinyes' demand for justice—their (Antigonean?) claim—and the BLM protests, setting the terms, I suggest, for a consideration of the conceptual relation between "fury" and "fuming," between "rage" and "breath":

> The anger against a legal system that deals violence as it claims to transcend violence is a sound of fury that we are hearing all the time. It is perhaps why the demonstrations mobilized by the movement for Black lives were at once acts of mourning and protest, exposing racial violence, acting nonviolently to demand . . . a less violent world, but also calling for a justice by which the legal system itself can be judged.[148]

Referring to Frantz Fanon—and, in particular, to his idea of rage and resentment that can initiate "a coming to consciousness through which the colonized recognize the precarious position of the colonizers and can break free of their subjugation"[149]—Thompson suggests that "the expression of so-called negative emotions such as anger, resentment, and rage, when used to highlight racial injustice, seek to construct a different kind of democratic politics." As she continues:

> The discourse of postracialism was easily employed as a liberal, socially palatable alternative that appealed to the "universalism" of racial indifference and negated the enduring persistence of racial inequality—until BLM explicitly, angrily challenged both the morality of racial indifference and the claim that racism no longer exists. . . . The expression of anger occurs precisely because we hope for a more just and equitable society; in fact, we *furiously* demand it.[150]

Thompson's "furiously demand[ing]" brings us back to Butler's "critical fury" and the BLM protests against an undifferentiated postracial universalism, a homogenizing, erasing operation that suppresses Black lives by folding them into a disingenuous (human? white?) reparative whole, purporting to bestow an ever-refused privilege of humanization while occluding the continuing traumas of slavery and systemic racism.[151] The rage of the protest, the agitation of bodies assembled on the streets, is the bodily affect that expresses and protects Black breath. What the white imagination construes as Black rage is, in fact, Black breath as such.[152] In the last moments of the play, when the Erinyes shout to Athena, "I *breathe out* (*pneô*) *fury* (*menos*) and total *anger* (*koton*)" (840 and 873), the strong sense of *menos* as an aerial substance hearkens back to Athena's earlier command (800–803):

> Don't hurl your *heavy anger* (*barun koton*) against this land, and don't *be enraged* (*thumousthe*), and don't bring sterility, letting go … *drops* (*stalagmata*), *uncontrolled spears that devour seeds* (*brôtêras aichmas spermatôn anêmerous*).

Deploying the dichotomies of life and death, reproduction and sterility—which she herself, the virgin goddess of war, problematizes through her more intuitive alignment with the poles she disdains—Athena does not simply domesticate the Erinyes, but divests them of the right to breathe, construing their breath, materialized in the rhoticity of the repeated *êr/er* (almost *aêr*), as condensing into drops that arrest the dissemination of life. The verb *thumousthe* drifts between the two interrelated meanings of *thumos* (Latin *fumus*; English "to fume"): "smoke" and "anger." In the Iliadic micro-context verbally crafted by war-loving Athena, the epic relation of both *thumos* and *menos* with breath acquires particular relevance:

> It makes great sense to think of *thumos* as breath, and so as life, when we think for instance of Peiros, leader of the Thracians, "breathing out his *thumos*" at the moment of his death (*thumon apopneiôn, Il.* 4.524): and *thumos* in that physical understanding goes well with the idea of *menos* as life's vital element—warriors in their epic state of battle rage are typically "breathing *menos*," as in the formulaic phrase *menea pneiontes Achaioi*.[153]

I am using this philological point to argue that the insistent invocation of rage contributes to the effort to criminalize the Erinyes, equating the fact of their existence, as reflected in their breathing, to a danger, to the diffusion of toxic air. The Erinyes cannot breathe, it seems, without *fuming*, without infecting their surroundings, contaminating a human world that strives to extricate itself from the messiness, the soil of aliveness by enclosing itself in a hierarchical fantasy of purity and self-protective, self-exculpatory detachment. If we heed the obvious racist implications of this line of thinking, we cannot ignore the resonance of the Erinyes' "I *breathe out* (*pneô*) *fury* (*menos*) and total *anger* (*koton*)" with Eric Garner's, Elijah McClain's, and George Floyd's "I can't breathe," which proclaims that, as Ashon Crawley has put it, "breathing is not just a sign of life but . . . an irreducibly irruptive critique of the normative world."[154] We may think similarly of bombarded and suffocated Palestinians in Gaza.[155]

Making the right to breathability integral to the affective and political performance of rage means moving justice from the domain of judgment to that of critique. In *What World Is This?* Butler says that "for Merleau-Ponty, the dyadic relation between you and me is both conditioned and exceeded by tangibility itself, by language, but also, we might add, by breathability—the social character of air."[156] Breathability is one of the terrains on which we measure the gap between equity and inequity—it is, in Butler's words, "what we share and what we share differently, and also that which exceeds us and comprehends or embraces us at every instance of touch and breath."[157] The law instituted at the end of *Eumenides* is the breath that denies its volatility in the violent "cuts" (or de-cisions) of recorded judgments, disavowing its own perishability, monumentalizing itself. It becomes inscriptional, wounding pliable surfaces (a stone, a wall, paper, or the skin), transforming not just public rage—which democracy promises as a right for its documented citizens—but also breath, of which rage is just a coded denomination, into a privilege, the property of some rather than all. Yet "air . . . belongs to no one and everyone" and "breath is intermingled with the world's breath, where that exchange of breath, syncopated and free, becomes what is shared—our commons."[158] Judgment, the domain of ostensibly dispassionate, unemotional, responsible justice, is a willful performance of self-possession, an imposition of individuation against the unbounded subject of the (under)commons. In the 2010 interview with Vikki Bell, Butler speaks of their long-standing investment in "an ethics without judgment," an investment motivated by the worry that "the . . . over-determination of judgment within the contemporary political field has produced a kind of high morality, a suspicion of any . . . thinking that makes us try to rethink our moralism, or rethink the fixity of our normative judgments of a certain kind."[159] In the classic 2002 intervention "What is Critique? An Essay on Foucault's Virtue," Butler observes, through discussions of Adorno and Foucault, that "judgments operate . . . as ways to subsume a particular under an already constituted category, whereas critique asks after the occlusive constitution of the field of categories themselves."[160] In other words, critique does not shy away from the "incoherence" and "unspeakability" that the rationalization inherent in judgment spurns or neglects. It is, in fact, from "the *tear* in the fabric of our epistemological web, that the practice of critique emerges, with the awareness that no discourse is adequate . . . or that our reigning discourses have produced an impasse."[161] To this *tear* Butler also gives the name of "desubjugation," which points to the collapse of the subject's sovereignty in the reckoning with epistemic limitations: "If the desubjugation of the subject emerges at the moment in which the episteme constituted through rationalization exposes its limit, then desubjugation marks precisely the fragility and transformability of the epistemics of power." In the 2010 interview, Butler refers to Hannah Arendt's notion of responsibility as predicated on a persistent state of self-division, which is pitted "against ideas of 'de-cision' that draw from the etymology of that term to suggest that a cut or rupture is overcome through decision."[162] This opposition between (liberal) judgment and critique is homologous, I would argue, to the schism between justice and rage that *Eumenides* seeks to enforce. The way in which justice (*dikê*) can be transformed by rage is through the division, the tear that, as we have seen, is expressed by the autonomous emergence and circulation of the syllable *di-* (the trace of a motion of *cutting through*) and the appearance of the almost homophonic *dich(a)* ("asunder, apart") in the Erinyes' initial self-presentation, an aspirated supplement of *dikê* that splits judgment, severs it from itself, roughens it with an irruptive breath.[163]

When Jean-Luc Nancy says that "anger concerns the inadmissible, the intolerable, and a refusal . . . to mark forth the possible ways of a new negotiation with what is reasonable,"[164] he concurs with Butler, who at the end of "Fury and Justice in the Humanities," evokes Lauren Berlant and the notion of "staying with the unbearable" as "the space of heterotopia."[165] Citing Berlant in *On the Inconvenience of Other People*, Butler says that "the disturbance that is life bears the possibility of new forms at the edge of the unbearable,"[166] bringing to mind for me the *thumos*, air-as-rage, breath-as-*jouissance*, whose unboundedness makes life possible, shaking any notion of egological boundedness that would freeze life (and livability) in Apollinean monumentality, in the enclosure of Athena's epistemic mastery. Placed in relation to and in contrast with *dikê*—the judgment that marginalizes rage, that aspires to purify itself of it—the negativity of *dicha* identifies justice with the discomfort of the "unthought," the aesthetic dread of "the not-yet-thought," the generative inconvenience of "that which is not-yet-recovered for the present"[167]—to reuse phrases that Butler employed in a recent intervention on academic freedom, on the need for critique, or "critical fury," against governmental attacks against the humanities and their political potentialities.[168]

Incandescent Abolition

> One cannot oppose violence without opposing the law, and yet the law is said to deliver us from violence. If one is angered by this operative contradiction, this formulation that exposes its own lie, then perhaps that fury is justified, even tied to an alternative view of justice.[169]

With these words Butler tracks the affective power of the last play of the trilogy, which spreads the Erinyes' anger to us, inducing us to emulate them, to expose ourselves to, and internalize, their fury. Butler notes that the basic structure of the play's finale—its "chain of command"— conjures "the specter of violence": "Apollo wields the power of destruction, and Athena … is backed by some seriously destructive thunderbolts she can unlock as she wishes. In this way, violence is already in the scene as an injunction to follow the law and to accept its binding power."[170] At the beginning of their re-reading of Aeschylus's play, Butler wonders why, after describing "their anger as infinite," the Erinyes "give up their violent ways, their eternal vows of vengeance and destruction." Discussing the finale, Butler comments:

> Rage is subsumed but not negated, in the image of the "torch devoured by fire" … or "the flamesprung torchlight." Has the rage become part of the law, its fiery light, its violent illumination? Can we read the rageful torch of the Furies re-instated now within the very terms of law? As the Furies are enclosed within the earth, so their burning light now fuels the law that put them there.[171]

We can add to the list of questions: can the Erinyes still set Athens on fire? Are they cast as latent arsonists? Is this another expression of the reactionary paranoia that we also read into *Bacchae* in the second chapter? In a recent talk, J. T. Roane explores the figure of the Black arsonist, considering, for example,

"Odessa Bradford, the woman charged with instigating the 1964 [Philadelphia] riot through her refusal and self-defense against violent policing and arrest."[172] Bradford was accused of having "vindictively lit fires." As Roane explains, in this and other cases, it is not "whether the case and its resolution are recoverable that interests" him, but rather the reification, "instigated through uncontainable anger and rage," of this woman as an arsonist. The threat of arson was incorporated into "a transitory grammar of the everyday actions of working-class Black women condemned first by a social order built on their violent delimitation, containment, and exploitation and, second, in the sense of their containment . . . by landlords, police, journalists, and courts."[173] As a metaphor of general collapse, a conflagration of urban structures and infrastructures used by government to maintain inveterate logics of inequality and oppression, arson manifests the thanatopolitical state's displacement of its own destructive power onto the fury of protesters, onto the rage of those who are making a claim for justice beyond the distorted logic of judgment, beyond naturalized dynamics of introjected guilt and self-criminalization, beyond the PIC's legitimized abuse, its customary practices of dehumanization. Dismissed by Apollo with the invocation "you *totally loathsome beasts* (*pantomisê knôdala*), *hated things* (*stugê*) of the gods" (644), the Erinyes seem to have set aflame Apollo's aesthetic edifice through their sparks of rage. In assimilating them to *knôdala*, "biting, scratching, scraping"[174] creatures, Apollo performs the buccal exscription and suffers the articulatory discomfort of the harsh consonant phonesthemes *kn-* and *st-* in the same line. He is stripped of divinity and even humanity in his very practice of dehumanization. In the course of the play, as rage "become[s] part of the law, its fiery light, its violent illumination," and "as the Furies are enclosed within the earth," "their burning light . . . fuel[ing] the law that put them there," we can say that the law is cast as that which contains an incendiary force, as that which stays with and derives energy from the "wild," as that which can craft justice only in the close experience and under the influence of "unbearable" proximity with the fiery undoing kindled by the elemental counterpart of sociability, the inhuman support of livability and unlivability alike—air itself.

Apollinean dehumanizing is a speech act that demands, in its making, the self-dehumanizing buccal act of spitting. This buccal act, which confronts Apollo with—and disperses him into—the material, recalcitrant inhumanity of breath, conveys the point that the 'human' is, as Butler maintains, a continually contested and rearticulated term. Those whom the Symbolic afflicts, in Lee Edelman's words, with "the burden of figuring nothing"[175]—women, Black people, queer and trans people, the disabled, the undocumented, and the list continues—are, as Butler continues, "not only outside some conception of the 'human' and requesting inclusions, but . . . are also establishing that precarious 'outside' as the site from which certain kinds of claims can and should be made."[176] Modeling justice as the law's recognition of this outside, of its precarious self-constitution alongside this space for a counterclaim, the Erinyes—figurations of the "so-called subjects who are subject to de-production," of "those who never get to enter into the process of being explicitly produced as subjects"—demonstrate that "their reiterated exclusion from the domain of a recognizable subject is central to the production of the recognizable *subject*."[177] The recognizable subject asking Athena to lay down the law that has already produced him, Apollo is re-produced not as the anti-Erinys, but as the one who in the very act of distancing himself from them is drawn into a process of assimilation. This point brings us back to the question of "self abolition" that we broached in the first chapter. Justice, *dikê* bordering on *dicha* ("asunder"), consists in taking stock of the ethico-political implications of the uncanny homophony between *menein* ("staying," that is, "stability, permanence, status quo") and *mênin* ("anger").

As we heed the pervasive role of "critical fury" in unmaking the formal texture of *Eumenides*, in pushing and stretching verbal relations, in recrafting the possibilities of meaning and non-meaning—how critical fury becomes tragic language's insistent power of unbecoming—we can perhaps also view justice as a coming to terms with the fact that "there are forms of suffering or de-realization, or unintelligibility ... that are not just there, but produced, enforced and managed over time, that get lived out, or that set a limit to what can be lived out."[178] The Erinyes, the anti-Muses of tragedy, make us affectively aware that there "can be an entire mode of living in the mode of non-living";[179] that an aestheticized encounter with the modes of stereotyped non-living that shake up our convictions of what constitutes life or livability can offer the language for "a struggle, transnational and stubborn, calling for the rethinking of all the categories bound up with the prospect of continuing devastation."[180] The Erinyes bid us to overcome the oppositions of "rage" and "law," "fury" and "justice," to contemplate conceptual intertwinings, unscripted ethico-political infiltrations and encounters—the breath of rage disturbing the law's narcissistic aspiration to exceed the mere materiality of breath, the smoke of fury obfuscating the dichotomous boundaries between legal and illegal, legitimate and illegitimate, that lend conventional justice the status of ontological given.[181] As the Israeli government pursues its revenge against Gaza, "we see," says Butler "that language has been stolen and abused, especially when those who cry for justice"—even non-violently—"are accused of being terrorists."[182] Discussing the stretching of grammar at the very end of *Black Skins, White Masks* (1967) as an attempt to undo the epistemic categories responsible for the racist foundations of Western society, Butler, in "Endangered Scholarship, Academic Freedom, and the Life of Critique," suggests that Fanon is "calling into questions obligatory categories . . . in order to see, to know, what kind of life is still possible, what kind of world might yet be habitable."[183] Commenting on Fanon's famous words, "At the end of this book, we would like the reader to feel with us the open dimension of every consciousness," Butler suggests that "being for an elsewhere, being for something else . . . breaks out of the self-referential ontology of being, figured as encasement"—the Being that is a priori denied to Blackness[184]—"and insists upon an ecstatic trajectory of consciousness in the midst of intimate equality." The end of the *Oresteia* upsets and enrages us with the "encasement" of the Erinyes, but the ecstatic language of tragedy, which I have placed in dialogue with Butler's own language throughout this book's analysis of their trilogy, performs a Niobean buccal agitation that rejects the containment of the speech act. The "furious justice," the *dicha*, that *Eumenides* enables us to envision by pressuring us, in spite of itself, to regard protests, demonstrations, and radical, dissensual critical thinking as the counter-institutional supplementations of the law, is justice that "seeks to imagine life beyond the confines of detention"[185]—the prison, the border, the tribunal, but also the family, kinship, gender, the self. This is where, as Butler's trilogy shows, critical theory and tragedy come together—in pushing us to face the limits of the intelligible, in forcing us to deal with the unbearability of the unintelligible, while assisting us in ecstatically negating "the idea that the world as constituted is the only possible version of the world, that [what we call] the human is the only possible version of life."[186]

Afterword

Regarding Vengeance, Vulnerability, Grievability, and a Future for Israel-Palestine

The following comments by Judith Butler were recorded in a conversation on December 13 and revised on December 27, 2023.

Law and Vengeance

Most students expect to see in Greek tragedy the realization of the idea that law will somehow put an end to vengeance or so-called cycles of vengeance—that's, at least, what we are taught in grade school, that this is what Greek tragedy will demonstrate for us. But does law really put an end to vengeance, or is it equally possible that it becomes a tool for vengeance? And then another question is, Who is figured as vengeful in Greek tragedy, and who has the potential to reach for a sense of justice beyond vengeance? I am hardly alone in noting that women are vengeful, as are barbarians. And maybe I am wrong, but let's just say that there is a preponderance of women and barbarians found throughout these plays who don't understand law, who are not Greek enough to *get* the law. They are neither Greek enough nor masculine enough; that is, they do not comport with the masculine norms of being Greek in this sense. A vengeful spirit, of course, has to be tamed, but who has the capacity to tame it? Now, as for revenge itself, it responds to the occasions in which an oath is broken or perhaps a law, but there is a difference between the two. It is interesting to think about oaths and promises that are broken, neither of which is codified as law. Vengeance proceeds from there, but all this is pre-legal, or preparatory to law. And if I remember correctly, that sort of vengeance can be linked with expiation and the restoration of some relationship between a community and the gods or the community and its own history of customary morals. All of that happens to the side of law, one might say, or even prior to law. It is important to remember that in such matters law is not everything; law has not even emerged as a form of adjudication. When law does emerge as an apparent counter to vengeance, it seems to be sequestered from that kind of rhythm, belonging to another domain. So, if law does not overcome vengeance but can, in some circumstances, become its instrument, it becomes important to ask whether law is ever fully sequestered or separated from vengeful rhythm.

If we go back to the question of why we want law to stop cycles of violence or vengeance, we might be fantasizing about an idea of justice that would be free of those kinds of passions: a reasonable dream, as it were. And I am not sure how to pursue that notion in Greek tragedy (I am outside the field and the language, and so rely on those who know better to guide me here). Oddly, even though we don't find unambiguous instances of the law emerging free of vengeance, we are always being told tragedy shows that justice is not vengeance, and that true justice is not vengeance, but consists, in fact, in its overcoming. As you well know, we're living in a time in which many legal operations are authorizing massive "retaliation" in the name of "self-defense," although we have many reasons to question why these are the terms that are being used by Israel, and whether a new crime, the crime of genocide, is being committed through the use of such legal terms. Many who call for the end of violence are also accused, and in ways that have led to students losing fellowships, and artists, faculty, and other workers losing jobs. If one tries to invoke an international law to stop the killing or to impose a ceasefire, one is considered to be outside the law, a partisan in the war itself. It is shocking to me that those who call for ceasefire, the cessation of violence, are sometimes figured as supporting Hamas, that is, as violent actors in the scene. *You are Hamas; you are the cultural wing of Hamas, a terrorist group. Therefore, you are a terrorist.* But if the law is invoked to stop violence (and we are imagining that laws can effectively be invoked for such purposes), that is taken to be an act expressing terrorist sympathy or alliance. Once construed as such, the speech that calls for the end to violence is suppressed by legal means, activating censorship and national security provisions, and thus that kind of censorship proves to be a military instrument: the law as a wing of the military. I am not sure we can call that vengeance, but perhaps it is a form of vengeance that knows no limit, infinite vengeance. It claims to be responding to an attack, and in some ways it is. But as the response turns out to be annihilating, then we have to ask, is this vengeance, a response to a crime, or is it the commission of a fresh crime, a tactical inversion of retaliation into aggression for the purposes of erasing from the earth the very existence of a people, the Palestinian people, in Gaza, if not elsewhere?

Let's remember that the law becomes enforceable through police and military powers. So, if the targeted murder of stateless people is undertaken in the name of "self-defense" or, in a racist twist, "the defense of civilization," or of the nation-state, through a retaliatory trajectory, which is called law or civilization or democracy or the nation-state, and the name for what it is fighting is "terrorism," then the targeted population monopolizes all the barbaric otherness that threatens that legal regime. The law is pitted against the barbaric threat, but barbarism, if we still use that term, is taking place through the law.

Vulnerability

If we reflect on the unbearable vulnerability that the United States briefly felt on September 11, 2001, when the Twin Towers and the Pentagon were attacked, there was the sense that national boundaries had been trespassed. There had been a smug sense that the US was impermeable, that no direct attack on its mainland was possible, and that no one would dare to come across our airspace or train internally in our country to attack monuments and to kill that many people. Analogies are always difficult, and I tend not to like them very much, but surely Israelis did feel that they were protected by the military against an incursion such as the one that happened on October 7, that they were protected against murderous violence, that it was their prerogative to use such violence against Palestinians, and their privilege to be protected from it. This epistemic economy, of course, based on collective denial and a truly necropolitical distribution of lethal power, generally leads to war, for what targeted population would agree to such a deal? Implicitly Israelis felt that they were the ones who could inflict murderous violence (it is their power and their right!), even though that's not the term most of them would use, but that such lethal violence would never be inflicted on them. A corollary of that belief would be simply that they must inflict lethal violence precisely never to have it inflicted on them. For some incredible reason, Israelis thought that military-epistemic economy would work. And there was, as we know, general shock in the face of Hamas's incursion and the atrocities that they committed, and they were surely atrocities—there is no doubt. There was shock that permeability had been exposed, as if it could have been denied or ruled out, or should have been. The events clearly ran contrary to the sense of their impermeability upon which they had relied. Ideological chanting played a role: Israel has a discourse of being "the most powerful military in the region"; they built their dome, and all of that. But I think that when a nation-state, a militarized nation-state, understands itself as having achieved impermeability while it gives itself license to inflict violence with impunity, they have fooled themselves into thinking that they have successfully cast permeability to the outside, that permeability is permanently secured as the outside. It's a shared fantasy that serves as an epistemic condition of militarization: the state not only has the power to defend itself but to distribute permeability, precarity, and vulnerability such that it is always and only to be found outside its border. The border, that very material structure infused and structured by fantasy, is the instrument by which permeability is constantly cast outside: it is that propulsive casting outward. At the same time, those who live in such fantasy zones know somewhere that they are in a fantasy, and they resist whatever wakefulness would make that all too clear. The only way to become protected from violence is to institute the conditions for a nonviolent world. But when one starts to talk about radical equality, a new constitution, freedom for all—basic democratic values—one is accused of anti-Zionism and antisemitism, as if to be a Jew is to embrace without question the long-standing injustice and violence of the Zionist legacy. Such a view not only narrows the definition of who is a Jew but denies the history and complexity of Judaism itself—it's arguably an antisemitic argument in favor of a reductive caricature: Jew = Zionist.

Again, it's not exactly a perfect analogy, but can we not say that when certain kinds of violence are considered "barbaric," the barbarians or the terrorists are then figured as vessels of violence who have to be tamed or suppressed or contained or civilized? In the classical Greek context, they need to be made more Greek, made more part of the *polis*, or if they are by nature, by the nature of their soul or body or passions, unable to be or become Greek, then they need to be properly subordinated so that Greekness can stay intact, defined in part by its powers of domination and conquest. And let's remember that it's not just the barbarians who are invested with this murderous violence that is considered pre-civilizational. It's also women and children and all those who haven't yet attained to the level of the Greek citizen understood as having those required capacities. The disavowed violence of the state comes back as a kind of haunting through the figure of the barbarian other or the undeveloped other or the "undevelopable" other, the one who by nature can never be developed but only held in check. It comes back as a pure vessel pointed at the speaker: *Oh, look at what's coming at us!* I do think that when the Palestinians in Gaza are killed en masse—children, women, people following directions to flee, killed while they are fleeing and following directions, killed in the hospital or in their homes sleeping—and Israelis see and know that, "self-defense" works in their minds by assuming that all those lives have to be eradicated in order for Israeli life to be protected. So, what we are seeing is a genocidal precondition and consequence of self-defense: *we will be killed if we do not kill; we have been killed, and will not be killed again; they are killers, who look to kill us, so we must kill them, kill them first.* That's also clearly a racial fantasy in this context, as it was in the Greek context, as we know from the enormous work that has been done on the institution of slavery in ancient Greece, the figure of the non-Greek as barbarian, but here and now, it seems that there is no possibility in the Israeli dominant culture and media of grieving the lives that have been killed by Israel, only Israeli lives killed by Hamas. For those who believe Israeli self-preservation and self-defense depend on the obliteration of Palestine, Palestinians are not living beings, but purely animate threats to life itself.

Life, human life, thus becomes coextensive with Israeli life, so whatever these "lives" are living in Gaza, they are all threats to life itself, which is Israeli life, and it doesn't matter if they are children, or aging people, or if they are sick in hospital beds, or clearly unarmed. It just doesn't matter, because if they themselves are not fighting or if they themselves did not vote for Hamas, they are still, within this mindset, operating as human shields or being instrumentalized by Hamas. I wish I did not know the voice of this logic so well, but it is the one to which I was exposed as a young person, and it is, sadly, familiar to me, as familiar as it is utterly wrong.

There is a disavowal of the violence at the same time that there is a disavowal of Palestinian life as living. The fact that they have to be killed, according to this logic, presupposes that they are alive. You don't kill non-living creatures, because they are already dead. How, then, is the living dimension of those non-lives accounted for? There is something animate about them, but whatever it is that is animate is murderous or potentially so, so their life is nothing other than potential death for Israelis. They are animated figures of murder that have to be murdered. So, even in the act of murder, there is a kind of confession: *Actually, we do murder, we have murdered, or we are capable of murder. We are showing ourselves as murderous, but that is possible only because we have defined the murderous impulse as outside ourselves. So, in murdering murder, what we are doing is preserving life*. And yet, as the world sees, they are simply making themselves into the very murderous nation that arrogates to itself the status of being the only human life in the region.

Grief and Grievability

It's interesting how many people from Gaza do say, when interviewed under the condition of bombardment, *I hope I will be buried, I hope my son will be buried, I hope my son will see me buried, and that there might be some way of honoring this life as it is on the verge of being destroyed*. Refaat Alareer's poem "If I must die" adopts the future anterior on his own life. The title is the first line, and I am stopped by the "must" of "If I must die"—it is not that there is an obligation to die, but some kind of necessity. He does not say, "If I am killed"—no, the dying is itself a final act, one undertaken under necessity. He does not write, "If it comes to that," suggesting a kind of accident. "If I must" has as its implied contrary, "against my desire, my desire to live, to live for you." Or so it seems. It is followed by the imperative not only to live, but to make something, a kite, a kite for a child who looks to heaven to find his lost dad:

> you must live
> to tell my story

> to sell my things
> to buy a piece of cloth
> and some strings,
> (make it white with a long tail)
> so that a child, somewhere in Gaza
> while looking heaven in the eye
> awaiting his dad who left in a blaze—
> and bid no one farewell
> not even to his flesh
> not even to himself—
> sees the kite, my kite you made, flying up above,
> and thinks for a moment an angel is there
> bringing back love

He asks the child, the one who survives him to make the kite for another who has undergone such a brutal and unspeakable loss. *Let that kite be "for a moment" an angel. Let that crafted object, endowed with transient angelic form, bring back love, since clearly love has vanished from this earth if someone can be killed in the way that I am killed.*

> If I must die
> let it bring hope
> let it be a tale

The poet does not ask that the story praise his life, but that it be sent into the air, like the kite, the angel, as a token of love, connecting the one child's loss to another's as they try to fathom a world that has become so brutally loveless. In Gaza, we see pictures of the mass graves. Few are given the decency of a burial; few family members have time as they respond to new orders to drive further south, crowding the Rafah gate. Burials are not just a way to honor or mourn the dead. They are the gatherings where people must regenerate themselves for living on, for being there for the traumatized, for the story that emerges from this brutal history. Burials are meant to acknowledge that this *dead body belongs to this earth*. It is the dust and dirt of the earth that covers the body and that is, at least, a form of belonging to that land through prosopopoeia: in other words, a way for the dead to say, *I will become this earth, this earth, which is the only one we have*. The politics of burial are there very often in the final utterances of any number of people who have in fact been killed in Gaza, whether journalists or poets. It's so unbearably sad. It pushes us to the limits of the thinkable.

When we say that someone is regarded as ungrievable, we are not always talking about someone who has lost life; we are talking about those whose living status has been de-realized or denied. The ban on grievability comes before the death—it is what is felt by the living who are so designated. And this has always been hard for me. Maybe because Antigone is the example to which I return. We think about a death, the death of her brother, and we think about how she defies Creon's interdiction against public burial in order to give her brother a public burial and even, obviously, risks her own life in doing so. Defying the interdiction is punishable by death. She'd rather die than not bury her brother, which says something about what makes life livable for her, the passion for which she lives. But if we try to analogize from that scene, we have to shift the temporality of our explanation. For when we look at genocidal bombardments in Palestine, as we do, today the ban on grievability is there prior to the commencement of war. In other words, a whole population is first cast as ungrievable in the midst of its living, and they are aware, of course, that they have been marked as ungrievable by the Israeli state. That doesn't mean that they don't grieve each other; they do. They do not accept this designation, but it is there, as a threat, if not a death sentence. Within their own community, Palestinians grieve one another openly and defiantly, and also to keep each other alive and to form networks that will sustain life and sustain all of those who must survive the loss of those they love. It's not a question of whether or not they have internalized this ungrievability. They are, at least from the Israeli point of view, cast as ungrievable prior to their lives being lost, which makes those lives eligible for elimination. For instance, limiting the amount of water that comes in—that is a sign that Israel is willing to deprive Gazans of the fundamentals of life. The Israelis allocate calories; they allocate water; they allocate electricity, which is needed for heat. They allocate medicine. They decide the minimal level that it takes to keep that population alive. And they calculate how many losses are acceptable to them. So they are in a necropolitical way distributing life and death in Gaza prior to the bombardment, which is exactly the intensification of that budget. These are figured as ungrievable lives in the minds of those who are deciding who lives and dies, whose practices have since the outset of occupation sought to be effective ways of distributing grievability.

Of course, the loss of Israeli life very quickly becomes Jewish life in general because without identifying Israeli life as Jewish life, no one can call upon the Nazi genocide in the same way. Zionists increasingly insist that the State of Israel represents the Jewish people, which means that those Jews not represented by the state are increasingly less thinkable as Jews. As a friend at Hebrew University, who recently resigned after being persecuted for her critique of Israel's military assault on Gaza, puts it: "These young people who are nineteen, twenty, twenty-one and in the army learn the Holocaust, learn the Nazi genocide in schools, and then they are sent to Auschwitz or another concentration camp, and the grief over the 6 million plus who died is quickly converted into nationalism and militarism." It is hard to call attention to grief and grievability under these conditions. The Israeli military machine is called by some anti-Zionist Jews "a grief machine." But if we think that grief has been monopolized by the state to justify its own campaign of slaughter, then we have given over a key notion that we need for thinking both about equality and resistance. For the State of Israel to exploit the grief over the Holocaust to feed the war machine is a defilement of grief. Grief, understood as grief for Jewish life only, is instrumentalized for the purposes of shoring up a state that is fundamentally based on dispossession, land theft, imprisonment, occupation, and violence, including forms of life-taking that predated, and prepared for, these bombardments. This is a perverse instrumentalization of grief that happens to justify killing, genocidal killing, to usher ever more loss into the world.

Appalling as it is, it is almost impossible to argue with those who are convinced that another genocide against the Jews is underway, that it is around the corner or already there, and that the only way to avoid that genocide is to commit genocide—and then not to acknowledge it by invoking legal justifications: self-defense, national security. Of course, even if all the people in Gaza were wiped out, the memory of that genocide and the justified anger, the infinite rage about that, would produce an indefinite intifada for the future. Peace cannot be secured through genocide, but only by co-habitation achieved through decolonization, in conditions of equality, freedom, and nonviolence. But who is thinking about that?

Vengeance—or Democracy?

Is it right to say that on October 7, Hamas was "vengeful" in its actions? Is it right to use "retaliation" to describe the Israeli bombardment of Gaza? When we use these terms now, we tend to imagine a static scene in which one party is harmed and the other reacts. But no history of Zionism, dispossession, rights destruction, or occupation can properly take place within that framework. If we use such terms to psychologize these actions, we tend to set aside the settler-colonial structure that has belonged to Zionism, and still does. Palestinians, especially in Gaza, are stateless, and they don't have the fundamental right to live. So though we may disagree with Hamas, and I have and do, we would be foolish to agree to the characterization that they are barbarians or terrorists or animals, when, in fact, they are rising up in a very human way against a settler power with enormous, potentially genocidal, military strength. Similarly, Israel is not just retaliating for the acts that Hamas committed on October 7. The story does not start there. Israeli state violence, and settler rogue violence, both continue forms of violence that have been underway, in different forms, since 1948, when people in villages were massacred or forced to flee under the threat of military force. What we are seeing now is not new, and I worry that there is a misuse of Greek tragedy when people move to vengefulness or retaliation: *We were hurt, so we responded this way; we couldn't respond in a different way*—as if it were a question of finding the right moral disposition. It's rather a question of finding a political form that honors grievability and allows for the state formation to change fundamentally so that equal grievability is actually embodied by whatever form of governance emerges.

People say, *Oh, if you are not a Zionist, that means you don't think Israel has a right to exist.* Consider that what the anti-Zionist is saying is the following: *It's not a question of a right to exist; there are different ways for states to exist, some of them more legitimate and democratic than others. Surely there are ways of opening up the laws of citizenship, ways of demilitarizing the country, ending occupation, honoring the Palestinian right of return through reparation or resettlement, ways of rethinking territory, taking apart the settlements.* None of those proposals are calls for destruction, yet under some conditions, they are imagined to be precisely that. To ask for a change in those conditions so that another imaginary is possible—that's not violent destruction. It is rather a restructuring of the state in full response to the demand for equality and freedom and justice, all of which rely on equal grievability as part of their very meaning. Hence, it's very important to resist that kind of inquisition that recites the question, *You think Israel has the right to exist? Yes or no?* The simple response, the nonviolent response, would be, *In what form do you think Israel's existence would be legitimate, and would it still be called Israel, or something else?* Or ask the question, *What state form, if any, do Palestinians want for that land? And why does that not exist? Is there a form that could decolonize the land and the practices of life? What about a state formation that established constitutionally equal freedom, equal citizenship for all people with the right to inhabit that land?* If one suggests that radical democracy in whatever form would institute rights of equality over against colonial rule, the answer that comes back is, *What? We cannot be equal with those people (or those animals) since we are destroyed by them.* Or, *No, democracy as we know it has always been based on civilizational racism, which is why Israel has been able to say that it is the only democracy in the Middle East.* I understand the Left skepticism about democracy, for there is a fear that democracy is a lie, a mode of justifying radical economic and racial inequalities. But what if we could take the lie out of democracy and make it true, maybe for the first time?

Notes

Introduction

1 Butler 2019a.
2 On agitation, see esp. Chen 2018 and 2023 (ch. 2).
3 See Butler 2005, 69, on "the breakage, the rupture, that is constitutive of the 'I.'" As they put it, "The 'I' finds that, in the presence of an other, it is breaking down."
4 See Butler and Athanasiou 2013, 26: "Being dispossessed by the other's presence and by our own presence to the other is the only way to be present to one another. . . . Being present to one another takes place at the limits of one's own self-sufficiency and self-knowability, in the wake of the endless finitude of the human."
5 On the *Oresteia* and Hegelian dialectic, see, e.g., Rose 1992 (ch. 4); see also Critchley 2019 (ch. 7) and Njoya 2020.
6 On the form of the tragic trilogy, see Scodel 1980, 11–19. On thematic and imagistic intertwinements in the *Oresteia*, see the foundational studies of Peradotto (1964 and 1969) and Lebeck (1971).
7 "Slide of identifications" and "improvisational solidarit[ies]" are two Butlerian phrases, used in reference to Antigone and Iphigenia respectively (Butler 2000 and Butler in Telò 2023c), which will often appear in the book.
8 For a global approach to the *Oresteia* that privileges the synchronic intricacies of reading, see Goldhill 1984; Porter (1990) unfolds the complex nexus of imagery and perception in *Agamemnon*; for a return to the practice of close reading of the trilogy in light of the interplay of language and sound, see Nooter 2017; on the emancipatory politics of anti-narrative, see Rancière 2004, 2014, and 2017. See also Telò 2020a (ch. 4) on the *Oresteia*'s death-driven political aesthetics as a challenge to linear narrative.
9 On Greek tragedy and contemporary philosophy, see Leonard 2015 (especially on Hegel, Nietzsche, Freud, Marx, and Arendt); see also, among others, R. Armstrong 1998 and 2012 (on Freud); A. Benjamin 2015 and Billings 2015 (on W. Benjamin); Billings 2014 (ch. 6, on Hegel); Bowlby 2010 (on Derrida); Chanter 2014 (on Derrida's Antigone); Felman 1983 (on Freud); Fleming 2015 (on Heidegger); Fletcher 2013 (on Freud); Goldhill 2015 and 2022 (on Hegel); Lecznar 2020 (on

Nietzsche); Leonard 2000 (on Cixous), 2005 (ch. 1, on Oedipus between Foucault and Deleuze and Guattari), 2006 (on Lacan and Irigaray), 2013 (on Freud), and 2018 (on Arendt); Porter 2000 and 2005 (on Nietzsche); Sjöholm 2009 (on Kristeva); Stocking 2008 (on Nancy and Antigone). On Lacan's and Žižek's Antigone and Zupančič 2023 (the most recent book-length treatment of Antigone), see chapter 1; on Foucault's Oedipus, see Miller 2021, Telò 2022b, and Toscano 2022.

10 On Sartre and Cixous, see Francobandiera 2018.

11 In the Norton anthology of texts on Sophocles' *Antigone* edited by Murnaghan (2023), Butler's *Antigone's Claim* is placed among the "modern responses"—rather than in the "criticism" section—together with Virginia Woolf's *Three Guineas* and Athol Fugard, John Kani, and Winston Ntshona's *The Island*. On Honig's interventions on *Antigone* and *Bacchae*, see esp. the papers collected in Leonard and Porter 2014 and Conybeare 2022.

12 In the essay on *Eumenides*, Butler (2023a, 17) observes that "we can, and must, read [ancient] texts against and beyond themselves, so that they can continue to speak to us."

13 See Butler and Athanasiou 2013, 26, on the entanglement of "presence"—the aspiration of historicist positivism and intentionalism—and "self-identity."

14 See the reference, in *Gender Trouble*, to the "impossibilities" that "certain kinds of 'gender identities'" open up "within the very terms of [the] matrix of intelligibility" (1990a, 17). See also Butler and Athanasiou 2013, 185: "The point of solidarity is . . . to make space for dismantling the social conventions and foreclosures that render some lives and desires impossible." See also Keeling 2019, xii, on Audre Lorde.

15 "Intertwinement," a key term for Butler, marks a transformation of Merleau-Ponty's phenomenology into an ethics of social ecology: see Butler 2022a.

16 See Ferreira da Silva 2014, 91.

17 See, e.g., Butler 2004b, 49: "If I am confounded by you, then you are already of me, and I am nowhere without you. I cannot muster a 'we' except by finding a way in which I am tied to 'you.'"

18 See Sanyal, Telò, and Young 2022, 4: "Butler refashions the perspective of the 'I' that is moved to write as that of a chorus of voices whose alternating convergence and divergence is the very means of their solidarity. The 'I' is plural, and proximity—or the work of thinking and writing—is not a simple harmony, but embodies the dissonant complexity of relationality itself."

19 We can say that *reading with* "open[s] up to others . . . the selves that are left over and that exceed the onto-epistemological typologies of the proper and proprietary self" (Butler and Athanasiou 2013, 76). See also Sanyal, Telò, and Young 2022, 4: "Reading enables a proximity that reflects the proximity of language's own metonymic process."

20 See, e.g., Butler's use of the notion of crisis in *Undoing Gender* (2004a) in relation to the category of "women," which "as a unitary category cannot hold" and "must undergo crisis and expose its fractures to public discourse"; see also Butler 1999, xxiv. See Butler 2022c, 419, on critique and "crisis," which "ope[n] up a practice of questioning and linking what happens in the university to the broader struggle for democracy."

21 See Henao Castro 2022, 147: "If there is a militant principle that runs throughout all of Judith Butler's work, it is the anti-liberal idea that [we] are [not] self-sufficient sovereign subjects but rather . . . socially interdependent ones."

22 This "being in non-being" is in line with Dienstag's notion of "pessimism," "describ[ing] the fundamental ontology of the human condition—one of radical insecurity, and radical possibility, freedom, and terror—that is the potential ground of tragedy" (2004, 98).

23 Butler 2019a.

24 In the phrase of Dean (2009). For Butler, the point of (democratic) politics is precisely the opposite of conventional harmony—it "is not to assemble a 'we' who can speak or, indeed, sing in unison. . . . The question of politics resides instead in the encounter with what troubles the norm of sameness" (2009c, 298).

25 See Peppiatt 1996, 91. Bacon attributes to Aeschylus the capacity to "produc[e] . . . a sort of stimulation in itself . . . a sort of excitement, perhaps even like sexual excitement, like something very strong anyway, a sort of very powerful urge" (Archimbaud 1993, 102–3).

26 For a different reading of line 253, see Lather 2018, 46. As I say elsewhere, "jaw-breaking laughter" can "tragically hollo[w] out the face, wrinkl[e] it, and freez[e] it into a grin" (Telò 2020b, 58).

27 On the "buccal," a concept elaborated by Jean-Luc Nancy, see chapter 3.

28 See Deleuze 1994.

29 In *What World Is This?* (2022a, 71), Butler refers to the definition of critical phenomenology supplied by Guenther (2012, xiii): "By critical phenomenology I mean a method that is rooted in first-person accounts of experience but also critical of classical phenomenology's claim that the first-person singular is absolutely prior to intersubjectivity and to the complex textures of social life." On Butler's influence on critical phenomenology, see Garland-Thomson 2020 and Sid Hansen 2020. Coole (2008, 17) characterizes Butler's philosophical orientation as "existential phenomenology," marked by the "enduring sense of an active, expressive body with the visceral capacities sometimes to resist the constraints imposed upon it, and of everyday lives wherein contestation is nurtured."

30 On this phrase, see chapter 2.

31 There is a Bataillean coloration in this description of laughter: see Bataille 2014, 40.

32 Butler 2022a, 8: "No bounded entity . . . no discrete body is by definition immune in advance."

33 On the "laughing god" in *Bacchae*, see Billings 2017. See the compound *dia-phoreô*, used of Pentheus's dismemberment in lines 739, 746, and 1210. In a play about *Dio*-nysus and his father Zeus (declined as *Dios, Dii, Dia*), *dia-* compounds acquire special significance.

34 See the occurrence of the adverb *di-ampax* ("through [his throat]"), in lines 992–96 (=1011–16), where it indicates the "cut" of Justice (*Di-kê*)—that is, the dismemberment of Pentheus—as a remedy against his ethical "mutilations" (*a-theon a-nomon a-dikon* "impious, lawless, unjust"); for a different way of conceptualizing the nexus between "justice" and "division," see chapter 3.

35 On the *kômos*, see Rossi 1971 and Olsen 2016, 101–11. Butler's description more closely recalls the so-called *paraklausithuron*, a serenade in front of a lover's door: see F. Cairns 2020.

36 Neyra (2020b) offers an inspiring analysis of the protest enacted through retching and laughing in Xandra Ibarra's *Nude Laughing* (2016).

37 Butler 2012b.

38 My emphasis.

39 Antigone reappears in *Precarious Life* in two moments. In one of them, Butler's writing approximates choral lyricism: "There will be no public act of grieving (said Creon in *Antigone*). If there is a 'discourse,' it is a silent and melancholic one . . . one in which there have been no lives, no losses; there has been no common bodily condition, no vulnerability that serves as the basis for an apprehension of our commonality; and there has been no sundering of that commonality" (2004b, 36).

40 Butler 2004b, xi.

41 See esp. Taxidou 2004, Rabinowitz 2014, Wiener 2015, Weiss 2017, and Eberwine 2019; see also McIvor 2016.

42 Honig 2013, passim.

43 Henao Castro 2020, 96. See also Henao Castro 2022 (ch. 2).

44 Butler 2012a, 21. Butler's essay on Benjamin's Niobe was originally published in 2006 (2006b). On Niobe in Palestine, see Telò 2023a, 138–42. On Butler's Benjaminian Niobe and her relationship with the Erinyes, see chapter 3.

45 Butler 2004b, xiv.

46 Butler 2023k. Elsewhere, Butler writes that the Israeli assault on Gaza has already "tak[en] away [Palestinians'] rights to mourn" (2023g). See also "Some Palestinian Americans Say They're Afraid to Mourn Their Loves Ones Out Loud" (https://www.npr.org/2023/10/17/1206601875/some-palestinian-americans-say-theyre-afraid-to-mourn-their-loved-ones-out-loud).

47 Butler 2009a, 38: "The differential distribution of public grieving is a political issue of enormous significance. It has been since at least the time of Antigone." As Murnaghan (1999–2000, 109) puts it, "Tragedy is . . . a song of survivors" and "those who survive are understood to live because others have died and thus to live at others' expense."

48 Butler 2009a, 14–15.

49 See Butler 2020c, 96, on grievability as a notion of "radical equality." For a treatment of Greek tragedy in conjunction with BLM protests, see McIvor (2016), who, however, approaches antiquity with traditional historicism.

50 Butler (2022a, 102–3), who calls these protests a "movement of counter-contagion." See Kilby 2023, 6, commenting on Butler 2020b, 59: "In asking what it means for lives to matter, we should simultaneously attend to how lives are grieved, how lives are valued and how they are safeguarded."

51 Butler 2004b, 25.

52 See Telò 2020a. As duBois (2008, 132) puts it, Aristotle's "views of catharsis . . . refer to the disciplining of the social body," which aims at curtailing "social disruption and disorder."

53 As we read in the introduction of the video on the website of PEN America: https://pen.org/multimedia/opening-night-on-the-edge-judith-butler/

54 Butler 2014.

55 See Butler 2015b, 64–65: "The dependency of human and other creatures on infrastructural support exposes a specific vulnerability that we have when we are unsupported, when those infrastructural conditions start to decompose, or when we find ourselves radically unsupported in conditions of precarity."

56 On these lines, a "sputter[ing] in rage by way of pounding labials," see Nooter (2017, 265–66), who notes that the repetition is "so insistent as to act as a mere extension of the repetition of nonverbal grunts of grief." On the etymological connection of "grief" with *gravis* ("heavy"), see Brinkema 2014 (ch. 4).

57 Sommerstein 1989, 110: " 'Unbearable' [*aphertos*] seems to be a word coined for the use in the *Oresteia*: it occurs nine times in the trilogy and nowhere else in extant Greek literature."

58 On emetic anti-teleology, see Brinkema 2011. The unbearable creates what from a philologically normative viewpoint is considered grammatically unbearable: see Fraenkel 1950, 756: "The question must be asked whether μόρον ἄφερτον is really an admissible expression here."

59 On Thyestes' perverted pregnancy, see, esp. Littlewood 1997 and Gowers 2006.

60 In *Undoing Gender*, we read: "The critique of gender norms must be situated within the context of lives as they are lived and must be guided by the question of what maximizes the possibilities for a livable life, what minimizes the possibility of

unbearable life or, indeed, social or literal death" (2004a, 8 [my emphasis]). Rescuing oneself from "unbearable life" means pursuing "the 'unrealism' of mania," that is, pushing against the "self-beratement" that introjected super-egotic structures of normativity impose on the ego as these structures present "a refusal to accept the status quo" as "unbearable": see Butler 2020b, 170.

61 On "unbearable dependency," see Butler 2020b, 94. In *The Force of Nonviolence* (2020b) Butler cites Berlant and Edelman's *Sex or the Unbearable* (2013, 90), which discusses "the subject's unbearable encounter with her radical incoherence, her trembling out-of-synchness with her fantasy of herself in the world." See also the discussion of the "unbearable" in Berlant 2022.

62 That is, those for whom the abandonment of a position of invulnerability is "unbearable": see Butler 2015b, 147. For Butler, "the very unbearability of exposure" is "the sign, the reminder, of a common vulnerability, a common physicality and risk" (2005, 100), while the lack of protection for demonstrators can be "a concrete form of political exposure and potential struggle, at once concretely vulnerable, even breakable, and potentially and actively defiant, even revolutionary" (2015b, 186).

63 There are resonances with Spillers's important essay on flesh (1987): see Telò 2024b.

64 See Harney and Moten 2021, 142: "Nationalism and individuation go together . . . since weirdness has to be individuated, and then collected, in order to be calmed." See chapter 1.

65 See Butler 1994, 6: "The institution of the 'proper object' takes place . . . through a mundane sort of violence."

66 See Butler 2020b, 198: "Life requires infrastructure, not simply as an external support, but as an immanent feature of life itself." On Cassandra's commodification, see Wohl 1998, 85 and 87.

67 I owe this phrase to Prins (2017, 37); the emphasis is mine. "Unintelligibility" is a Butlerian term: see section 3.

68 Woolf 1925, 48 (my emphasis). On this passage, see Prins 2017, 37–38, and Worman 2018, 61.

69 See Butler 2020b, 200: "Both the 'I' and the 'you' require a *sustaining* world. These social relations can serve as a *ground* for thinking about the broader global obligations of nonviolence we *bear* toward one another" (my emphasis). For Butler, "the political concept of self-preservation . . . does not consider that the preservation of the self requires the preservation of the earth, and that we are not 'in' the global environment as self-subsisting beings, but subsist only as long as long the planet does" (2020b, 199).

70 On this point, see chapter 3.

71 Butler 2022a, 24; the citation within the passage is from Scheler 1954.

72 Butler 2020b, 41: "No one moves or breathes or finds food who is not *supported* by a world that provides an environment . . . a world that sustains the environment that makes possible air of a quality that we can breathe" (my emphasis).

73 See Butler in Butler and Worms 2023, 51: "For some people living in the middle of climate change, in Indigenous lands in Brazil . . . human interventions into their life worlds have produced toxic soil and the inability to drink the water that is available to them or grow the crops they require, the ones they have grown for generations." For Butler, "we are vulnerable to those environmental and social structures that make our lives possible" (2020b, 45).

74 Butler 2022a, 34.

75 Butler 2022a, 34.

76 Worms in Butler and Worms 2023, 21.

77 On the intertextual relationship between *Alcestis* and *Antigone*, see Gregory 2006.

78 Butler in Butler and Worms 2023, 26.

79 Butler in Butler and Worms 2023, 55.

80 Butler in Butler and Worms 2023, 58.

81 Butler (2020b, 190) notes that the losses provoked by *feminicídio* "belong to a social structure that has deemed women ungrievable." Wohl (1998) sees *Alcestis* as an act of matricide, the act that, in *Eumenides*, demands the intervention of the law, a resolution or reparation coinciding with the repetition of mother-killing: see chapter 3.

82 See Wohl 1998, 126: "Alcestis, although dead, lives on as a part of Admetus . . .; Admetus, on the other hand, though still alive, loses a part of himself with Alcestis."

83 In line 350, "I will fall *toward* [the statue] and, folding my arms *around* it (*hôi pros-pesoumai kai peri-ptussôn cheras*) /, calling your name . . .," the "I" seems to be made and unmade by the prepositionality of *pros-* ("toward") and *peri-* ("around"), by the "threshold[s] of the body" (Butler 2020b, 16), which unsettle the individuation pursued by the "name," with its interpellating force. On Admetus's cold attachment to the statue, see esp. Wohl 1998, 154, and K. Bassi 2018, 37.

84 Thus Butler (2004c, 99), commenting on Bracha Ettinger's cycle of Eurydice paintings. See Sanyal, Telò, and Young 2022, 8: "Butler urges us to read Eurydice's appearance in disappearance . . . as a figuration of the (com)prehension, ethical and epistemological, that generates the loss it disavows. This (com)prehension amounts to a quasi-predatory clinginess striving to stretch out the instant of epiphany into the fantasy of a repaired, restored time, a time devoid of trauma, of trauma's intermittent, disruptive insistence."

85 The sequence of alphas also suggests a sequence of interjections (ἆ. . .ἆ. . .ἆ), an outburst of sorrow.

86 See, e.g., the classic treatment by Segal 1978.

87 According to Helmreich (2017, 45), "The turn to materiality . . . does not banish older genderings and racializations of the sea," but places "such analytics as gender,

sexuality, and/or queerness . . . freshly at sea, wavering, and, perhaps, available to new kinds of gender trouble and turbulence." See chapter 2.

88 "Intertwinement" is a word that Butler repeatedly uses in *What World Is This?* (2022a): it links up with "bond" and "kinship," two other Butlerian concerns: see chapter 2. The language of intertwinement (*desis*) and loosening (*lusis*) is central to both *Hippolytus* and *Bacchae.*

89 See Butler 2020b, 141: "Human creatures living somewhere, requiring soil and water for the continuation of life, are also living in a world where non-human creatures' claim to life clearly overlaps with the human claim."

90 See Butler 2015b, 131: "If we cannot really speak about bodies at all without the environments, the machines, and the complex systems of social interdependency upon which they rely, then all of these nonhuman dimensions of bodily life prove to be constitutive dimensions of human survival and flourishing."

91 The chiasmus is a quintessentially Butlerian figure, since at least *Bodies That Matter* (1993, 38 and 84), where it is used to cast "language and materiality" as "fully embedded in each other, chiasmic in their interdependency" and to characterize the subject as "a crossroads of cultural and political discursive forces" à la Gloria Anzaldúa; in *Senses of the Subject* (2015a), the chiasmus has Merleau-Pontian associations. On the pervasive imagery of entanglement and loosening in *Hippolytus*, see the important studies of Goff 1990 and Zeitlin 1996 (ch. 6).

92 See Butler in Aquilina and Borg 2017, 128: "The human is already an animal, and . . . when we say humans are over here and animals are over here, we miss the fact that there is a chiasmic relation between them. . . . Thinking about conditions of livable life . . . puts humans and animals in alliance, or it brings out some of their convergent concerns." See also Butler 2015b, 131. See also chapter 2.

93 On the semantic connection between waves and laughter in the Greek imaginary, see Lipari and Sirna 2023.

94 Butler in Butler and Worms 2023, 75.

95 The name is usually translated as "the one who stampedes, loosens horses," but the ambiguity of the syntactic relation between the two parts of the name (*hippo-* and *-lytos*) allows for another reading: that is, "the one who is loosened by the horses" as a result of his "loosening himself from the horses." Zeitlin (1996, 266) notes that, at the end of the play, "the horses with whom [Hippolytus] identified himself prove to be creatures alien to the self, although, as he reproaches them, they were his own, 'reared and nurtured by his own hand.'" This reproach is part of an apostrophe to the assemblage of chariot and horses, "Hateful equine chariot, *nurtured thing of my hand* (*emês boskêma cheros* 1355–56)," in which the formal disjunction between the two elements of the possessive phrase (*emês . . . cheros*) underscores the deindividuating force of the "intertwinement."

96 See Butler 2015b, 213: "I cede some part of my distinctively human life in order to live, in order to be human at all." See also Butler 2019c, 15: "Any project of social justice that is critical, that seeks to stop the acceleration of ecological destruction, has to begin with the presumption that . . . all lives . . . are bound to the living world at the level of need, desire and obligation."

97 See Butler in Aquilina and Borg 2017, 116.

98 Butler in Aquilina and Borg 2017, 117.

99 Discussing their investment in the practice of close reading, Butler says: "When Shoshana Felman used to teach at Yale, she would sometimes look at the graphic dimension of the page, which meant that you actually had to take into account the white space, as well as the print and the formatting and where a paragraph begins and ends" (Aquilina and Borg 2017, 120); in the same discussion, Butler lingers on the relation between close reading and critical theory: "I do work closely—I mean, I grew up in a time of close textual reading and I still do that, and I want to do that and that's important to me—but that does not mean that you cannot develop large questions on the basis of close textual analysis" (ibid.).

100 On radical and resistant formalisms, see Telò 2023b and Nooter and Telò 2024.

101 The "experiential imbrication (precarious, imperfect, tendentious)" that I see as central to my approach to reading tragedy can be understood as Butlerian. As I have said, "I conceive the interpretive process as an interobjective being acted-upon, in which the notional interpreter lets herself/itself be undone by the effects of reading that the textual object alluringly, tantalizingly tenders, dissolving the mastery it ostensibly bestows" (Telò 2023a, 5; see also Telò 2023b, 28–29, on interpretation and Levinas). My goal is to "launch the speculative potential of texts, one only available through readings that proceed without guarantee" (Brinkema 2022, 260). On hypersensitive reading and overanalysis, with which I sympathize, see Neyra 2020a and McEleney 2021, respectively.

102 Olson and Worsham 2000, 732. See also Salih 2003.

103 Kornbluh 2024.

104 See Emre and Kornbluh 2022.

105 Olson and Worsham 2000, 732.

106 So Ahmed (2023a), paraphrasing the beginning of the preface of the first edition of *Gender Trouble* (Butler 1990a, xxix). See Ahmed 2023b.

107 Butler 2005, 136. In the aforementioned interview with Olson and Worsham, Butler confesses that "reading Heidegger as a young person and trying to figure what it is he was trying to do with his neologisms and his coinages also influenced me. Some people, such as Bourdieu, have dismissed it completely, but I think there was and remains a rather profound effort there to call into question ordinary language and the ways in which we structure the world on its basis" (2000, 732).

108 "In *Minima Moralia* [Adorno] talks about the painfulness of passing through difficult language but how it is absolutely essential to developing a critical attitude toward the constituted social world if we're not to take the constituted social world . . . as it is given" (Olson and Worsham 2000, 734). Here Butler is probably referring to Adorno 2020, 108: "A writer will find that the more precisely, conscientiously, appropriately he expresses himself, the more obscure the literary result is thought, whereas a loose and irresponsible formulation is at once rewarded with certain understanding." See Hamilton 2003 on the "soliciting"—that is, disruptive, unsettling, and, thus, critical—force of Pindar's obscurity.

109 Olson and Worsham 2000, 728.

110 Olson and Worsham 2000, 728.

111 Reynolds 2021, 59, referring to *Specters of Marx* (Derrida 1994, 64) and *Of Hospitality* (Derrida and Dufourmantelle 2000, 77).

112 Porter 1990, 46. See also Goldhill 1984.

113 On the complexities and ambiguities of Sophocles' syntax, see esp. Ferrari 1983 and Goldhill 2012, esp. 13–37; see also Budelmann 2000. Ferrari observes that, because of "overlapping constructions" and "syntactical symmetries and asymmetries," Sophocles' diction "spurns obviousness while apparently pursuing effects of unaffected naturalness": thus, "under the compact crust, the Sophoclean text defies capture" (7). On the density of Euripides' "late" style, see esp. Said 2006, 137. On problems with Aristophanes' dichotomizing of Aeschylus's and Euripides' style, see Rosen 2004.

114 See Butler 2020b, 29, on imagination and "what is imaginable" as means of thinking "beyond what are treated as the realistic limits of the possible."

115 Butler in Olson and Worsham 2000, 728, 740, and 765.

116 On the syntactictal minutiae of this passage, see Hiscock 2018, 9–10.

117 "Suspension" is an important concept in Butler's theorizations: "*Suspending* the demand for self-identity . . . seems to me to counter a certain ethical violence, which demands that we manifest . . . self-identity at all times" (2005, 42 [my emphasis]); "If a life is produced according to the norms by which life is recognized, this implies neither that everything about a life is produced according to such norms nor that we must reject the idea that there is a remainder of 'life'—*suspended* and spectral—that limns and haunts every normative instance of life" (2009a, 7 [my emphasis]).

118 See Butler 2015b, 119: "No one escapes the precarious dimension of social life—it is, we might say, the joint of our nonfoundation." Forced to bear the corpses of his son, his wife, and Antigone herself, Creon becomes, despite himself, the ground—"a commonly held ground" (2015b, 119): see Telò 2023a (ch. 6), and

chapter 1. On "standing," see Butler 2021c, 47: "Standing can only figure self-sufficiency by eliding the infrastructural conditions of its very possibility. This means . . . that the sort of standing that humans do is conditioned and formed by objects and material conditions that are constituent moments of standing upright as a human." On the refusal of standing, see Harney and Moten 2015; see also Shirazi 2022.

119 Butler 2004b, 151. In a more recent intervention, Butler (2022b, 37) declares: "I am in favor of aesthetic experimentations, sustained hypotheticals, political imaginaries, and critical fabulations," that is, "forms of wishful elaboration, experiments in the possible . . . that help provide a counterpoint to the exceedingly rough times we are in." We can hear an echo of Antigone in Butler's op-ed in *The New York Times* in June 2023. Regarding their youth, Butler writes: "Formulating a question freed me momentarily from what felt like *an authoritarian grip of the throat*. Yet I could not answer the question of who I thought I might be without a mighty struggle to counter the force that would *throttle* the right to be at all" (2023f, my emphasis).

Chapter 1

1 Butler in Antonello and Farneti 2009.

2 Butler 2000, 5.

3 Lloyd 2005, 454.

4 Henao Castro 2021, 97.

5 Butler 2000, 72: "Although not quite a queer heroine, Antigone does emblematize a certain heterosexual fatality that remains to be read."

6 Sjöholm 2002, 28.

7 On this point, see also Orrells 2023.

8 Henao Castro 2021, 101.

9 As Henao Castro (2021, 99) puts it, for Butler "ethics refers to a non-sovereign ontological condition of vulnerability and inter-dependency," while politics concerns "a confrontation with the ways in which social orders make livable or unlivable those conditions." Dahms (2020) describes Butler's project as the construction of "a speculative social ontology." The phrase "radical heterology" is from Derrida 2008, 82; it has a strong Blanchotian coloration, as I will discuss later; on Butler and Blanchot, see Secomb 2007. I use the concept to connect Butler's social ontology with other theoretical contestations of the sovereign self, especially Fred Moten's deindividuation and Marquis Bey's self abolition. James

Porter has drawn my attention to a passage of Jacques Rancière in which he says: “The logic of emancipation is heterology” (Rancière 1992, 59). See Porter 2024.

10 Eng (2011, 565), who refers to the famous passage in *Giving an Account of Oneself* (2005, 135) in which Butler says, “We must recognize that ethics requires us to risk ourselves precisely at moments of unknowingness, when what forms us diverges from what lies before us, when our willingness to become undone in relation to others constitutes our chance of becoming human.”

11 Butler 2000, 67.

12 Butler 2000, 59 and 67.

13 Butler 2000, 67.

14 Coetzee 2019, 467; cf. Butler 2000, 20.

15 See Butler’s definition of the Real in *Bodies That Matter* (against Žižek): “What counts as the ‘real,’ in the sense of the unsymbolizable, is always relative to a linguistic domain that authorizes and produces that foreclosure, and achieves that effect through producing and policing a set of constitutive exclusions. Even if every discursive formation is produced through exclusion, that is not to claim that all exclusions are equivalent: what is needed is a way to assess politically how the production of cultural unintelligibility is mobilized variably to regulate the political field, i.e., who will count as a ‘subject,’ who will be required not to count” (1993, 207). On the oscillation of Butler’s Antigone between inside and outside, see esp. Kramer 2014.

16 See Carver and Chambers 2007, 431: “Antigone and her three siblings—and indeed her entire family as it devolves from the tragedy of Oedipus—represent a figural challenge to intelligible kinship. Even in fictional terms, they are that which cannot be, the unintelligible.” For McRobbie (2003, 132), Butler’s Antigone “is the unimaginable in culture; by virtue of her incestuous parentage, her abject status produces a shudder across the social field, but she also resists this status by defying the state and asserting a human bond that she is not expected to dare to acknowledge.”

17 Lloyd 2005, 466.

18 Coetzee 2019, 468. As Henao Castro (2020, 100) observes, it is “the transcendental separation of the Symbolic structure from the historically contested field of social norms” that Butler primarily takes issues with in Lacan’s position and in Irigaray’s Lacanian feminism.

19 The death drive is central to Butler’s thought, with various emphases and inflections: see esp. 1990b; 1997, 187–94; 2006a, 2020b, 84–86, 151–52 and 155–57; 2019b; and 2023e.

20 See Butler 2000, 47–48, and esp. 53.

21 Žižek (1992, 76–77) exemplifies what Butler considers the “anti-political” stance of the Lacanian Antigone when he compares her to Gudrun Ensslin, “leader of the

'Red Army Faction,' a Maoist 'terrorist' organization, who killed herself in a maximum security prison in 1978." For Žižek, Antigone's dissent is (only) realized in and as death; any form of identification of Antigone with dissent in life, with a deterritorialization of the Symbolic from within, entails "domestication." See below on Edelman and the "liberal" Antigone.

22 Butler (2000, 53) clarifies the death-driven position of Antigone in terms that recast Lacan: "It seems that one reason that standing for her brother implicates her in a death in life is that it abrogates precisely the kinship relations that articulate the Lacanian symbolic, the intelligible conditions for life. She does not merely enter death by leaving the symbolic bonds of community to retrieve an impossible and pure ontology of the brother." As Butler continues, "What Lacan elides . . . is that she suffers a fatal condemnation by virtue of abrogating the incest taboo that articulates kinship and the symbolic."

23 See, e.g., Žižek 2004 and 2005, 344; see also 2015. In 2012, Žižek observed: "As Stalin would have put it, [Antigone and Creon] are both worse (than what? Than the power of the people!), part of the same hierarchic power machine" (323). The important intervention of Copjec (2004) on Antigone and the death drive offers substantial elements of differentiation from Lacan, while operating in a strongly Lacanian framework: see, for discussion, Henao Castro 2021, 81–87. Still operating in a Lacanian framework, Badiou (2013, 162) sees Antigone and Creon as participating together in "the subject-process through the combined categories of anxiety and the superego," where "superego" does not equate to "law" but "the senseless excess of linguistic tautology," that is, "the ferocity of the superego injunction, reduced to a pure *You must*, or to redundancies of the type *The law is the law*" (Bosteels 2008, 1910).

24 Edelman 2004, 103–4.

25 Zupančič 2023, 26.

26 Butler 2000, 67.

27 Butler 2000, 6.

28 On "underlife," see Wynter 1979, and below.

29 On self abolition, see esp. Bey 2022a, on which see below.

30 Butler 2000, 30: "The psychic relation to social norms can, under certain conditions, posit those norms as intractable, punitive, and eternal, but that figuration of norms already takes place within what Freud called 'the culture of the death drive.'"

31 Butler 2000, 30. In *The Psychic Life of Power* (1997, 194), Butler reflects on germs of the theorization of the death drive in Freud's *Mourning and Melancholy* (1917): "Although in 1917 Freud does not yet distinguish between the pleasure principle and the death drive, he does note that melancholy has the power to force the ego

into death. . . . In mourning, the claim of life does not triumph over the lure of death; on the contrary, the 'death drives' are marshalled in the service of breaking with the object, 'killing' the object in order to live."

32 See chapter 3.

33 My emphasis.

34 On the semantic overlap between *mania* and *anoia*, see Padel 1995, 21.

35 See also, in the first part of line 90, *ei kai dunêsêi g'*, which Griffith (1999 ad loc.) translates as "Yes (γε), if in fact (καί) you succeed"; a series of limitative particles almost turn "possibility" (*dunamis* in *dunêsêi*) into impossibility. As Wohl (2009, 129) puts it, an "impossible, destructive desire metaphorizes Antigone's status as outlaw, playing out in an erotic key the theme of her repudiation of both the gender norms and the laws of the city." See Butler 1987, 98, on Sartre: "Caught in the paradox of determinate freedom . . . human beings are forced to desire the impossible. And impossibility guarantees the continued life of desire, the paradoxical striving that characterizes human beings essentially." See Stanley 2021, 26: "To be radical is . . . not to want to go back to a prelapsarian image of perfection, but rather to seek that which can be possible—or maybe even to seek that which is *im*possible."

36 Martínez Ruiz (2019) underscores the entanglement of the death drive with—or even its subordination to—Eros as "not simply 'binding'" but "hold[ing] within it the very disturbance allocated to the death drive," as Butler puts it in the preface to the book (viii). In Butler's reading of Martínez Ruiz, "Eros contains within it the potential to dismantle sovereignty in favor of a different sociality, one that prizes heterogeneity without seeking recourse to a unifying principle or the goal of harmony" (xi). On the term lifedeath, see Derrida 2020.

37 Freud 1920, 41.

38 Jebb 1900, 115.

39 Butler 2000, 53. See Edelman 2023, 179–80: "Antigone appeals to an absolute authority, a Truth, beyond that of the state."

40 Butler in Antonello and Farneti 2009.

41 Lacan 1992, 243–56. For further discussion of Lacan's Antigone, see, among others, Leonard 2005, 101–30, 2006, and 2015 (ch. 5); Miller 2007; Eagleton 2010; Buchan 2012; Harris 2013; and Edelman 2023, 179–80. On horror as a tragic emotion, see D. Cairns 2015.

42 For an anti-cathartic reading of tragedy—a critique of Aristotle through psychoanalysis, deconstruction, and queer theory—see Telò 2020a.

43 On dust and water, see Marder 2016, 4–5; see also Telò 2020a, 175.

44 In emphasizing the political-theoretical implications of "foam," I am influenced by Sloterdijk (2016); for a reading of Sloterdijk from the perspective of radical politics that places him in dialogue with Butler, see Janicka 2017.

45 Some of the material in *The Postcard* is borrowed from the seminar.

46 The full quotation is drawn from an unpublished 1981 statement reported in various publications, including Nestor 2021: "My art is the way I re-establish the bonds that unite me to a universe. It is a return to the maternal source. Through my earth/body sculptures, I become one with the earth."

47 Unpublished statement, cited in Blocker 1999, 34.

48 Raine 1996; Derrida 1996. In the preface to Martínez Ruiz 2019, xii–xiii, Butler comments on Freud's essay on the mystic pad (1925), in terms that recall the emphasis on ground and the supporting surface, especially in *Notes toward a Performative Theory of Assembly* (2015b): "The writing instrument requires pressure, and the writing surface always resists this inscription. . . . Without that resistance, writing itself could not take place. Writing requires resistance to make its mark."

49 Derrida 1978, 228. Nestor (2021) analyzes Mendieta's work in light of Derrida's *Cinders* (2014), noting that "*The Silueta Series* particularly binds the temporal, ephemeral, and self-subject trace explicitly, where Mendieta's body is both marked and always in a state of disappearance, self-effacement." The ephemerality exhibited by Mendieta's silhouettes, "always dispersing and changing, becomes an object of revisitation, restlessness." Pushing against some "presentist" feminist readings of Mendieta, Kwon (1996, 169) points out that "as delayed relays, photographs of Mendieta's work register at another level an absence already contained *within* her work"; in other words, "the appropriation of distance in time and space engendered by photographs never delivers on its promise of contact." For Boetzkes (2010, 151), "the imprint demarcates a gesture of receiving and thereby opens itself to its own disassembly as natural activity distorts the shape of the body and overtakes the parameters of the *silueta*."

50 Callus (2020, 361) significantly defines Derridean autothanatoheterography as "the realization that giving an account of oneself (to cite a title of Judith Butler's), whether to oneself or others, is ineluctably a relating of being-toward-death and of alterities within and without": see also Weinmann 2018. Hyacinthe (2019, 57) maintains that Mendieta's " 'act of disappearance' is more a process than a finality."

51 Here I draw on Muñoz 2011.

52 Boetzkes 2010, 150. For Boetzkes, "the body, in Mendieta's artworks . . . acts as both an overflowing receptacle and a surface that registers the point at which sensation abounds beyond the body's capacity to organize and interpret it" (151).

53 Hiscock 2018.

54 Uribe 2016, 35.

55 "Antigone does not precisely signify a blood line but something more like 'bloodshed'—that which must be remaindered for authoritarian states to be maintained" (Butler 2000, 4).

56 Butler 2000, 24; on the aesthetic unconscious—*pathos* infiltrating the *logos* of representation—see Rancière 2009. Holmes (2012, 171) defines Butler's Antigone as "the outside that is always already inside," a heroine "*silhouetted* against the horizon of political potentiality" (my emphasis).

57 In the blurb that Butler wrote for Uribe's book.

58 On Sara Uribe, see esp. Morales 2020, 149–50, and Henao Castro 2023, 72–73.

59 https://queenmobs.com/2016/06/the-silence-is-our-most-unyielding-creon-five-questions-for-sara-uribe-john-pluecker-about-antigona-gonzalez/

60 Uribe 2016, 119.

61 Butler 2000, 8.

62 In *Undoing Gender*, Butler returns to this scene from Sophocles' *Antigone*, observing that "although it reads as guiltless defiance," Antigone's confession implies "a suicidal act propelled by an obscure sense of guilt," which "in retrospect illuminate[s] a desire for punishment, a final relief from guilt" (2004a, 170). This point seems to me to indicate an attempt to connect Antigone with the death drive in a novel, non-Lacanian fashion; the word "relief" makes one think of *Beyond the Pleasure Principle.*

63 In lines 901–2 (*elousa kakosmêsa kapitumbious / choas edôka* "I washed and adorned [the corpse], and I gave tombal libations"), the double crasis in *kakosmêsa* (*kai ekosmêsa* "*and* I adorned") and *kapitumbious* (*kai epitumbious* "*and* tombal [libations]") assimilates Antigone's action of caring for Polynices' corpse ("*and* I adorned") to the "product" of the libations; in lines 902–3 (*nun de, Poluneikes, to son / demas peristellousa toiad' arnumai* "And now, Polynices, I obtain this while covering your body"), an enjambment separates *to son* ("your") and *demas* ("[Polynices'] body").

64 Butler 2000, 11.

65 "The prohibition against incest in the play *Antigone* requires a rethinking of prohibition itself, not merely as a negative or privative operation of power but as one that works precisely through proliferating through displacement the very crime that it bars. The taboo . . . delineates lines of kinship that harbor incest . . . establishing 'aberration' at the heart of the norm" (Butler 2000, 67)

66 Butler 2000, 67.

67 "K-incoherence" is the term that Bradway and Freeman (2022) coin to capture various theoretical attempts to contest, reimagine, and queer kinship, exposing it to the subversive force of aesthetic incoherence. Butler (2022b, 41) suggests that "kinship is a site of queer coinage, of a performative re-elaboration, and the recognition of binding ties made and remade."

68 "Consider that in the situation of blended families, a child says 'mother' and might expect more than one individual to respond to the call. Or that, in the case of

adoption, a child might say 'father' and might mean . . . the absent phantasm she never knew as well as the one who assumes that place in living memory. The child might mean that at once, or sequentially, or in ways that are not always clearly disarticulated from one another" (Butler 2000, 69).

69 Derrida 2020, 257 and 259; cf. Derrida 1987, 333 and 336.

70 On the aesthetics of Greek tragedy and the death drive, see Telò 2020a.

71 Derrida 2020, 315 (my emphasis).

72 Butler 1997, 149.

73 On this crucial point in Butler's psychoanalytic theorization, see chapter 2.

74 Butler 1997, 168.

75 Butler 1997, 169.

76 Suggesting that Butler construes Antigone "as a sign that confounds the very symbolic system in which she exists, and yet goes unrecognized," Appel (2014, 188 and 198–99) sees her as a "figure for deixis, indexicality," but reminds us that pronouns and deictic markers, "always about to be refigured around a different center of discourse," are "empty forms" à la Emile Benveniste. The radical heterology I am positing goes further by imagining a contradictory deixis, a simultaneous presence of mutually exclusive positionalities emblematized by Antigone's role as synchronically brother and sister.

77 Butler 2005, 42. Stocking (2014; cf. 2008) sees Sophocles' *Antigone* as depicting the auto-immunity that accompanies the subject's "attempt to protect its self-identity . . . against the threat of finitude" (78); in his view, tragedy contributes to forging a sense of community not as a fusion into a totality, but as a sharing of finitude and difference.

78 Butler and Connolly 2000.

79 On Oedipus and Freud, see esp. Rudnytsky 1987, passim; on Antigone and Anna, see, among others, Derrida 1996, 43; Stewart-Steinberg 2011; and Telò 2017, 100–101.

80 Freud and Fliess 1986.

81 See Edelman 1995, 189.

82 See Bersani 2010.

83 Derrida and Dufourmantelle 2000. See Telò 2022a.

84 Featherstone 2022, 1023.

85 Derrida 2020, 258.

86 Derrida and Dufourmantelle 2000. See Weismann 1892.

87 Featherstone 2022, 1029.

88 Featherstone 2022, 1029.

89 Derrida 2020, 320.

90 Butler 2022a, 12.

91 See this passage from *Precarious Life*: "If I am confounded by you, then you are already of me, and I am nowhere without you. I cannot muster a 'we' except by finding a way in which I am tied to 'you'" (2004b, 49).

92 Butler 2006a, 121; see Butler 2015a, 77. See also Butler in Kirby and Butler 2006, 152, on Spinoza as a precursor of psychoanalysis.

93 Blanchot 1988, 6.

94 Butler 2022a, 12.

95 Derrida 2020, passim. See also Butler 2006a, 118; as Porter (2006, 136) puts it, *Beyond the Pleasure Principle* expresses "a desire to see death as a permanent element in the logic of life."

96 Butler 2022a, 106.

97 Butler 2022a, 43.

98 Butler 2022a, 44.

99 Butler 2020b, 11–12.

100 Bey 2022a, 33.

101 Bey 2022a, 34.

102 Bey 2022a, 33 (my emphasis).

103 See also the concept of "auto-repugnancy" that Deutscher (2020) has elaborated in her reading of *Beyond the Pleasure Principle*.

104 On the "anti-social thesis" in queer theory, see, after Edelman 2004 and 2023, Caserio, Edelman, Halberstam, Muñoz, and Dean 2006; Weiner and Young 2011; Bernini 2016; and Ruti 2017.

105 Hartman 2020a and Du Bois 1999, 149–60.

106 Sanyal, Telò, and Young 2022, 12.

107 Hartman 2020a and Telò 2023a, 111–12.

108 Hartman 2022a, 40. These words seem to connect Antigone with slavery, a topic that, as underscored by Chanter (2011) as well as Henao Castro (2021)—who focuses on the neglected "coloniality of gender"—the critical-theoretical reception of Antigone has failed to consider. In *Undoing Gender* (2004a, 103), Butler, referring to a statement of Hartman in a 2001 private conversation ("slavery is the ghost in the machine of kinship"), says that "it is not possible to separate questions of kinship from property relations (and conceiving persons as property), and from the fictions of 'bloodline' as well as the national and racial interests by which these lines are sustained." See also Saha 2022, 124: "Kinship depends on an impossible unconditionality: the false name of family reveals structures of obligation, conditionality, and contract."

109 Cohen 2023, 9.

110 Walker 2000, 24.

111 Wynter 1979, 149: "As the self-confidence of the axiomatic culture weakened, the stigmatized cultures began to counterdefine themselves, in terms of the larger

world, moving from the *underlife* into the mainstream to extend the work of cultural transformation" (my emphasis). Hartman (2008, 2) refers to Foucault's "Lives of Infamous Men" (2000): "An act of chance or disaster produced a divergence or an aberration from the expected and usual course of invisibility and catapulted her"—a figure whom Hartman calls Black Venus—"from the *underground* to the surface of discourse" (my emphasis). Moten 2013, 739: "Blackness is the anoriginal displacement of ontology . . . it is ontology's anti- and ante-foundation, ontology's *underground*, the irreparable disturbance of ontology's time and space" (my emphasis). See also Moten and Harney 2013. Fanon 1967, 8: "There is a zone of nonbeing, an extraordinarily sterile and arid region, an utterly naked declivity where an authentic upheaval can be born. In most cases, the black man lacks the advantage of being able to accomplish this descent into a real hell." For discussion of all these passages and their connections, see esp. Cohen 2023, 46–57.

112 See Butler 2015a, 189: "Colonization is the deadening of sense, the establishment of the body in social death, as one that lives and breathes its potentiality as death."

113 Du Bois 1999, 151.

114 See Telò 2023a, 116–17.

115 On geopower—"the force, the forces, of the earth . . . which we as technical humans have tried to organize, render consistent and predictable"—see Grosz et al. 2017, 135.

116 Hartman 2022a, 40 (my emphasis).

117 On support and infrastructure, see Butler 2016a, 19: "All action requires support and . . . even the most punctual and seemingly spontaneous act implicitly depends on an infrastructural condition that quite literally supports the acting body"; see also Butler 2015b (ch. 4) and the many other passages cited in the Introduction.

118 Hartman 2020a.

119 See Telò 2023a, 122–23.

120 Hartman 2020a.

121 See Rifkin 2022, 156–57.

122 Marriott 2021a and 2021b.

123 Marriott 2021b, 111.

124 Marriott 2021b, 121.

125 Marriott 2021b, 111.

126 Hartman 2022, 43.

127 This position perhaps recasts as an equalizing or egalitarian desideratum Edelman's notion, enunciated in his 2023 book, that the Symbolic "reproduces the world as sense" by "imposing on certain persons"—women, queer, trans,* Black

people, and others—"the burden of figuring nothing," the task of embodying "the absenting of meaning from being."

128 Ricco 2023, 162.

129 Moten 2018b.

130 Moten 2018b.

131 Moten 2018b. Moten refers to Édouard Glissant's exhortation against individuation, *consent à n'être plus un seul*, which we also find in *Stolen Life* (2018a, 263), where what Moten calls "our consent to that (nonsingle, paraontic) sociality" is cast as part of an "erotics of fugitivity." Moten pits these erotics against "freedom's drive," a "death drive" consisting of "sovereignty's continual (dis)establishment . . . the repetition . . . of subjectivity's failure to launch." Deindividuation is self abolition, a death drive of sorts, as I have been arguing, which opposes the death-driven compulsion to repeat the failure of individuation.

132 Moten 2018b.

133 Uribe 2016, 103.

134 See Butler 2020b, 46: "The relational understanding of vulnerability shows that we are not altogether separable from the conditions that make our lives possible or impossible. . . . Because we cannot exist liberated from such conditions, we are never fully *individuated*" (my emphasis).

135 Morrison 1955.

136 Davis and Morrison 2010, 42–43.

137 Danticat 2010, 16.

138 My emphasis.

139 Morrison 1955, 1. On Morrison's classicism, see esp. Roynon 2013, esp. 62–63.

140 Knox 1964. Knox, a socialist, served in the military, an experience that presumably influenced his consideration of Sophoclean characters from the perspective of "heroism": see McDonald 2010, 143. See Worman 2012 for an approach to the Sophoclean hero that emphasizes abjection, unheroism, and vulnerability.

141 Morrison 1955, 35.

142 Morrison 1955, 25 and 28.

143 See esp. Worman 2018, 26–34.

144 Yergeau 2018, 34; see Knox 1964, 24, 44, 58, and 71.

145 Yergeau 2018, 18.

146 Yergeau 2018, 19.

147 Yergeau 2018, 27.

148 Moten in Manning 2019, 10; Moten 2008, 188.

149 Manning 2019, 11.

150 Yergeau 2018, 15–16 and 169: "Whereas autism is represented as compulsions toward the self (*autos*), allism is fashioned as a turning-toward the other (*allos*)"; "In constructing pathological theories of nonautism or allism, autistic rhetors work to define allism as something more than absence of autism, as a means to unmask cognition that has become so naturalized as default or normal that its substance goes unquestioned."

151 Yergeau 2018, 16.

152 On "difficulty," see the Introduction.

153 My emphasis.

154 The phrase "mineralogy of being" is borrowed from Nancy (1994, 171).

155 Yergeau 2018, 71–72.

156 Carson 2012, 29.

157 Yergeau 2018, 19.

158 Yergeau 2018, 170–71.

159 Griffith 1999, ad loc.

160 We can thus say that the characterization of Antigone as *auto-nomos* reveals the disavowal behind the modern notion of autonomy. See Butler 1992, 12: "The subject is constituted through an exclusion and differentiation, perhaps a repression, that is subsequently concealed, covered over, by the effect of autonomy. . . . Autonomy is the logical consequence of a disavowed dependency, which is to say that the autonomous can maintain the illusion of its autonomy insofar as it covers over the break out of which it is constituted."

161 On the "farmer," the *autourgos*, in Euripides' *Electra*, see esp. Rosenbloom 2002, 321–22, and Wohl 2015.

162 Yergeau 2018, 24.

163 Morrison 1955, 33.

164 The rhythm or pace of neuroqueer life is typically, that is, neurotypically, perceived as out of touch, out of joint. As Pyne (2021, 348 and 350) observes, referencing Maxfield Sparrow (2013, 148), autistic being is seen as "out of step with life's procession," and, thus, "too slow" for "the economic growth of the family and the nation." Discussing Pauline Hopkins's first novel, *Contending Forces: A Romance Illustrative of Negro Life North and South*, Knadler (2022, 306 and 319) has noted a tension "between a neurotypical politics of racial uplift and . . . moments of neurodiverse Afro-fabulation that create . . . neurodiverse enchantment." In particular, in the novel, "the rhythm, volume, and tempo of Ophelia's singing are more than a disrupting, deforming, and silencing Black noise to the social order of things: they are 'paralyzing.'"

165 Morrison 1955, 6.

166 Morrison 1955, 22.

167 See Knox 1964, 27: "Time and its imperative of change are . . . what the Sophoclean hero defies; here is his real adversary, all-powerful time. Time is the condition and frame of our human existence, and to reject it is 'to be in love with the impossible.'"

168 See, esp. Savarese 2014. In the stunning *The Secret Life of a Black Aspie* (Prahlad 2017), a chapter is entitled "The Pillows Are Crying"; we also read the subtitle "Never Let People Know that Objects Are Alive."

169 See Worman 2018, 28–29.

170 Morrison 2007, 73–74.

171 Cavarero 2016. On Butler's reponse to Cavarero, see chapter 2.

172 See, e.g., Butler 2015a, 12: "I am a being in need of support, dependent, given over to an infrastructural world in order to act, requiring an emotional infrastructure to survive"; see also 2015b, 21 and 147: "Precisely because bodies are formed and sustained in relation to infrastructural supports . . . and webs of relation, we cannot extract the body from its constituting relations."

173 Berlant 2022, 180–81.

174 Williams 2018, 93.

175 Morrison 2007, ix (my emphasis).

176 Williams 2018, 93.

177 Morrison 2007, x.

178 Morrison 2007, ix–x.

179 Williams 2018, 103.

180 This phrase, which I borrow from Manning (2013, ch. 1), reminds me of Butler's use of the adjective "porous" in *What World Is This?* (2022a): see, e.g., "If my life is never fully my own; if life names a condition and trajectory that is shared, then life is the place where I lose my self-centeredness and discover the porous character of my embodiment" (43); "As porous, the body is neither pure boundary nor pure opening but a complex negotiation between the two" (108–9).

181 Williams 2018, 97.

182 Dittmar 1990,141.

183 See esp. Wong 1990.

184 Morrison 2007, 110.

185 Butler and Taylor 2010.

186 Butler and Taylor 2010, 188.

187 Butler and Taylor 2010, 190–91.

188 Butler and Taylor 2010, 198.

189 Butler 2012b.

190 Morrison 1955, 23.

Chapter 2

1 Loebl 2022.

2 On *Bacchae* and its many queer adaptations since at least *Dionysus in 69*, see, among others, Zeitlin 2005; Fusillo 2006, esp. 67–70; Powers 2018, 121–54; and Pauly 2023.

3 Butler 2021a. My citation is from S. Bassi and G. LaFleur's commentary on the interview (2022, 325); see also Butler 2021b. In 1992, Butler argued that "any effort to give universal or specific content to the category of women . . . will necessarily produce factionalization" and "identity categories are never merely descriptive, but always normative, and as such, exclusionary" (15–16). See Ruffell 2022, 240: "[Pentheus] models an aggressive patriarchal authority and an obsessive but fantastical heteronormativity including the espousing of transphobic tropes and outright violence—all of which are made to rebound upon him."

4 Butler 2017a, 11. Cf. Honig 2021.

5 On horrorism, see Cavarero 2009.

6 See Butler 2022d: "We have a new constellation of authoritarianism that feeds on economic distress, migration, demographic changes, family structures, gender relations."

7 Butler 2004a, 205. See also https://www.npr.org/2023/05/29/1178718092/uganda-anti-gay-law

8 See Butler 2022a, 86: "The police violence against Black and brown people, women and men, trans people, the Indigenous and *travestis* . . . coincides with the systematic forms of allowing death, promoted and accepted by market enthusiasts who operate under the guise of economic realism."

9 Butler 2004a, 113; see also Butler 2002.

10 Cited in Jaschik 2017. In the same article Butler explains: "The performative theory of gender that I proposed then accepted that we are all born into social norms and conventions that define our genders, but that we can also craft our genders within that scene of constraint. The aim of the theory was to offer more language and recognition to those who found themselves ostracized because they did not conform to restrictive ideas of what it means to be a man or a woman. But that theory never denied the existence of constraints, and as I developed it in later years, I sought to show how it served the moral purpose of creating a more livable life for all people who span the gender spectrum." See also Butler 2023b.

11 Butler in Jaschik 2017.

12 In 2021b, Butler points out that "the anti-gender movement is . . . a fascist trend," for "it mobilizes a range of rhetorical strategies from across the political spectrum to maximize the fear of *infiltration* and destruction that comes from a diverse set

of economic and social forces" (my emphasis). On Butler's trans-inclusive feminism, see Butler 2004a, 4–6, 9, and ch. 3. According to M. A. Thompson (2022), positioned "as an infiltration, usurpation, and corruption of feminism . . . transness comes to exist as an endemic threat to women's rights and, by extension, women's bodies."

13 See Butler 2022b, 33; on the guest as enemy, see esp. Derrida and Dufourmantelle 2000. Citing Beauchamp 2012, 72, Galarte (2019) observes that "the border wall that Trump fetishizes and the policies that seek to translate the fantasy it represents into a social reality can be understood as attempts to protect the nation from 'gendered and racialized bodies that move through borders of all sorts, from the metaphorical gender boundaries so often invoked in transgender transition narratives to the national borders involved in immigration.'" See Butler 2020b, 142, on "state violence, fueled by racism and paranoia . . . directed against the migrant population."

14 On the "wild" as "a foil to civilization, . . . the dumping ground for all that white settler colonialism has wanted to declare expired, unmanageable, undomesticated, and politically unruly," see Halberstam 2018b, 454; see also Halberstam 2023. Hartman's theorization of "wild and wayward" Black femininity (2018; 2020b) can be productively applied to *Bacchae*: see Honig 2021 and 2022. On the feral, see below.

15 Butler 2017a, 12.

16 Butler 2017a, 4.

17 Butler 2017a, 12.

18 Butler 2017a, 21.

19 See Bradway and Freeman 2022.

20 Butler 2017a, 5.

21 Butler 2017a, 5–6.

22 In *Precarious Life*, we read: "When we undergo what we do, something about who we are is revealed, something that delineates *the ties* we have to others, *ties or bonds* that compose us" (2004b, 22; my emphasis). See also the important discussion of kinship in *Undoing Gender*, published in the same year, where Butler declares: "Changes at the level of kinship . . . demand a reconsideration of the social conditions under which humans are born and reared, opening up new territory for social and psychological analysis" (14).

23 Butler 2017a, 15.

24 Butler in Antonello and Farneti 2009.

25 Butler in Antonello and Farneti 2009.

26 Butler in Antonello and Farneti 2009. See, e.g., Butler 2009a, 19: "Animality is a precondition of the human, and there is no human who is not a human animal." See also Butler 2015b, 121.

27 On the co-implication of the social and the ecological in Butler's thought, see esp. Barnett 2017: "Human life and political agency are always made possible by conditions that precede them. Those prior conditions are nothing if not ecological conditions. 'We' affect and are affected by not only the condition of exposure but by the many 'others' who find themselves similarly exposed. The more-than-human world often serves as infrastructure for human life in its own right." See Butler discussing *Precarious Life* (2004b) in Kirby and Butler 2006, 153: "One problem with using the framework of humanization and dehumanization is that it leaves the question of the animal to the side, and it tends to effect that separation of human from other sentient beings that contributes to an anthropocentrism of a worrisome kind." See Stanescu 2012. See also Butler 2019c, 14: "Nature is organic . . . in itself, but considered from the human perspective, it starts to become inorganic once it starts to sustain the human at which point it is the human life that is sustained and animated by nature."

28 Szendy 2023, 111.

29 See Butler 2022b, 33: "The reduction of kinship to genetic tie . . . is one way that the government evacuates the affective character of the bond of kinship. On the other hand, that same affective tie is presumed and exploited by the exact same policy."

30 For a survey of all the sources before and after Euripides on the "scandal" of Zeus's uterine transformation of his thigh, see Leitao 2012 (ch. 3), who connects the Euripidean play's interest in Dionysus's trans-birth with the 451 BCE Periclean law that only "a union of *astê* and *astos* [a female and a male Attic citizens] could produce a citizen, a requirement that was frequently the basis upon which demesmen rejected a man's request that his son be inducted into the deme."

31 On Butler and Deleuze and Guattari, see below.

32 Bradway and Freeman 2022.

33 *Gender Trouble* (1990a) can be read as an overall investigation of the ways in which "*regulatory practices* of gender formation and division constitute identity, the internal coherence of the subject" (1999, 23; my emphasis). See also Butler 2004b, 216: "It is important . . . to trace the moments where the binary system of gender is disputed and challenged, where the coherence of the categories is put into question, and where the very social life of gender turns out to be malleable and transformable."

34 Here I echo Moten 2003.

35 Zeitlin 1985 and 1996. Among the many post-Zeitlin readings of Greek tragedy influenced by Butler's gender trilogy—*Gender Trouble* (1990a), *Bodies That Matter* (1993), and *Undoing Gender* (2004a)—see, esp. K. Bassi 1998, Wohl 1998, Ormand 2003, Griffith 2005, Cawthorn 2013, and Worman 2020.

36 See Telò 2022a on the disavowed queerness of Freud's Oedipus complex.

37 Wohl 2005, 146.

38 Wohl 2005, 147.

39 Wohl 2005, 145. On the Deleuzian-Guattarian molecularity of sexuality, see Rosenberg 2014.

40 Bell 2010, 150. As Butler concludes: "So there are people who have suggested that I am Deleuzian in that way—one is not born a woman but becomes one, therefore woman, the category, and all categories of gender, are modes of becoming."

41 See Stryker 2008, 45; Bey 2017, 2022b, and 2022c; Halberstam 2018a; and Preciado 2018 and 2021. This position is controversial within trans studies: see Keegan 2020. Butler encapsulates the terms of this controversy in an interview with *The Transadvocate* (2017b), from the same year as their lecture on *Bacchae*, observing that while the refusal of gender assignment by "many genderqueer and trans people . . . opens the way for a more radical form of self-determination . . . one problem with that view of social construction is that it suggests that what trans people feel about what their gender is, and should be, is itself 'constructed' and, therefore, not real."

42 Gabriel 2018, 317.

43 Explaining Maxe Crandall and Hope Mohr's intention to make *Bacchae Before* "as trans as possible," Silk Worm (2021) elaborates on the close attention that the directors paid to the robing scene, "imbuing it with as much tender love and care for the curious Pentheus as possible." As Silk Worm continues, "It is a gentle, if murderous, seduction; dressing as a woman might be the first step in Dionysus's scheme to punish Pentheus, but it doesn't have to be a humiliating one. Pentheus's excitement at the prospect of cross-dressing serves here as an especially poignant note to the end he meets, rather than an indignity he suffers along the way."

44 Ruffell 2022, 242–43.

45 Ruffell 2022, 248.

46 Ruffell (2022, 239) says that "while it is the culmination of a trans-relevant thematic" the robing scene "is not in itself the most decisive scene for a trans reading."

47 Butler 2017a, 13.

48 Wohl (2005, 148) observes that "the riddle of sexual reproduction is not scripted as a family romance—the loving union of man and woman, two becoming one—but instead is understood as a series of unexpected and *transitory* conjunctions: the unexplained coincidence of Zeus's thunderbolt and the mother's womb, the violent blow that kills Semele and expels the baby from her body, his instantaneous transfer from one birth-chamber to another" (my emphasis).

49 Pezaro, Crowther, Pearce et al. 2023, 126.

50 Pezaro, Crowther, Pearce et al. 2023, 126. See Preciado 2021, 88: "The designation of heterosexuality as the only normal reproductive sexuality together with patriarchal depictions of fatherhood and biopolitical depictions of motherhood

seem . . . anachronistic when faced with the many possible ways of managing reproduction, and assisted procreation: . . . trans paternity . . . surrogacy . . . and research projects in womb transplant, the possibility of creating artificial wombs." See Gay and Butler 2022 on reproductive inclusivity.

51 Toze 2018, 204.

52 Cited in Toze 2018, 202.

53 Radi 2020, 402.

54 Kage was inspired by the 2015 picture of Evan Hempel, an American transgender man breastfeeding his son: https://www.gay.it/rimini-cancellato-il-murale-delluomo-trans-che-allatta-il-sindaco

55 On *mothering* as an open, non-biological alternative to maternity or motherhood, see Gumbs, Martens, and Williams 2016 and Lewis 2021 and 2022.

56 https://www.corriereromagna.it/rimini-sgarbi-e-il-murale-cancellato-una-bestemmia?

57 Cavarero 2016, 99 and 104.

58 The haptic dynamics of the painting are complex. An imagistic intertwinement of arms forges a parallelism between Mary and baby Jesus, on the one hand, and baby Jesus and a baby lamb on the other. Jesus is in the same position as the animal destined, like him ("God's lamb"), to be sacrificed. Jesus's self-sacrifice seems almost intimated by his grip on the lamb. Mary's self-sacrifice—the loss of her child—can be read as eerily homologous to Jesus's self-sacrifice through the threatening scenario of his possible (inevitable?) violence against the animal. As Freud relays in the essay "Leonardo da Vinci and a Memory of His Childhood" (1910, 115n1), one of his students, Oskar Pfister, spotted the outline of a vulture in Mary's orientation toward Jesus, a sign of "the menace which laces all motherly affection" (Leonard 2016, 320). Honig (2021, 85) pursues the possible connection between the Leonardo painting and *Bacchae*: "a *Bacchae* reading of the painting sees inclination in a range of kinship roles and postures in which care and/as murderousness are inextricably intertwined."

59 Butler 2021c, 56–57: "She is dealing with generalizations that do not always fit the instance. So it makes no sense to find examples of uncaring mothers and caring fathers, since all that is surely possible without the dominant norms becoming fully dislodged from their place." Butler's warning against generalization is formulated here only implicitly and indirectly.

60 Butler 2021c, 47–48.

61 Butler 2021c, 49–50.

62 https://www.thenation.com/article/culture/josh-hawley-manhood?

63 These are the Antigonean words that, in the preface of the 2021 reissue of *Excitable Speech* (2021d, xxiii), Butler uses to describe the speech act of Paul Preciado as he

fearlessly declares to the Psychoanalytic Society, "I am a monster who is speaking to you." See Preciado 2021.

64 https://ballotpedia.org/Michigan_%22Dismemberment_Abortion_Ban_Act%22_Initiative_(2020)

65 https://necatholic.org/news-events/newsroom.html/article/2020/03/06/-it-is-what-it-is/

66 Cavarero 2009, 8.

67 See chapter 3.

68 Segal (1997, 187–88) observes that Agave "tears [Pentheus] limb from limb . . . and then *takes* his body back *into* herself in a monstrous 'feast'" (my emphasis). The Hippocratic corpus and the late-antique medical tradition record gruesome abortion procedures: see Kapparis 2002, 22–27.

69 Carson 2015, 70.

70 Butler 2023d.

71 On somatechnics as "a shorthand label for a robust ontological account of embodiment as process," see Stryker 2015, 229; see also Sullivan (2014), who observes that "transgender, like forms of bodily being commonly presumed not to be technologically produced, is a heterogeneous somatechnological construct" (188).

72 On unbecoming and transness, see Halberstam 2018c; on transness and interspecies unbecoming, see Barad 2014 and 2015, Chen 2015, Hayward and Weinstein 2015, and Kelley 2014 and 2017. See also below.

73 On "intertwinement," see Butler 2022a. In *The Force of Nonviolence* (2020b, 57 and 111), Butler reaches a position close to a contestation of species division through the ethics of social ecology: "If the interdiction against killing rests on the presumption that all lives are valuable . . . then the universality of the claim only holds on the condition that value extends equally to all living beings. This means that we have to think not only about persons, but animals; and not only about living creatures, but living processes, the systems and forms of life"; "If racism is a way of 'introducing a break into the domain of life that is under power's control,' as [Foucault] claims, then perhaps we can think of that break as distinguishing not merely between superior and inferior types within the idea of the species, but also between the living and the nonliving."

74 Butler 2022a, 38.

75 When Segal (1997, 82) notes that line 3 is marked by a "dense cluster of four key words: Σεμέλη λοχευθεῖσ' ἀστραπηφόρῳ πυρί," he implicitly suggests that the line is in itself saturated, perhaps "pregnant."

76 See Diggle 1994, 453–56.

77 Wohl 2005.

78 See below.

79 On the epidemic "threat" of transness, see M. A. Thompson 2022.

80 See K. Bassi 2017.

81 Quint 2011, 274 (my emphasis).

82 Butler 2015a, 51 and 56.

83 My emphases.

84 Weil 2017, 199 (my emphasis).

85 Weil 2017, 199. In the 2010 interview with Vikki Bell, Butler declares: "I've become more and more interested in modes of agency that don't reside in human subjects, and I think there can be institutional modes of agency that are distributed throughout institutional scenes. When we talk about agency, we in fact need to divorce it from the idea of the subject and allow it to be a complex choreographed scene with many kinds of elements—social, material, human—at work." Here Butler also refers to her engagement with the work of Karen Barad (2007), Rayna Rapp (2000), and Charis Thompson (2005).

86 Weil 2017, 199.

87 See esp. Sullivan (2006, 552), who "rather than seeing transmogrification as a negative process that produces disavowed and abjected monstrous others" sees it as "the expression of a fundamental human condition, part of the process through which we all negotiate the boundary between self and other, and through which we perpetually transform ourselves in relation to an Other." See Butler 2015a, 29, on the detachability of the body: "If one can pose the question whether one's hands and one's body are not one's own, then what has happened such that the question has become posable? In other words, how is it that my hands and my body became something other than me, or at least appeared to be other than me, such that the question could even be posed whether or not they belong to me?"

88 See Telò 2023b (ch. 4) on trans-form.

89 On the relation between Butler and Catherine Malabou's notion of plasticity, see Helberg (2020), who suggests that "the form of transformation Butler associates with a subject's resistance to the power that forms it involves a plastic movement" (601).

90 Most recently, Ruffell (2022, 242) dismisses the pun as something that "looks more like the rationalisms of contemporary speculative thinkers than it does the insight of a prophet with a hotline to the divine."

91 Aspiration produces an effect of phonetic blurring, which we can consider homologous to that of diphthongs, seen as phonetic figurations of transness by Avesani (2023).

92 On fugitive ungendering, see Bey 2022b. In a book dedicated to Butler, Preciado (2021) asserts: "I prefer my new condition as monster to that of man or woman, because his condition is like a foot stepping forward into the void, indicating the path to another world" (41); "The trans body is a life force, it is the inexhaustible Amazon flowing through the rainforest" (43); "The trans experience is a whirlwind of transformative energy that recodifies all political and cultural signifiers, preventing a clear . . . delineation between yesterday and today, between the feminine and the masculine" (46). See Szendy (2023) on air as a "sympneumatic texture that interleaves all (living beings)." When Szendy says that "sympnea, when and if it happens, is only possible on the condition of dyspneic finitude," I perceive an echo of Butler's theorization of ecological interdependence in *What World Is This?* (2022a).

93 Butler 2022a, 59.

94 Dodds (1960, 114) observes: "Pentheus speaks of Bacchism as if it were a physical infection transmissable by contact. . . . His violent horror of such contact is a fine psychological stroke: something in him knows already the fascination and the mortal peril which the new rites hold for him."

95 On the stuttering of language, see Deleuze 1994.

96 "Transcorporeality means that all creatures, as embodied beings, are intermeshed with the dynamic, material world, which crosses through them, transforms them and is transformed by them" (Alaimo 2018, 435). See also Alaimo 2008, 2012, and 2021.

97 Butler 2022a, 39: "I am not fully sealed as a bounded creature but emit breath into a shared world where I take in air that has been circulating through the lungs of others." On breath and the ethics of alterity in Levinas, see Marder 2009.

98 Butler 1990a, 23: "The heterosexualization of desire requires and institutes the production of discrete and asymmetrical oppositions"; Butler 1999, xxiv: "Ideals . . . of proper and improper masculinity and femininity . . . are underwritten by racial codes of purity and taboos against miscegenation."

99 Wohl, forthcoming, on the conceptual link between air and the idea of sameness in Diogenes of Apollonia.

100 In the advance praise of Osmundson's *Virology* (2022), Butler writes: "The viral world is the ordinary world of life and death, of caring for one another in our vulnerability and persistence."

101 Deleuze 2003, 25.

102 On "reproductive communism," see Lewis 2021 and 2022.

103 See Segal 1997, 151–52: "The waters of Dirce receive the divine child either because they extinguish the lightning fire of his celestial father or else because they serve to wash the newborn in anticipated normal birth from the mother." In

structuralist terms, he writes: "Celestial fire, immortality, Olympus, and birth from the male contrast implicitly with earth, mortality, the chthonic regions, and birth from the female womb in sexual reproduction."

104 Enjambment is the linguistic figure of the "interruption" that Butler valorizes especially in *Giving an Account of Oneself* (2005): see, e.g., "It is . . . the case that I give an account *to* someone, and that the addressee of the account . . . also functions to interrupt the sense that this account of myself is my own" (36); "If the other is always there, from the start . . . then a life is constituted through a fundamental interruption, is even *interrupted prior to the possibility of any continuity*" (52).

105 See, e.g., Pugliese 2023, 26: "Water is at once a dispositional-conditioning element and a transitional element that is always becoming: it is effectively always in a state of transitional becoming through movements of ingestion, absorption, enfleshing, respiration, transpiration and evaporation."

106 On this debate, see esp. Keegan 2020. Chen (2013, 171) observes: "Just as gender and sex are unavoidably linked, so too are trans and queer. They can be considered as independent factors which participate in intersectional spaces."

107 The citation is from Pugliese 2023, 32.

108 The citation is from Hazard (2022, 220), who proposes a trans/queer theory of fluvial interconnection.

109 See Quashie 2021, 59–60.

110 Pugliese 2023, 22.

111 Pugliese (2023, 24), referring to Winona LaDuke and work on "Indigenous cosmoepistemologies."

112 See Butler in the 1999 edition of *Gender Trouble* on the "multiple and *diffuse* points of origin" brought out in their genealogical investigation of "phallogocentrism and compulsory heterosexuality" (xxxi [my emphasis]).

113 Lewis 2023, 75.

114 https://www.newstribune.com/news/2023/aug/08/indigenous-leader-inspires-amazon-city-to-grant/. The article adds: "The Komi Memem . . . is now the first among hundreds of rivers in the Brazilian Amazon to have a law that grants it personhood status. This is part of a new legislative approach to protect nature that has made inroads in many parts of the world, from New Zealand to Chile."

115 Butler 2020b, 141.

116 O'Donnell and Talbot-Jones 2018, 3.

117 duBois 2022.

118 Dodds 1960, 162.

119 See Jean-Luc Nancy on sleep and togetherness: "Everyone sleeps in the equality of the same sleep—all the living. . . . Sleeping together opens up nothing less than

the possibility of penetrating into the most intimate part of the other. . . . Sleeping together comes down to sharing an inertia, an equal force that maintains the two bodies together. . . . It is in effect the great equal sleep of the whole Earth that those who sleep together share. In their 'together' is refracted the entirety of all sleepers: animals, plants, rivers, seas, sands, stars set in their crystalline spheres of ether, and ether itself, which has fallen asleep" (2009, 17–19). On the sleep of the Maenads, see Honig 2021, 49–50.

120 On the "cage" of gender, see Preciado 2021, 39. On ungendering, see esp. Bey 2022b, 67: "Gender is that which is made to attach to bodies of a domesticized space, predicated on the integrity of an ontology constituted by a white symbolic order. The subjects contained in the 'lab' of the ship's hold, as malleable flesh, ungender subjectivity by way of refusing and being refused by the necessary symbolic ontology of gender. . . . Ungendering might be understood usefully as a refusal of an 'identity' and furthermore of an ontological grounding. Ungendering's undercurrent of blackness, an abolitionist feminist blackness, is to mobilize the flesh."

121 See Butler 1994 on the "proper" and "improper"; on the "wild," see Halberstam 2018a and 2020.

122 Preciado 2021, 41.

123 See Butler 2005, 26, on the structures "that enable my living to belong to a sociality that exceeds me"; see also Butler 2011, 382 and 385–86: "To be a body is to be exposed to social crafting and form. . . . That is what makes the ontology of the body a *social* ontology. . . . The boundary of who I am is the boundary of the body, but the boundary of the body never fully belongs to me."

124 Cavarero (2023) speaks of "the wild nourishing vitality of the maternal body," the "delirium of a hypermaternity that exceeds its own excess," and a "maternity absorbed in alimentary frenzy."

125 In lines 710–11, the *thursoi*, phallic objects, spurting milk, patently become breasts. On anatomopolitics—the "sophisticated technology" imposing "the context in which the organs acquire their meaning (sexual relationship) and are properly used in accordance with their nature"—see Preciado 2018, 29.

126 See Butler 1993, 172, 176–78, on heterosexist interpellation.

127 See Blackston 2017, 127: "Transplants—as in the movement of organs from bodies to other bodies—are themselves trans* movements that direct vitality from one body to another in neither an equal nor equalizing fashion. The act of unplanting and replanting is enacted through cuts in multiple fields (physical and social)."

128 Ruffell (2022, 245) comments on the Maenads' sparagmatic feat in these terms: "For the messenger, the women are displaying super*human* strength, but also

invert gender norms, putting the men to flight, despite being armed only with the thyrsus (731–35 and 759–65)." See also below.

129 Butler 1993 (ch. 2), on the lesbian phallus, which codifies "the displaceability of the phallus, its capacity to symbolize in relation to other body parts or other body-like things" (51).

130 See Butler 2005, 28: "An encounter with an other effects a transformation of the self from which there is no return. What is recognized about a self in the course of this exchange is that the self is the sort of being for whom staying inside itself proves impossible."

131 Berlant 2022.

132 "Other Maenads threw their thyrses through the sky / at Pentheus, an unfortunate aiming; for they missed the mark (*allai de thursous hiesan di' aitheros / Pentheôs, stochon dustênon; all'ouk ênuton* 1099–100)." The striking juxtaposition of the two genitives *aitheros Pentheôs*—an anomaly reinforced by the following accusative in apposition to the preceding clause—conveys the impression that the Maenads are not targeting just Pentheus, but the air itself, as though there were no distinction between the former and the latter.

133 Establishing a connection between Butler's ethics of interdependent ecology and Barad's deconstructive new materialism, founded on the notion of "intra-action," Bell (2012, 117) draws attention to the ethics of Barad's "cuts" in passages like this: "Cuts are agentially enacted not by willful individuals but by the larger material arrangements of which 'we' are a 'part.' . . . Ethics is not a geometrical calculation; 'others' are never very far from 'us'; 'they' and 'we' are co-constituted and entangled through the very cuts 'we' help to enact. Cuts cut things together and apart" (2007, 178–79). The break as/in the bond that Butler situates in *Bacchae* is comparable to this notion of the "cut."

134 Butler 2022b, 47.

135 Ruffell 2022, 245.

136 On this expression, see the Introduction.

137 Dodds (1960, 166) observes that this rhythmical phenomenon "occurs in only seven other tragic trimeters."

138 Line 1147 can be considered the "end" (or one of the two endings) of the Messenger's speech; the last five lines (1148–52) pivot from the reporting of the disaster to the preparation for Agave's impending arrival.

139 Butler and Taylor 2010, 190 and 195.

140 Butler in Butler and Taylor 2010, 200.

141 Butler 1993, 235–36. See, also, Butler in Kirby and Butler 2006, 147: "The normative account of the emergence of heterosexuality presupposes a melancholia over a lost and unavowed homosexuality."

142 This is a well-trodden path in the literary interpretation of the play: see esp. Zeitlin 1996 and Segal 1997.

143 Butler 2009a, 16.

144 Deutscher (2017, 157) borrows the term "responsibilization" from Foucault (1990, 105).

145 Deutscher (2017, 153–54), analyzing Butler's theorization of precarious lives in relation to reproductive rights.

146 I am indebted here to the discussion of reproductive rights and biopolitics offered by Deutscher (2017, 164), who refers to Brown 1983. See Barbara Johnson's commentary on a line from Gwendolyn Brooks's "The Mother" ("Believe that even in my deliberateness I was not deliberate") in her famous article "Apostrophe, Animation, and Abortion" (1986): "I have not chosen the conditions under which I must choose."

147 See again Deutscher 2017, referencing Memmi 2011. See also Berlant 1994 on the state's biopolitical affirmation of the fetus's rights over those of the mother.

148 Butler 2009a, 19. See McNeilly 2013.

149 Butler 2009a, 19.

150 Butler 2009a, 22.

151 Butler 2009a, 18.

152 See Z. Jackson (2020), on the racializing implications of any kind of anthropocentrism. See also the foundational essay by Spillers (1987). Rifkin (2022, 156–57) pushes against the default identification of kinship with "enfamilyment" as "the racializing means of (pre)qualifying for personhood and political subjectivity."

153 Butler 1999, xix and xx.

154 See Butler and Worms 2023 and the Introduction.

155 See also 1237: "hunting beasts with our hands (*cheroin*)."

156 Butler 2015a, 54.

157 Delgado Huitrón (2019, 167), referring to Derrida 2005, 81.

158 Vaccaro 2014, 96.

159 Delgado Huitrón 2019, 167.

160 Butler 2017a, 17.

161 Seaford 1996, ad loc.

162 On this caressing, see Telò 2023a, 49. On aspirated sounds and hairiness, see esp. Telò 2019.

163 See Butler 2005, 101: "Violence . . . delineates a physical vulnerability from which we cannot slip away, which we cannot finally resolve in the name of the subject, but which can provide a way to understand that none of us is fully bounded,

utterly separate, but, rather, we are in our skins, given over, in each other's hands, at each other's mercy."

164 See Dodds 1960, 224–25: "L. S. [=Liddell Scott] still seems to take μόσχος to be a lion's whelp here, as did most scholars before Wilamowitz. But although a boy or girl could be called a μόσχος (*anglice* 'kid'), it does not follow that a young lion could—particularly without λέοντος, and in a play where μόσχος has been used more than once in its literal sense." Battezzato (2022, 7) rightly points out that "(without realizing it?) Agave knows she has not simply killed a 'lion,' but a 'beast' that can be metaphorically read as a human that is both male (beard) and female ('calf'/'heifer')."

165 On ferality, see esp. Halberstam (2020), who elaborates "an epistemology of the feral" or "of the ferox"; for Halberstam, the feral "frames an orientation that turns away from the human and toward the animal"; in other words, "it offers approximate language for a wildness that exceeds human classification." See also Yoon 2017. On the function of satyrs in satyr drama, see esp. Hall 1998 and Griffith 2002.

166 Ferreday 2011, 219. See Austin 2021, 123: "Furries are more likely to identify themselves as transgender compared to other fandoms . . . and this may also be a reason why there is a plethora of gender-bending found in Furry pornography."

167 Ferreday 2011, 223.

168 Ferreday 2011, 223.

169 See Butler 2020d, 690–91: "The link with animality is not only internal to the human but entails a set of interdependent relations between humans and other animals. . . . For a human to be an animal . . . is to be an animal among animals, to have one's human life bound up with animal life, and to love as a being whose life should be freed of the degradations and exposures implied by the anthropocentric ideal that gives dignity to some physical, intellectual, and linguistic activities over the interdependent conditions among living creatures, if not over life itself. . . . If humans are led to differentiate themselves from animals to gain proper dignity, then they assume, and institute, the indignity of animal life, including their own lives. Under such conditions, striving to be human (and *not* animal) consists in the suppression and degradation of animality." Referring to Butler's "gender trilogy," Uhlig (2021) analyzes satyrs' drag performances, in particular, images, offered by vase painting, of juxtaposition of "the masculine and bestial attributes of the satyrs with their feminine dress." I am suggesting that in Agave we can see a "desire to become satyr" that exposes what we can call animal trouble, that is, the melancholic introjection of the lost object of animality that is necessary to become humananimal.

170 In lines 989–90, the Chorus says of the "cruel" Pentheus that he must have been born from "some lioness."

171 Thus, Zaman (2023), who continues: "The fursona . . . can be understood as a non/human drag performance of doing 'neutrality' that does not 'come to terms' with a static gender or racialized identity but instead resists the terms of domestication. This process is a performative tool for 'More Life' as it gives a way to embody indistinguishability as livability." In Klaus Michael Grüber's 1974 production of the play, Agave leaves the stage walking on four limbs while shouting and howling.

172 See Zaman (2023), referring to Spillers 1987 on the flesh: "We are less interested in joining the ranks of gendered femaleness than gaining the *insurgent* ground as female social subjects." Zaman also refers to Halberstam, who valorizes the wild as a way to engage with "chaotic force[s] of nature, the outside of categorization, unrestrained forms of embodiment, the refusal to submit to social regulation, loss of control, the unpredictable" (2020, 3).

173 On subjunctivity, see Quashie 2021.

174 See Dodds 1960, 235–36; see also Janan 2004, 144n46.

175 "Gender-critical" is a synonym of "transphobic": see Butler 2017b and, esp., 2021c, an interview with *The Guardian* in which Butler says that "anti-gender ideology is one of the dominant strains of fascism in our times," a statement that the newspaper later censured. See also S. Bassi and G. LaFleur 2022 and Lewis and Saresin 2022. In a book on "late fascisms," Toscano (2023, 99), referring to Butler (2021b), observes: "A planetary moral panic around transness has joined racist narratives of migration as ethnic substitution in a wellspring of fascistic energies."

176 Butler 2021a.

177 See esp. Hayward and Weinstein 2015.

178 See Steinbock, Szczygielska, and Wagner 2017, 3.

179 Stryker and Currah 2015, 189.

180 Morin 2017, 92.

181 Butler 2020d, 691.

182 Butler 2020d, 691.

183 Referring to Clark 2015, Kelley (2017) says that "Clark places tranimals beside Judith Butler's theories of gender performativity to argue that 'tranimals' are, in a way, 'dragging' the gendered human, causing a divergence from the heteronormative performance." As Kelley continues, " 'Dragging' evokes both a performance of gender and the work of carrying or crossing terrain with encumbrances." For Kelley, "the physical labour of trans*, movement across and between gendered and genetic taxonomies, facilitates posthuman becomings that develop hard-won social alliances across species."

184 Butler 2017a, 21.

185 Butler 2004b, xiv–xv.

186 See https://www.lastampa.it/la-zampa/2023/06/30/news/ministra_roccella_contro_nomi_bambini_cani_famiglia-406205169/

187 On queer theory and animal studies, see Freccero 2017 and 2021 (on attachments to pets as queer relations).

188 Butler 2022d. See also Butler 2023i.

189 Butler 2023g: "Hundreds of Palestinians children have died since Israel began its 'revenge' military actions against Hamas." In an interview with *Democracy Now!* Butler (2023k) says that "[Palestinians] are not just [considered] less than human . . . but a threat to what the idea of the human is, that is being defended by Zionist politics."

190 Butler 2023g.

191 Butler in Yancy 2023: "The vast number of children killed in Gaza will never have the kind of global attention and empathy that the Israeli child will have. We will know the Israeli's name and family, but we will only get a number for the Palestinian child, or thousands of children."

192 Butler 2023g.

193 Gosine 2021, 129.

194 Gosine 2021, 150.

195 Julien 2021, 17.

196 Butler in Telò 2023c, 13.

197 On the female deer in *Iphigenia in Aulis*, see Haselswerdt 2022. Caspers (2012) considers the thematic connections between *Bacchae* and *Iphigenia in Aulis*, without including the sacrificial animal.

Chapter 3

1 Butler 2023a, 16.

2 Butler 2020b.

3 Freud 1915, 279.

4 Cassandra calls herself an Erinys in Euripides' *Trojan Women* 457. See also the line in the finale of *Agamemnon*, discussed in the Introduction, in which Cassandra sees the Erinyes. See Loraux 2002, 80, 90, and 116n9. On the connection between the Furies and the figure of the *vates* in Seneca's tragedies, see Schiesaro 2003, 8–9 and 12.

5 Butler 2020b, 155.

6 Butler 2023a, 7.
7 See esp. Goldhill 1984, 279–83; Griffith 1995; Bacon 2001; Easterling 2008, 230–35; Zakin 2009; Toscano 2015 (on the play as a failure of Hegelian dialectic); and Nooter 2017 (ch. 5). In Telò 2020a, 217–30, I suggested an anti-cathartic, i.e., auto-immunitarian, reading of the politico-aesthetic imaginary of the play.
8 Prins 1991.
9 Butler 2023a, 7.
10 Butler 2023a, 6.
11 In the Derveni Papyrus, the Erinyes are presented as "guardians of Justice"—a characterization that goes beyond their Aeschylean role as agents of retribution: see Janko 2022, 177–79.
12 Deuber-Mankowsky (2016, 257) connects "Toward a Critique of Violence" with Benjamin's 1934 essay "Franz Kafka: On the Tenth Anniversary of His Death" (1999).
13 Butler 2020a and 2006b.
14 Morales (2022) valorizes *mania* in Euripides' *Bacchae*, influenced by important interventions in Black studies such as Bruce 2021.
15 Butler 2020b, 163.
16 Butler 2020b, 164.
17 Butler 2020b, 168.
18 As Butler (2020b, 171) adds, "Mania can never become a politics without becoming a dangerous form of destruction, but it introduces a vigorous 'unrealism' into the modes of solidarity that seek to dismantle violent regimes, insisting . . . on another reality." Commenting on Muñoz (1999), Butler (2018, 4) defines disidentification as "the exciting venture of departing from protocols of propriety that seek to shame a wide range of desires and to foreclose potential connections or . . . connections with potentiality."
19 See Butler 2002, 222.
20 Butler 2020b, 169.
21 Butler 2020b, 182 (my emphasis).
22 Freud 1915, 279.
23 Butler in Telò 2023b, 18 and 19.
24 On this explanation, see, esp., Siegel 1980; for a discussion of the many changes of mind in Euripides' play, see Gibert 1996 (ch. 5).
25 On the identification of the Erinyes with the *alastôr* ("demon"), see Padel 1992, 172.
26 See Telò 2023a (ch. 3).
27 Here I refer to Aristotle's conception of the tragic plot as discussed in *Poetics*: see esp. Rancière 2011, 97, and Panagia 2018, 42–51. Foucault (2023, 247) observes that "madness is . . . the site of impossibility" or, differently put, "crosses limits that

are usually insurmountable." See Butler 2023h, on the danger of being called "crazy" for thinking the impossible in relation to the Palestine and Israel conflict.

28 See, esp., Saxonhouse 1984, Zeitlin 1996 (ch. 3), Aristodemou 1999, and Schroeder 2000.

29 See Derrida 1992, 5, on the "force" of the law: "Law is always an authorized force, a force that justifies itself or is justified in applying itself, even if this justification may be judged from elsewhere to be unjust or unjustifiable . . . . It is the force essentially implied in the very concept of *justice as law* (*droit*), of justice as it becomes *droit*, of the law as '*droit*.'" Derrida's project is, in fact, to contemplate "the possibility of a justice, indeed of a law that not only exceeds or contradicts 'law' (*droit*) but also, perhaps, has no relation to law."

30 Goldhill (1984, 219) writes that "the grammar of this sentence . . . is, as Verrall notes, more forceful than regular."

31 Foucault and Simon 1991, 27.

32 Sommerstein 1989, 99–100 (my emphasis).

33 For the casting of the migrant as a contagious agent, see Butler 2022a, 10–11: "At the outset of the pandemic, the virus was figured by media reports as coming from a place, a 'foreign' place . . . and described as an unwanted immigrant, imported without proper papers into the body politic, at which point 'public health' within the US nation-state . . . was said to be imperiled by what is foreign." On the Erinyes as migrants, see Yi 2015.

34 Butler 2020a, 16. See also Butler 2020c, 88.

35 Butler 2020a, 19, where Butler also remarks that reading Kafka in current times "allows us to think [of] the brutal repetition of legal violence as a collapse of expected temporal sequence."

36 Butler 2020a, 19.

37 Butler 2006b, 22.

38 W. Benjamin 2021.

39 W. Benjamin 2021, 55–56. As Radcliffe (2024, 59) observes, the German word for violence, *Gewalt*, "can connote an illegal, destructive exercise of force" but also a "legitimate state power or authority, in expressions such as 'the power of the people' or the 'authority of the court.'"

40 Butler 2006b, 203

41 Butler 2006b, 207.

42 Butler 2006b, 208.

43 Butler 2006b, 208.

44 Butler 2006b, 208.

45 Butler 2006b, 208.

46 Butler 2006b, 208.

47 Butler 2006b, 208.

48 W. Benjamin 2021, 55 (my emphasis). As Radcliffe (2024, 61) notes: "What Niobe marks is not a spatial boundary between territories but a metaphysical boundary between the mortal and the immortal. The form of the marker preserves the ambiguity of the violence that produced it: petrification serves at once to institute a boundary and to punish Niobe for transgressing the same boundary, a semiotic murkiness redoubled by Niobe's enigmatic existence as a grieving stone."

49 Butler 2006b, 208.

50 Butler 2006b, 211.

51 Butler refers especially to the work of Angela Davis, Gina Dent, Beth Richie, and Ruth Ann Gilmore: see Davis et al. 2022.

52 Richie 2012, 124.

53 See Sanyal 2019.

54 See Telò 2023d.

55 On necrocitizenship, the necropolitical violence directed against citizens "who are subject to a . . . politics of exclusion and militarization," see Díaz-Barriga and Dorsey 2020, 48.

56 On the violence always implicated in the establishment of "property" and "decorum," see Butler 1994. According to Eagleton (2005, 50), in *Eumenides* "the law itself is simply a sublimated version of the very violence and terror which it seeks to contain."

57 On the strong semantic link between *di-airein* and *dikas* in this passage, see Goldhill 1984, 238–39.

58 In a tragedy that plays with the dialectal mixture of Doric and Attic, *dikas* is liable to be read as the Doric form of *dikês.*

59 Sommerstein 1989, 149.

60 There is an interesting convergence between Niobe and the Erinyes as tragic icons: the former employed as an implicit or explicit comparandum for many tragic characters (Antigone, Electra, Andromache, Heracles, etc.), the latter customarily used in vase painting to mark the tragic atmosphere of the depicted dramatic scene. Deuber-Mankowsky (2016, 259) notes that "the very title of chapter 5 of [Judith Butler's] *The Psychic Life of Power: Theories in Subjection*, 'Melancholy Gender/Refused Identifications,' recalls Niobe."

61 The interpretive upshot of this observation is, for Oliensis (2019), that "in Ovid's telling, her transformation into a perpetually weeping rock could accordingly be seen, not as a permanent expression of her grief, but as a humiliating reduction, part and parcel of her divinely imposed comeuppance."

62 Rimell 2024, 76.

63 See Hamilton 2024.

64 See esp. Taplin 1972, 60–62, and 2007, 74–79; Seaford 2005; and Telò 2023a (ch. 7) and 2024a.

65 Statius, *Thebaid* 4.575–78.

66 Comay 2024, 39.

67 On this interchangeability, see Derrida 1988.

68 The echo of this act is perceptible, through reversal, at the beginning of *Eumenides*, where Apollo presents the Erinyes as "those who are spat upon by the gods": *kata-ptustoi* (68) and *apo-ptustou* (191), whose referent is their "feast," a clear allusion to the banquet of Thyestes.

69 See Nooter 2017, 264: "Clytemnestra draws images of breath, wind, and blood into her vision of an attack, evoking the constellation of wind and breath imagery that blows through the choral song of Iphigenia's sacrifice in the parodos of *Agamemnon*."

70 I owe the phrase "buccal exscription" to P. Armstrong (2020), referring to Jean-Luc Nancy 2016. In *The Gravity of Thought* (1997, xiii), Nancy connects "ex-scription" with "the finite movement of the event of meaning as the inscription (ex-scription) of ex-propriation at the heart of appropriation."

71 See Nancy 2016, 111: "*Bucca* . . . is the puffed cheeks, the movement, the contraction/distention of breathing, eating, spitting, or speaking. Buccality is more primitive than orality. Nothing is yet taking place there, and . . . . an unstable and mobile opening forms at the instant of speaking."

72 See Nancy 2023; the picture on the cover of this book—Valérie Jouve, *Untitled (Characters with Josette)*, 1991–95—presents a woman's protesting buccality.

73 Analyzing Benjamin's "Theological-Political Fragment" (2002), Butler (2016b, 280 and 283) discusses "the soul of the living" as "messianic intensity," as the "rhythmic recurrence of loss" that results from "the loss of the radical singularity of [the] first-person *I*." This "rhythmic recurrence of loss," which "constitutes the unshackling of guilt and the release from cycles of debt, recrimination, and revenge," is, for Butler, "a specifically Jewish departure from the cycles of Greek tragedy." In a sense, the rocky and liquid deindividuation of Niobe herself defies its punitive function by bringing about an experience of the "rhythmic recurrence of loss," that is, "the very rhythm of destruction."

74 Nancy 2023, 7.

75 Nancy 2023, 8 and 9.

76 This is my reading of lines 840–43 ("I breathe out all the anger and wrath. / Oioi da pheu. / Which pain penetrates my side!"): *pneô toi menos <th'> hapanta te koton; / oioi da pheu / tis m' hupoduetai / pleuras oduna. Pheu* is, of course, a spitting sound—along with the other *p* sounds. See also below.

77 Butler 2009a, 58–59; speaking of a poem of another Guantanamo poet, Butler says that he is "dispossessed by these tears that are in him, but that are not exclusively his alone."

78 Butler 2009a, 61.

79 Butler 2009a, 61.

80 On the "whirlpool, blowing in a genuine wind of revolt" as an image of rage, see Fanon 1963, 90.

81 Roane 2021, 858.

82 Roane 2021, 858. The phrase "Black captive maternals" is borrowed from James (2016, 256), who explains it in these terms: "In transitioning a colony through a republic into a representative democracy with imperial might, the emergent United States grew a womb, it took on the generative properties of the maternals it held captive." In other words, "Western democracy, based in American Exceptionalism, merged Enlightenment ideologies with Western theories to birth a new nation (a nascent empire) that fed on black frames."

83 Roane 2021, 858.

84 Roane 2021, 868.

85 Roane 2021, 863.

86 Nancy 2016, 111. Gyenge and Ricco (2023, 102) observe that "it is not even that the 'I' opens the mouth but that the mouth in and as its opening makes the body (open), and in creating this stoma gives birth to an I that is always already exposed, cast out, and expropriated from itself." As they add, "The subject, ego, or I, does not preexist the mouth's opening, including in the form of enunciation, constative, or performative speech, or even breath, but instead is born from out of this abyss and its rhythmic gaping."

87 Butler 2004b, 132.

88 The quotes are from Butler (2004b, 133–34), who concludes, at the end of an analysis of Levinas's "Peace and Proximity" (1996), that "the face seems to be a kind of sound, the sonorous substratum of vocalization that precedes and limits the delivery of any semantic sense." In other words: "The face can stand for the sound precisely because it is *not* the sound. In this sense, the figure underscores the incommensurability of the face with whatever it represents" (144). Butler's discussion emphasizes how "the face can also be defaced to index the antihuman" (Sanyal, Telò, and Young 2022, 6). See Sanyal, forthcoming.

89 Guyer 2007, 90.

90 On this "ordinariness," see Gyenge (2018, 21), who refers to Derrida's comment on Nancy's "buccality" as a coming to terms with the fact that "mouth speaks but it does so among other things" and "has not always been an oral agency" (Derrida 2005, 20). In one of his poems, Nancy calls *os* and *bucca* twin sisters, or "the twin rims of your yawning gap / two lips two jaws / vestibule and cavity / resonating outward from within / from airy outside to visceral inside" (2023, 69).

91 See Butler 2016a, 14–15: "All action requires support and . . . even the most punctual and seemingly spontaneous act implicitly depends on an infrastructural condition that quite literally supports the acting body." See the Introduction. Citing Nancy 1989, Gyenge and Ricco (2023, 98) observe, "The mouth is the site of an originating intrusion, birth, and burst of presence, and thus 'not a foundation, but an opening—a serration, a wound.'"
92 On "breathability," see Butler 2022a, 77.
93 Roane 2021, 874 (my emphasis).
94 Deleuze and Guattari 1987, 171; see Gyenge 2018, 189.
95 Butler 2023c, 53.
96 Gagliardi 2020, 436.
97 Taussig 1999, 54.
98 Butler 2012a, 49.
99 Cf. the censoring violence of the white paint thrown onto a mural representing a breastfeeding trans man, as discussed in chapter 2.
100 Butler (2023c) observes that the environmental activists attacking works of art "say that the work is protected, that there is film or another sort of encasement that protects the work against actual damage." The point is that, while works of art are "naturally" given protection, the environment is left unprotected or is not protected enough.
101 Gagliardi 2020, 434, and Butler 2012a, 49.
102 Susan Hansen 2017, referring to Derrida 1993.
103 Roane 2021, 876 (my emphasis).
104 Martin 1920, 286.
105 Martin 1920, 286.
106 Martin 1920, 286.
107 Mason 2020, 104. See Butler 2015b.
108 Butler 2015b, 19 (my emphasis).
109 "Stuff" is cognate with the Greek verb *stuphô* (στύφω): "contract, draw together"; "to be astringent" (LSJ).
110 Butler 2015b, 20: "Gatherings . . . serve as one of democracy's incipient or 'fugitive' moments." Referring to Wolin 1994, Butler reads these gatherings as disidentificatory moments from the "we" of conformity that democratic governments seek to install: see Butler 2009c.
111 See Butler 2015b, 70 and 86: "Though these movements have depended on the prior existence of pavement, street and square . . . it is equally true that the collective actions collect the space itself, gather the pavement, and animate and organize the architecture"; "If we are living organisms who speak and act, then

we are clearly related to a vast continuum or network of living beings; we not only live among them, but our persistence as living organisms depends on that matrix of sustaining interdependent relations."

112 Mason 2020, 140.

113 In *Frames of War* (2009a, 182), Butler observes: "The claim of non-violence not only requires that the conditions are in place for the claim to be heard and registered . . . but that anger and rage also find a way of articulating that claim in a way that might be registered by others. In this sense, non-violence is a not a peaceful state, but a social and political struggle to make articulate and effective—the carefully crafted 'fuck you.'"

114 The prepositional use of *dikên* is exceptionally frequent in *Oresteia*; see O'Neill 1941, 295; Loraux 1990, 259–61; and Wilson (2006), who suggests that "senses of *dikê* make themselves felt even as we hear this seemingly innocuous prepositional *dikê.*" Referring to the Watchman and Iphigenia respectively, the phrases *kunos dikên* ("like a dog" *Agamemnon* 3) and *dikan chimairas* ("like a goat" or "like the Chimaera" *Agamemnon* 232) have led Wilson (2006) and Tralau (2016) to suggest that the play's primary violation of *dikê* is the overturning of the human animal vs. non-human animal hierarchy brought about by the assimilation of Iphigenia to a sacrificial animal. The interpretive uncertainty raised by *chimairas*—a goat? the Chimaera as a symbol of deindividuation or undifferentiation?—self-reflexively encapsulates a comparative disarray or the disarray constitutive of comparison as such, which I seek to connect with the affect of *dikê*. It is significant that the prepositional *dikên* is most frequently used of Cassandra, who, in *Agamemnon*, is compared to a swallow (1050), a dog (*kunos dikên* 1093), a wave (*kumatos dikên* 1181), a cow (1298), a swan (1444), and a crow (1472–73), in a shocking proliferation of sliding identifications, to use the Butlerian expression I discussed in the first chapter. Implicitly conjuring the Erinyes, the canine comparison, which hearkens back to the Watchman's prologue, makes the Erinyes spectrally present at the very beginning of the trilogy: on their imagistic omnipresence, see Bakola 2018; this canine, Erinys-like identity (see, e.g., *Eumenides* 132) also phonically emerges from the wave comparison.

115 North 2021, 15.

116 Nancy 2023, 24

117 Nancy 2023, 28.

118 See Nancy 2023, 21: "What is extended does not pass from inside to outside but is amplified, spread out, distended, disposed, or even dislocated. . . . Extension spreads apart of and from itself, it is its spreading and spacing apart—to which corresponds an intensification (or an 'in-tension') and therefore a plurality of

tensions." For Jean-Luc Nancy, justice "pulses" like blood and "can spurt out from a violent blow and coagulate."

119 According to Goldhill (1984, 216), "the image of the charioteer . . . seems to echo Orestes' description of his own rising madness"; as a result, "the depiction of [the Erinyes'] emotions in terms recalling Orestes' loss of wits stands in contrast to confuse the definition of the level of madness and sanity in the text."

120 Butler 2015b, 9.

121 Through deixis, the body "assert[s] its existence within readable terms." In fact, the body "acts as its own *deixis*, a pointing to, or enacting of, the body that implies its situation: *this* body, *these* bodies; *these* are the ones exposed to violence, resisting disappearance" (Butler 2020b, 197). See also Butler 2015b, 9, a passage commented on by S. Jackson (2022, 345): "The bodily assembly in public"—which deixis can draw attention to—"provokes awareness of public sector systems, the need for access to such systems to sustain the lives of those bodies." Appel (2014, 198) sees Butler's Antigone "as a figure for deixis, indexicality, and the structure, experience of subjectivity."

122 The connection of the term *keuthmôn* with the verb *keuthô* plays up the tombal connotations: see Telò 2020a, 212.

123 Butler 2023a, 11–12; Carson 2010, 16.

124 On the (in)visible presence of the Erinyes throughout the trilogy, even when and where they do not appear, see Bakola 2018.

125 As Hélène Cixous puts it (Fort 1997, 429), *Eumenides* demonstrates that "the invention of democracy is supposed to be seen as . . . progress, whereas it represses . . . the need to find by the side of law . . . *justice*, which is beyond the law."

126 See, among others, Lebeck 1971, 25–29; Di Benedetto 1978; Goldhill 1984, 28, 157–58; and Conacher 1987, 83–85.

127 Lorde 1981, 220–21.

128 Lorde 2020, 53. Cherry (2021, 5) writes that "Lordean rage has an important role to play in anti-racist struggle."

129 The same sibilant bookending is present in Lorde's line "swift in familiar dread and silence."

130 Lorde 1984, 145,

131 Bruce 2021, 159. Pickens (2016, 18) observes that "anger and insanity dovetail in what might be termed 'madness,' an echolalia of all of its resonances of excess, distress, irrationality, and inhumanity."

132 Bruce 2021, 152.

133 Butler 2023a, 12.

134 Butler 2023a, 15.

135 An important methodological reflection upon this point is offered by Gunderson (2020).
136 See the Introduction.
137 See Telò 2023b (ch. 2).
138 The phrase "poethical" is borrowed from Ferreira da Silva (2014, 91).
139 Butler 2023a, 16.
140 D. Thompson 2017, 460.
141 See Derrida and Dufourmantelle 2000.
142 D. Thompson 2017, 470. The citation is from Lyman 2004, 133–34.
143 On erotics and Athenian democracy, see Wohl 2002; on the eroticization of anger, see Allen 2003; on Athenian anger and Frederick Douglass, see duBois 2003.
144 D. Thompson 2017, 468.
145 D. Thompson 2017, 473.
146 Butler 2023a, 17.
147 Okiji, forthcoming
148 Butler 2023a, 17.
149 D. Thompson 2017, 474. See, e.g., Fanon 1963, 148: "Fully aware they are in the process of losing themselves, and consequently of being lost to their people, these men work away with raging heart and furious mind to renew contact with their people's oldest, inner essence, the farthest removed from colonial times. . . . Perhaps this passion and their rage are nurtured or at least guided by the secret hope of discovering beyond the present wretchedness, beyond this self-hatred, this abdication and denial, some magnificent and shining era that redeems us in our own eyes and those of others."
150 D. Thompson 2017, 476 and 477 (my emphasis).
151 See Moten 2018a, 112, on the "right to differ that difference bodies forth; the right to refuse right/s, the right to refuse . . . the etiolated citizenship and subjectivity that have been refused you, the right to refusal which is the first right."
152 See Fanon 1970, 50 on the colonized's "combat breathing": see esp. Perera and Pugliese 2011.
153 Bakker 2008, 72.
154 Crawley 2016, 42. According to Cox and Jean-François (2022, 100–101), when "the utterance 'I can't breathe' . . . is choked into this phrase by state violence," it becomes clear that "Black breathing is in abundance of, and despite of form, of the dead/alive dyad, of the symbolic." In his monograph *Breathing Aesthetics,* Tremblay (2022, 137) recalls his participation in Black Lives Matter protests after the murder of Eric Garner in these terms: "I was breathless—a production of exhaustion, rage, and hope. To some extent, the protesters who had assembled shared breathlessness. But my breathlessness couldn't be equated with the

breathlessness of protesters asphyxiated by environmental racism, police violence, or microaggressions."

155 https://twitter.com/MiddleEastEye/status/1718687049589350486. Discussing June Jordan's poem "Moving towards Home" ("I was born a Black woman / and now / I am become a Palestinian . . ."), Butler in Yancy 2023 observes: "Let us also remember that the same groups that teach how to produce a fully militarized police force, such as the Israeli-export Urban Shield, have targeted Palestinians and Black people, treating all uprisings and forms of resistance as 'terrorism,' domestic or foreign."

156 Butler 2022a, 59.

157 Butler 2022a, 77.

158 Butler 2022a, 37 and 109.

159 Bell 2010, 138.

160 Butler 2002, 213. See also Butler 2009b, 795: "Could it not be that critique is that revolution at the level of procedure without which we cannot secure rights of dissent and processes of legitimation?"

161 Butler 2002, 215 (my emphasis).

162 Bell 2010, 139

163 In a 2020 interview with Masha Gessen (Butler and Gessen 2020), Butler observes that "rage can be crafted—it's sort of an art form of politics." See also Sanyal 2020 on Kimberly Jones's "lucid rage" in the course of the protests after the murder of George Floyd, a rage which, as Claudia Rankine might put it, constitutes "a type of knowledge": as Sanyal notes, we need "to witness and hold on to Kimberly Jones's speech in its implicit call for creation out of destruction; to listen to its words, but also its rhythms, its registers, its embodiment, its resonance with the shouts and murmurs in the streets around us" and to heed "the choreography of unruly bodies in public spaces, the *chorus of fury*" (my emphasis). The adverb *dich(a)* appears only once in *Eumenides*, eight times in *Agamemnon* (323, 324, 349, 757, 815, 861, 1272, 1369), and once in *Libation Bearers* (778).

164 Nancy 1992, 375.

165 Butler 2023a, 17. See Berlant 2022, 225: "The unbearable points to a pressure we feel that points to a system at its limit, a structure or a mind being tested until it appears to bend to the point of nearly giving out."

166 Butler 2023a, 17.

167 Butler 2022c, 420–21.

168 Butler 2023a, 7.

169 Butler 2023a, 13.

170 Butler 2023a, 9.

171 Butler 2023a, 12.
172 Roane 2022.
173 Roane 2022.
174 LSJ s.v. κνάω.
175 Edelman 2023, 3.
176 Butler in Antonello and Farneti 2009.
177 Butler in Bell 2010, 133.
178 Butler in Bell 2010, 134.
179 Butler in Bell 2010, 134.
180 Butler 2022c, 420–21.
181 Cox and Jean-François 2022, 100: "(Black) breathing is the point where all laws collapse."
182 Butler in Yancy 2023.
183 Butler 2022c, 402.
184 Butler 2022c, 404.
185 Butler 2022c, 410.
186 Butler 2022c, 420.

Bibliography

Adorno, T. 2020. *Minima Moralia*. London.

Ahmed, S. 2023a. "Feministkilljoys: In Conversation with Judith Butler." https://feministkilljoys.com/

Ahmed, S. 2023b. *The Feminist Killjoy Handbook: The Radical Potential of Getting in the Way*. New York.

Alaimo, S. 2008. "Trans-Corporeal Feminisms and the Ethical Space of Nature." In *Material Feminisms*, edited by S. Hekman and S. Alaimo, 237–64. Bloomington, IN.

Alaimo, S. 2012. "States of Suspension: Trans-corporeality at Sea." *Isle* 19.3: 476–93.

Alaimo, S. 2018. "Trans-corporeality." In *Posthuman Glossary*, edited by R. Braidotti and M. Hlavajova, 435–38. London.

Alaimo, S. 2021. "Transcorporeality II: COVID–19 and Climate Change." In *More Posthuman Glossary*, edited by R. Braidotti, E. Jones, and G. Klumbytė, 147–48. London.

Allen, D. 2003. "Angry Bees, Wasps, and Jurors: The Symbolic Politics of *orgê* in Athens." In *Ancient Anger: Perspectives from Homer to Galen*, edited by S. Braund and G. Most, 76–98. Cambridge.

Antonello, P., and R. Farneti. 2009. "Antigone's Claim: A Conversation with Judith Butler." *Theory &Event*, n.p.

Appel, L. 2014. "Itinerant Antigone." In *The Returns of Antigone: Interdisciplinary Essays*, edited by T. Chanter and S. D. Kirkland, 187–203. Albany, NY.

Aquilina, A., and K. Borg. 2017. "The *CounterText* Interview: Judith Butler." *CounterText* 3.2: 115–29.

Archimbaud, M. 1993. *Francis Bacon*. New York.

Aristodemou, M. 1999. "The Seduction of Mimesis: Theater as Woman and the Play of Difference and Excess in Aeschylus's *Oresteia*." *Cardozo Studies in Law and Literature* 11.1: 1–33.

Armstrong, P. 2020. "Buccal Exscriptions: Ann Hamilton's *face to face* Photographs." *Parallax* 26.4: 366–83.

Armstrong, R. 1998. "Oedipus at Paris and Vienna: Freud and Sophocles in Performance." *Text and Presentation* 19: 1–15.

Armstrong, R. 2012. "Freud and the Drama of Oedipal Truth." In *A Companion to Sophocles*, edited by K. Ormand, 477–91. Malden, MA.

Austin, J. R. 2021. *Fan Identities in the Furry Fandom*. London.

Avesani, T. 2023. "Diphthongs: Trans and Norm." *TSQ* 10.1: 28–31.

Bacon, H. 2001. "The Furies' Homecoming." *CP* 96.1: 48–59.

Badiou, A. 2013. *Theory of the Subject*. London.

Bakker, E. J. 2008. "Epic Remembering." In *Orality, Literacy, Memory in the Ancient Greek and Roman World*, edited by E. A. Mackay, 65–78. Leiden.

Bakola, E. 2018. "Seeing the Invisible: Interior Spaces and Uncanny Erinyes in Aeschylus' *Oresteia*." In *Gaze, Vision, and Visuality in Ancient Greek Literature*, edited by A. Kampakoglou and A. Novokhatko, 163–86. Berlin.

Barad, K. 2007. *Meeting the Universe Halfway: Quantum Physics and the Entanglements of Matter and Meaning*. Durham, NC.

Barad, K. 2014. "Diffracting Diffraction: Cutting Together-Apart." *Parallax* 20.3: 168–87.

Barad, K. 2015. "Transmaterialities: Trans*/Matter/Realities and Queer Political Imaginings." *GLQ* 21.1–3: 387–422.

Barnett, J. T. 2017. "Thinking Ecologically with Judith Butler." *Culture, Theory, and Critique* 59.1: 1–20.

Bassi, K. 1998. *Acting Like Men: Gender, Drama, and Nostalgia in Ancient Greece*. Ann Arbor, MI.

Bassi, K. 2017. "Mimesis and Mortality: Reperformance and the Dead among the Living in *Hecuba* and *Hamlet*." In *Imagining Reperformance in Ancient Culture*, edited by R. Hunter and A. Uhlig, 138–59. Cambridge.

Bassi, K. 2018. "Morbid Materialism: The Matter of the Corpse in Euripides' *Alcestis*." In *The Materialities of Greek Tragedy: Objects and Affect in Aeschylus, Sophocles, and Euripides*, edited by M. Telò and M. Mueller, 35–48. London.

Bassi, S., and G. LaFleur. 2022. "TERFs, Gender-Critical Movements, and Postfascist Feminisms." *TSQ* 9.3: 311–33.

Bataille, G. 2014. *Inner Experience*. Albany, NY.

Battezzato, L. 2022. "Migrant Refusals: The Inoperativity of the Asian Bacchae in Euripides." *CA* 41.2: 4–15.

Beauchamp, T. 2012. "The Substance of Borders: Transgender Politics, Mobility, and US State Regulation of Testosterone." *GLQ* 19.1: 57–78.

Bell, V. 2010. "New Scenes of Vulnerability, Agency and Plurality: An Interview with Judith Butler." *Theory, Culture & Society* 27.1: 130–52.

Bell, V. 2012. "Declining Performativity: Butler, Whitehead and Ecologies of Concern." *Theory, Culture & Society* 29.2: 107–23.

Benjamin, A. 2015. "*Leben und Glück*: Modernity and Tragedy in Walter Benjamin, Hölderlin, and Sophocles." In *Tragedy and the Idea of Modernity*, edited by J. Billings and M. Leonard, 115–36. Oxford.

Benjamin, W. 1999. "Franz Kafka: On the Tenth Anniversary of His Death." In *Selected Writings 2, 1927–1934*, edited by M. W. Jennings, H. Eiland, and G. Smith, 720–22. Cambridge, MA.

Benjamin, W. 2002. "Theological-Political Fragment." In *Selected Writings 3, 1935–1938*, edited by H. Eiland and M. W. Jennings, 305–6. Cambridge, MA.

Benjamin, W. 2021. *Toward the Critique of Violence*, edited by P. Fenves and J. Ng. Stanford, CA.

Berlant, L. 1994. "America, 'Fat,' the Fetus." *boundary 2* 21.3: 145–95.

Berlant, L. 2022. *On the Inconvenience of Other People*. Durham, NC.

Berlant, L., and L. Edelman. 2013. *Sex, or the Unbearable*. Durham, NC.

Bernini, L. 2016. *Queer Apocalypses: Elements of Antisocial Theory*. London.

Bersani, L. 2010. *Is the Rectum a Grave? And Other Essays*. Chicago.

Bey, M. 2017. "The Trans*-ness of Blackness, the Blackness of Trans*-ness." *TSQ* 4.2: 275–95.

Bey, M. 2022a. "All In." In *Proximities: Reading with Judith Butler*, edited by D. Sanyal, M. Telò, and D. R. Young, *Representations* 158.1: 30–38.

Bey, M. 2022b. *Black Trans Feminism*. Durham, NC.

Bey, M. 2022c. *Cistem Failure: Essays on Blackness and Cisgender*. Durham, NC.

Billings, J. 2014. *Genealogy of the Tragic: Greek Tragedy and German Philosophy*. Princeton.

Billings, J. 2015. "Margins of Genre: Walter Benjamin and the Idea of Tragedy." In *Tragedy and the Idea of Modernity*, edited by J. Billings and M. Leonard, 266–84. Oxford.

Billings, J. 2017. "The 'Smiling Mask' of *Bacchae*." *CQ* 67.1: 19–26.

Blackston, D. M. 2017. "Monkey Business: Trans*, Animacy, and the Boundaries of Kind." *Angelaki* 22.2: 119–33.

Blanchot, M. 1988. *The Unavowable Community*. Barrytown, NY.

Blocker, J. 1999. *Where Is Ana Mendieta? Identity, Performativity, and Exile*. Durham, NC.

Boetzkes, A. 2010. *The Ethics of Earth Art*. Minneapolis.

Bosteels, B. 2008. "Force of Nonlaw: Alain Badiou's Theory of Justice." *Cardozo Law Review* 29.5: 1905–26.

Bowlby, R. 2010. "Derrida's Dying Oedipus." In *Derrida and Antiquity*, edited by M. Leonard, 187–206. Oxford.

Bradway, T., and E. Freeman. 2022. "Introduction: Kincoherence/Kin-aesthetics/Kinematics." In *Queer Kinship: Race, Sex, Belonging, Form*, edited by T. Bradway and E. Freeman, 1–24. Durham, NC.

Brinkema, E. 2011. "Laura Dern's Vomit, or, Kant and Derrida in Oz." *Film-Philosophy* 12: 51–69.

Brinkema, E. 2014. *The Forms of the Affects*. Durham, NC.

Brinkema, E. 2022. *Life-Destroying Diagrams*. Durham, NC.

Brown, W. 1983. "Reproductive Freedom and the Right to Privacy: A Paradox for Feminists." In *Families, Politics, and Public Policy*, edited by I. Diamond, 322–38. New York.

Bruce, L. J. 2021. *How to Go Mad without Losing Your Mind*. Durham, NC.

Buchan, M. 2012. "Sophocles with Lacan." In *A Companion to Sophocles*, edited by K. Ormand, 492–504. Malden, MA.

Budelmann, F. 2000. *The Language of Sophocles.* Cambridge.

Butler, J. 1987. *Subjects of Desire: Hegelian Reflections in Twentieth-Century France.* New York.

Butler, J. 1990a. *Gender Trouble: Feminism and the Subversion of Identity*. New York.

Butler, J. 1990b. "The Pleasure of Repetition." In *Pleasure beyond the Pleasure Principle*, edited by R. Glick and S. Bone, 259–75. New Haven, CT.

Butler, J. 1992. "Contingent Foundations: Feminism and the Question of Postmodernism." In *Feminists Theorize the Political*, edited by J. Butler and J. Scott, 3–21. New York.

Butler, J. 1993. *Bodies That Matter: On the Discursive Limits of Sex.* New York.

Butler, J. 1994. "Against Proper Objects." *differences* 6.2–3: 1–26.

Butler, J. 1997. *The Psychic Life of Power*. Stanford, CA.

Butler, J. 1999. *Gender Trouble: Feminism and the Subversion of Identity*, second edition. New York.

Butler, J. 2000. *Antigone's Claim: Kinship between Life and Death*. New York.

Butler, J. 2002. "What Is Critique? An Essay on Foucault's Virtue." In *The Political: Readings in Continental Philosophy*, edited by D. Ingram, 212–27. Oxford.

Butler, J. 2004a. *Undoing Gender*. New York.

Butler, J. 2004b. *Precarious Life: The Powers of Mourning and Violence*. London.

Butler, J. 2004c. "Bracha's Eurydice." *Theory, Culture & Society* 21.1: 95–100.

Butler, J. 2005. *Giving an Account of Oneself.* New York.

Butler, J. 2006a. "The Desire to Live: Spinoza's Ethics under Pressure." In *Politics and the Passions, 1500–1850*, edited by V. Kahn, N. Saccamano, and D. Coli, 111–30. Princeton.

Butler, J. 2006b. "Critique, Coercion, and Sacred Life in Benjamin's 'Critique of Violence.'" In *Political Theologies*, edited by H. de Vries, 201–19. New York.

Butler, J. 2009a. *Frames of War: When Is Life Grievable?* New York.

Butler, J. 2009b. "Critique, Dissent, Disciplinarity." *Critical Inquiry* 35.4: 773–95.

Butler, J. 2009c. "Finishing, Starting." In *Derrida and the Time of the Political*, edited by P. Cheah and S. Guerlac, 291–306. Durham, NC.

Butler, J. 2011. "Remarks on 'Queer Bonds.'" *GLQ* 17.2–3: 381–87.

Butler, J. 2012a. *Parting Ways: Jewishness and the Critique of Zionism*. New York.

Butler, J. 2012b. "Can't Stop Screaming." *Public Books*. https://www.publicbooks.org/cant-stop-screaming/

Butler, J. 2014. "On the Edge: Grief." https://pen.org/on-the-edge-grief/

Butler, J. 2015a. *Senses of the Subject*. New York.

Butler, J. 2015b. *Notes toward a Performative Theory of Assembly*. Cambridge, MA.

Butler, J. 2016a. "Rethinking Vulnerability and Resistance." In *Vulnerability in Resistance*, edited by J. Butler, Z. Gambetti, and L. Sabsay, 12–27. Durham, NC.

Butler, J. 2016b. "One Time Traverses Another: Benjamin's 'Theological-Political Fragment.'" In *Walter Benjamin and Theology*, edited by C. Dickinson and S. Symons, 272–85. New York.

Butler, J. 2017a. "Breaks in the Bond: Reflections on Kinship Trouble." UCL Housman Lecture. https://www.ucl.ac.uk/classics/sites/classics/files/housman_butler_2017.pdf

Butler, J. 2017b. "Gender Performance: *The Transadvocate* Interviews Judith Butler." https://www.transadvocate.com/gender-performance-the-transadvocate-interviews-judith-butler_n_13652.htm

Butler, J. 2018. "Solidarity/Susceptibility." *Social Text* 36.4: 1–20.

Butler, J. 2019a. "Out of Breath: Laughing, Crying at the Body's Limit." https://hemisphericinstitute.org/en/encuentro-2019-keynote-lectures/item/3084-keynote-lectures-004.html

Butler, J. 2019b. "Genius or Suicide." *London Review of Books* 41.20 (October 20). https://www.lrb.co.uk/the-paper/v41/n20/judith-butler/genius-or-suicide

Butler, J. 2019c. "The Inorganic Body in the Early Marx: A Limit-Concept of Anthropocentrism." *Radical Philosophy* 2.6: 3–17.

Butler, J. 2020a. "Indefinite Detention." *Qui Parle* 29.1: 15–24.

Butler, J. 2020b. *The Force of Nonviolence*. London.

Butler, J. 2020c. "The Radical Equality of Lives: Judith Butler Interviewed by Brandon M. Terry." In *On Anger*, edited by A. Callard, 85–100. Cambridge, MA.

Butler, J. 2020d. "Companion Thinking: A Response." *NLH* 51.4: 687–94.

Butler, J. 2021a. "We Need to Rethink the Category of Woman." https://www.theguardian.com/lifeandstyle/2021/sep/07/judith-butler-interview-gender

Butler, J. 2021b. "Why Is the Idea of 'Gender' Provoking Backlash the World Over?" https://www.theguardian.com/us-news/commentisfree/2021/oct/23/judith-butler-gender-ideology-backlash

Butler, J. 2021c. "Leaning Out, Caught in the Fall: Interdependency and Ethics in Cavarero." In *Toward a Feminist Ethics of Nonviolence*, edited by T. J. Huzar and C. Woodford, 46–62. New York.

Butler, J. 2021d. *Excitable Speech*. London.

Butler, J. 2022a. *What World Is This? A Pandemic Phenomenology*. New York.

Butler, J. 2022b. "Kinship beyond the Bloodline." In *Queer Kinship: Race, Sex, Belonging, Form*, edited by T. Bradway and E. Freeman, 25–47. Durham, NC.

Butler, J. 2022c. "Endangered Scholarship, Academic Freedom, and the Life of Critique." *Critical Times* 5.2: 399–425.

Butler, J. 2022d. "I Am Hopeful that the Russian Army Will Lay Down Its Arms." https://en.ara.cat/culture/am-hopeful-that-the-russian-army-will-lay-down-its-arms_128_4353851.html

Butler, J. 2023a. "Fury and Justice in the Humanities." *CA* 42.1: 1–18.

Butler, J. 2023b. "Categories by Which We Try to Live." *European Journal of Philosophy* 31.1: 283–88.

Butler, J. 2023c. *Perdita e rigenerazione. Ambiente, arte, politica*. Venice.

Butler, J. 2023d. "Who's Afraid of Gender?" https://fempers.se/2023/2023-04-21/whos-afraid-of-gender/

Butler, J. 2023e. "La pensée politique de Freud: la guerre, la destruction et le pouvoir de la critique." In *Pulsion de mort: destruction et créations*, edited by M. David-Ménard and B. Santos, 161–84. Paris.

Butler, J. 2023f. "I Question, Therefore I Am." *New York Times* (June 13). https://www.nytimes.com/2023/06/13/special-series/question-identity-judith-butler.html

Butler, J. 2023g. "The Compass of Mourning." *London Review of Books* 45.20 (October 13). https://www.lrb.co.uk/the-paper/v45/n20/judith-butler/the-compass-of-mourning

Butler, J. 2023h. "Solo una democrazia radicale può porre fine alla violenza in Medio Oriente." *Il Manifesto* (October 16). https://ilmanifesto.it/judith-butler-solo-una-democrazia-radicale-puo-porre-fine-alla-violenza-in-medio-oriente

Butler, J. 2023i. "Who Is Afraid of Gender?" Lecture given at the Scuola Normale Superiore in Pisa on October 20.

Butler, J. 2023k. "On Hamas, Israel's Collective Punishment of Gaza and Why Biden Must Push for Ceasefire." https://www.democracynow.org/2023/10/26/judith_butler_on_hamas_israels_collective

Butler, J. 2024. *Who's Afraid of Gender?* New York.

Butler, J., and A. Athanasiou. 2013. *Dispossession: The Performative in the Political*. New York.

Butler, J., and W. Connolly. 2000. "Politics, Power, and Ethics." *Theory & Event* 4.2: 24–36.

Butler, J., and M. Gessen. 2020. "Judith Butler Wants Us to Reshape Our Rage." *The New Yorker* (February 9). https://www.newyorker.com/culture/the-new-yorker-interview/judith-butler-wants-us-to-reshape-our-rage

Butler, J., and S. Taylor. 2010. "Interdependence." In *Examined Life: Excursions with Contemporary Thinkers*, edited by A. Taylor, 185–213. New York.

Butler, J., and F. Worms. 2023. *The Livable and the Unlivable*. New York.

Cairns, D. 2015. "The Horror and the Pity: *Phrikê* as a Tragic Emotion." *Psychoanalytic Inquiry* 35.1: 75–94.

Cairns, F. 2020. "The Terms *Komos* and *Paraklausithyron*." *GRBS* 60: 262–71.

Callus, I. 2020. "Autothanatography and Contemporary Poetry." In *The Routledge Companion to Death and Literature*, edited by W. M. Wang, D. K. Jernigan, and N. Murphy, 361–71. London.

Carson, A. 2010. *An* Oresteia*: Agamemnon by Aiskhylos; Elektra by Sophokles; Orestes by Euripides*. New York.

Carson, A. 2012. *Antigonick (Sophokles)*. New York.

Carson, A. 2015. *Euripides: Bakkhai*. New York.

Carver, T., and S. A. Chambers. 2007. "Kinship Trouble: *Antigone* and the Politics of Heteronormativity." *Politics & Gender* 3: 427–49.

Caserio, R., L. Edelman, J. Halberstam, J. E. Muñoz, and T. Dean. 2006. "The Antisocial Thesis in Queer Theory." *PMLA* 121.3: 819–27.

Caspers, C. L. 2012. "Diversity and Common Ground: Euripides' *Iphigenia in Aulis* and *Bacchae* as Companion Plays." In *Greek Drama IV: Texts, Contexts, Performance*, edited by D. Rosenbloom and J. Davidson, 127–48. Warminster.

Cavarero, A. 2009. *Horrorism: Naming Contemporary Violence*. New York.

Cavarero, A. 2016. *Inclinations: A Critique of Rectitude*. Stanford, CA.

Cavarero, A. 2023. "Donne che allattano cuccioli di lupo: zoontologia del materno nelle *Baccanti* di Euripide." Lecture given at the Scuola Normale Superiore in Pisa, March 7.

Cawthorn, K. 2013. *Becoming Female: The Male Body in Greek Tragedy*. London.

Chanter, T. 2011. *Whose Antigone? The Tragic Marginalization of Slavery*. Albany, NY.

Chanter, T. 2014. "Antigone as the White Fetish of Hegel and the Seductress of Derrida." In *A Companion to Derrida*, edited by Z. Direk and L. Lawlor, 378–411. Malden, MA.

Chen, M. Y. 2013. "Animals without Genitals: Race and Transsubstantiation." In *The Transgender Studies Reader 2*, edited by S. Stryker and A. Z. Aizura, 168–77. London.

Chen, M. Y. 2015. "Tranimacies." *TSQ* 2.2: 317–23.

Chen, M. Y. 2018. "Agitation." *SAQ* 117.3: 551–66.

Chen, M. Y. 2023. *Intoxicated: Race, Disability, and Chemical Intimacy across Empire*. Durham, NC.

Cherry, M. 2021. *The Case for Rage: Why Anger Is Essential to Anti-Racist Struggle*. Oxford.

Clark, J. 2015. "Art and the Subversion of Heteronormativity: A Proposal toward a Post-Hetero Aesthetics." Thesis, UNSW Australia, Art & Design.

Coetzee, A. 2019. "Antigone, Empire, and the Legacy of Oedipus: Thinking African Decolonization through the Rearticulation of Kinship Rules." *Hypatia* 34.3: 464–84.

Cohen, L. L. 2023. *Going Underground: Race, Space, and the Subterranean in the Nineteenth-Century United States.* Durham, NC.

Comay, R. 2024. "*Nihil est in imagine vivum.*" In *Niobes: Antiquity, Modernity, Critical Theory*, edited by M. Telò and A. Benjamin, 36–53. Columbus, OH.

Conacher, D. 1987. *Aeschylus'* Oresteia: *A Literary Commentary*. Toronto.

Conybeare, C., ed. 2022. "Honig's *Bacchae* / Euripides' Theory of Refusal." *CA* 41.2.

Coole, D. 2008. "Butler's Phenomenological Existentialism." In *Judith Butler's Precarious Politics: Critical Encounters*, edited by T. Carver and S. A. Chambers, 11–27. New York.

Copjec, J. 2004. *Imagine There's No Woman: Ethics and Sublimation.* Cambridge, MA.

Cox, J., and I. Jean-François. 2022. "Aesthetics of (Black) Breathing." *liquid blackness* 6.1: 98–117.

Crawley, A. T. 2016. *Blackpentecostal Breath: The Aesthetics of Possibility*. New York.

Critchley, S. 2019. *Tragedy, the Greeks, and Us*. New York.

Dahms, I. 2020. "Always Trouble: Gender before and after *Gender Trouble*." *Radical Philosophy* 2.9: 41–54.

Danticat, E. 2010. *Create Dangerously: The Immigrant Artist at Work*. Princeton.

Davis, A., and T. Morrison. 2010. "Literacy, Libraries, and Liberation." https://www.nypl.org/audiovideo/angela-davis-and-toni-morrison-literacy-libraries-and-liberation

Davis, A., et al. 2022. *Abolition. Feminism. Now*. Chicago.

Dean, J. 2009. *Democracy and Other Neoliberal Fantasies: Communicative Capitalism and Left Politics.* Durham, NC.

Deleuze, G. 1994. "He Stuttered." In *Gilles Deleuze and the Theater of Philosophy*, edited by C. V. Boundas and D. Olkowski, 23–29. London.

Deleuze, G. 2003. *Francis Bacon: The Logic of Sensation*. Minneapolis.

Deleuze, G., and F. Guattari. 1987. *A Thousand Plateaus: Capitalism and Schizophrenia.* Minneapolis.

Delgado Huitrón, C. C. 2019. "Haptic Tactic: Hypertenderness for the [Mexican] State and the Performances of Lia García." *TSQ* 6.2: 164–79.

Derrida, J. 1978. *Writing and Difference*. Chicago.

Derrida, J. 1987. *The Post Card: From Socrates to Freud and Beyond*. Chicago.

Derrida, J. 1988. *The Ear of the Other: Otobiography, Transference, Translation*. Lincoln, NE.

Derrida, J. 1992. "Force of Law: The 'Mystical Foundation of Authority.'" In *Deconstruction and the Possibility of Justice,* edited by D. Cornell, M. Rosenfeld, and D. G. Carlson, 3–67. New York.

Derrida, J. 1993. "Le Toucher: Touch/To Touch Him." *Paragraph* 16.2: 122–57.

Derrida, J. 1994. *Specters of Marx*. London.

Derrida, J. 1996. *Archive Fever: A Freudian Impression*. Chicago.

Derrida, J. 2005. *On Touching—Jean-Luc Nancy*. Stanford, CA.

Derrida, J. 2008. *The Gift of Death & Literature in Secret*. Chicago.

Derrida, J. 2014. *Cinders*. Minneapolis.

Derrida, J. 2020. *Life Death*. Chicago.

Derrida, J., and A. Dufourmantelle. 2000. *Of Hospitality*. Stanford, CA.

Deuber-Mankowsky, A. 2016. "Rhythms of the Living, Conditions of Critique: On Judith Butler's Reading of Walter Benjamin's 'Critique of Violence.'" In *Walter Benjamin and Theology*, edited by C. Dickinson and S. Symons, 253–71. New York.

Deutscher, P. 2017. *Foucault's Futures: A Critique of Reproductive Reason*. New York.

Deutscher, P. 2020. "Auto-Repugnancy: In-Between Freud's *Beyond the Pleasure Principle*." *Psychoanalysis, Culture & Society* 25.4: 518–36.

Díaz-Barriga, M., and M. E. Dorsey. 2020. *Fencing in Democracy: Border Walls, Necrocitizenship, and the Security State*. Durham, NC.

Di Benedetto, V. 1978. *L'ideologia del potere e la tragedia greca: ricerche su Eschilo*. Rome.

Dienstag, J. F. 2004. "Tragedy, Pessimism, Nietzsche." *New Literary History* 35.1: 83–101.

Diggle, J. 1994. *Euripidea*. Oxford.

Dittmar, L. 1990. "'Will the Circle Be Unbroken?': The Politics of Form in *The Bluest Eye*." *Novel* 23.2: 137–55.

Dodds, E. R., ed. 1960. *Euripides: Bacchae*. Oxford.

Du Bois, W. E. B. 1999. *Darkwater: Voices from within the Veil*. Mineola, NY.

duBois, P. 2003. *Slaves and Other Objects*. Chicago.

duBois, P. 2008. "Toppling the Hero: Polyphony in the Greek City." In *Rethinking Tragedy*, edited by R. Felski, 127–47. Baltimore.

duBois, P. 2022. *Democratic Swarms: Ancient Comedy and the Politics of the People*. Chicago.

Eagleton, T. 2005. *Holy Terror*. Oxford.

Eagleton, T. 2010. "Lacan's Antigone." In *Interrogating Antigone in Postmodern Philosophy and Criticism*, edited by S. E. Wilmer and A. Zukaskaite, 101–9. Oxford.

Easterling, P. E. 2008. "Theatrical Furies: Thoughts on *Eumenides*." In *Performance, Iconography, Reception: Studies in Honor of Oliver Taplin*, edited by M. Revermann and P. Wilson, 219–36. Oxford.

Eberwine, P. 2019. "'Music for the Wretched': Euripides' *Trojan Women* as Refugee Theatre." *Classical Receptions Journal* 11.2: 194–210.

Edelman, L. 1994. *Homographesis: Essays in Gay Literary and Cultural Theory*. New York.

Edelman, L. 2004. *No Future: Queer Theory and the Death Drive*. Durham, NC.

Edelman, L. 2023. *Bad Education: Why Queer Theory Teaches Us Nothing.* Durham, NC.

Emre, M., and A. Kornbluh. 2022. "Bootstrapping across Dystopia: Autofiction, Autotheory, Autoeverything." https://marktwainstudies.com/autoeverything/

Eng, D. 2011. "Reparations and the Human." *Columbia Journal of Gender and Law* 21.2: 561–83.

Fanon, F. 1963. *The Wretched of the Earth*. New York.

Fanon, F. 1967. *Black Skin, White Masks*. New York.

Fanon, F. 1970. *A Dying Colonialism*. Ringwood, Victoria.

Featherstone, M. 2022. "Viral Law, Death, Difference, and Indifference from the Spanish Flu to Covid-19." *International Journal for the Semiotics of Law* 35.3: 1019–37.

Felman, S. 1983. "Beyond Oedipus: The Specimen Story of Psychoanalysis." *MLN* 98.5: 1021–53.

Ferrari, F. 1983. *Ricerche sul testo di Sofocle*. Pisa.

Ferreday, D. 2011. "Becoming Deer: Nonhuman Drag and Online Utopias." *Feminist Theory* 12.2: 219–25.

Ferreira da Silva, D. 2014. "Toward a Black Feminist Poethics: The Quest(ion) of Blackness toward the End of the World." *The Black Scholar* 44.2: 81–97.

Fleming, K. 2015. "Heidegger's *Antigone*: Ethics and Politics." In *Tragedy and the Idea of Modernity*, edited by J. Billings and M. Leonard, 178–93. Oxford.

Fletcher, J. 2013. *Freud and the Scene of Trauma*. New York.

Fort, B. 1997. "Theater, History, Ethics: An Interview with Hélène Cixous on *The Perjured City, or the Awakening of the Furies*." *NLH* 28.3: 425–56.

Foucault, M. 1990. *The History of Sexuality*, vol. 1 (*An Introduction*). New York.

Foucault, M. 2000. "Lives of Infamous Men." In *Power: Essential Works of Foucault 1954–84*, edited by J. D. Faubion, 157–75. New York.

Foucault, M. 2023. "Literature and Madness: Madness in the Baroque Theatre and the Theatre of Artaud." *Theory, Culture & Society* 40.1–2: 241–57.

Foucault, M., and J. K. Simon. 1991. "Michel Foucault on Attica: An Interview." *Social Justice* 18.2: 26–34.

Fraenkel, E., ed. 1950. *Aeschylus: Agamemnon*. Oxford.

Francobandiera, D. 2018. "Le retour des Érinyes." *Pallas* 108: 79–92.

Freccero, C. 2017. "Queer Theory." In *Edinburgh Companion to Animal Studies*, edited by L. Turner, U. Sellbach, and R. Broglio, 430–43. Edinburgh.

Freccero, C. 2021. "Death Do Us Part." In *Long Term: Essays on Queer Commitment*, edited by S. Herring and L. Wallace, 117–33. Durham, NC.

Freud, S. 1910. "Leonardo da Vinci and a Memory of His Childhood." *SE* 11: 63–137.

Freud, S. 1915. "Thoughts for the Times on War and Death." *SE* 14: 273–300.

Freud, S. 1917. "Mourning and Melancholia." *SE* 14: 239–60.

Freud, S. 1920. *Beyond the Pleasure Principle*. *SE* 18: 1–64.

Freud, S. 1923. *The Ego and the Id*. *SE* 19: 1–66.

Freud, S. 1925. "A Note upon the 'Mystic Writing Pad.'" *SE* 19: 225–32.

Freud, S., and W. Fliess. 1986. *The Complete Letters of Sigmund Freud to Wilhelm Fliess (1887–1904)*. Cambridge, MA.

Fusillo, M. 2006. *Il dio ibrido: Dioniso e le* Baccanti *nel Novecento*. Bologna.

Gabriel, K. 2018. "Specters of Dying Empire: The Case of Carson's *Bacchae*." *Tripwire* 14: 315–23.

Gagliardi, C. 2020. "Palestine Is Not a Drawing Board: Defacing the Street Art on the Israeli Separation Wall." *Visual Anthropology* 33.5: 426–51.

Galarte, F. J. 2019. "General Editor's Introduction." *TSQ* 6.4: 467–71.

Garland-Thomson, R. 2020. "Misfitting." In *50 Concepts for a Critical Phenomenology*, edited by G. Weiss, A. V. Murphy, and G. Salamon, 225–30. Evanston, IL.

Gay, R., and J. Butler. 2022. "Why 'Pregnant People' and Other Gender-Inclusive Language Matters." https://www.kqed.org/news/11920528/roxane-gay-and-judith-butler-on-why-pregnant-people-and-other-gender-inclusive-language-matters

Gibert, J. 1996. *Change of Mind in Greek Tragedy*. Göttingen.

Goff, B. E. 1990. *The Noose of Words: Readings of Desire, Violence, and Language in Euripides'* Hippolytus. Cambridge.

Goldhill, S. 1984. *Language, Sexuality, Narrative: the* Oresteia. Cambridge.

Goldhill, S. 2012. *Sophocles and the Language of Tragedy*. Oxford.

Goldhill, S. 2015. "The Ends of Tragedy: Schelling, Hegel, and Oedipus." In *Tragedy and the Idea of Modernity*, edited by J. Billings and M. Leonard, 231–50. Oxford.

Goldhill, S. 2022. "Sophocles' *Antigone*, Feminism's Hegel and the Politics of Form." In *The Politics of Form in Greek Literature*, edited by P. Vasunia, 49–64. London.

Gosine, A. 2021. *Nature's Wild: Love, Sex, and Law in the Caribbean*. Durham, NC.

Gowers, E. 2006. "Noises Off: The Thyestes Theme in Tacitus's *Dialogus*." In *Roman Drama and Its Contexts*, edited by S. Frangoulidis, S. J. Harrison, and G. Manuwald, 555–71. Berlin.

Gregory, J. 2006. "Genre and Intertextuality: Sophocles' *Antigone* and Euripides' *Alcestis*." *BICS* 87: 113–27.

Griffith, M. 1995. "Brilliant Dynasts: Power and Politics in the *Oresteia*." *CA* 14: 62–129.

Griffith, M., ed. 1999. *Sophocles: Antigone*. Cambridge.

Griffith, M. 2002. "Slaves of Dionysos: Satyrs, Audience, and the Ends of the *Oresteia*." *CA* 21.2: 195–258.

Griffith, M. 2005. "Antigone and Her Sister(s): Embodying Women in Greek Tragedy." In *Making Silence Speak: Women's Voices in Greek Literature*, edited by A. Lardinois and L. McClure, 117–36. Princeton.

Grosz, E., et al. 2017. "An Interview with Elizabeth Grosz: Geopower, Inhumanism, and the Biopolitical." *Theory, Culture & Society* 34.2–3: 129–46.

Guenther, L. 2012. *Solitary Confinement: Social Death and Its Afterlives*. Minneapolis.

Gumbs, A. P., C. Martens, and M. Williams, eds. 2016. *Revolutionary Mothering: Love on the Front Lines*. Oakland.

Gunderson, E. 2020. "Theology's Shadow." In *Classical Philology and Theology*, edited by C. Conybeare and S. Goldhill, 119–224. Cambridge

Guyer, S. 2007. "Buccality." In *Derrida, Deleuze, Psychoanalysis*, edited by G. Schwab, 77–104. New York.

Gyenge, A. 2018. *Res Oralis: Mouths of Philosophy*. Ph. D. dissertation, University of Minnesota.

Gyenge, A., and J.-P. Ricco. 2023. "Afterword to *Stoma*." In J.-L. Nancy, *Corpus III:* Cruor *and Other Writings*, 97–108. New York.

Halberstam, J. 2018a. *Trans*: A Quick and Quirky Account of Gender Variability*. Oakland, CA.

Halberstam, J. 2018b. "Introduction: Theory in the Wild." *SAQ* 117.3: 453–64.

Halberstam, J. 2018c. "Unbuilding Gender: Trans* Anarchitectures in and beyond the Work of Gordon Matta-Clark." *Places* (October). https://placesjournal.org/article/unbuilding-gender

Halberstam, J. 2020. *Wild Things*. Durham, NC.

Hall, E. 1998. "Ihyphallic Males Behaving Badly, or Satyr Drama as Gendered Tragic Ending." In *Parchments of Gender: Deciphering the Body of Antiquity*, edited by M. Wyke, 13–38. Oxford.

Hamilton, J. 2003. *Soliciting Darkness: Pindar, Obscurity, and Classical Tradition*. Cambridge, MA.

Hamilton, J. 2024. "Tears from Stone." In *Niobes: Antiquity Modernity Critical Theory*, edited by M. Telò and A. Benjamin, 98–113. Columbus, OH.

Hansen, Sid. 2020. "Queer Performativity." In *50 Concepts for a Critical Phenomenology*, edited by G. Weiss, A. V. Murphy, and G. Salamon, 283–88. Evanston, IL.

Hansen, Susan. 2017. "The Right to Write the City: Breaking the Law of Untouchability." *Nuart Journal* 1: 28–30.

Harney, S., and F. Moten. 2015. "Michael Brown." *boundary 2* 42.4: 81–87.

Harney, S., and F. Moten. 2021. *All Incomplete*. Oakland.

Harris, O. 2013. "The Ethics of Metamorphosis or a Poet between Two Deaths." In *Classical Myth and Psychoanalysis: Ancient and Modern Stories of the Self*, edited by V. Zajko and E. O'Gorman, 251–64. Oxford.

Hartman, S. 2008. "Venus in Two Acts." *Small Axe* 12.2: 1–14.

Hartman, S. 2018. "The Anarchy of Colored Girls Assembled in a Riotous Manner." *SAQ* 117.3: 465–89.

Hartman, S. 2020a. "The End of White Supremacy, an American Romance." *Bomb* 152. https://bombmagazine.org/articles/the-end-of-white-supremacy-an-american-romance/

Hartman, S. 2020b. *Wayward Lives, Beautiful Experiments: Intimate Histories of Riotous Black Girls, Troublesome Women, and Queer Radicals*. New York.

Hartman, S. 2022. "Litany for Grieving Sisters." In *Proximities: Reading with Judith Butler*, edited by D. Sanyal, M. Telò, D. R. Young, *Representations* 158: 39–44.

Haselswerdt, E. 2022. "*Iphigenia in Aulis*: Perhaps Not." In *Queer Euripides: Re-readings in Greek Tragedy*, edited by S. Olson and M. Telò, 53–64. London.

Hayward, E., and J. Weinstein. 2015. "Introduction: Tranimalities in the Ages of Trans* Life." *TSQ* 2.2: 195–208.

Hazard, C. W. 2022. *Underflows: Queer Trans Ecologies and River Justice*. Seattle.

Helberg, N. 2020. "Insubordinate Plasticity: Judith Butler and Catherine Malabou." *Hypatia* 35: 587–606.

Helmreich, S. 2017. "The Gender of Waves." *WSQ* 45.1–2: 29–51.

Henao Castro, A. F. 2020. "Can the Palestinian Antigone Grieve? A Political Reinterpretation of Judith Butler's Ethical Turn." *Settler Colonial Studies* 10.1: 94–109.

Henao Castro, A. F. 2021. *Antigone in the Americas: Democracy, Sexuality, and Death in the Settler Colonial Present*. Albany, NY.

Henao Castro, A. F. 2022. *The Militant Intellect: Critical Theory's Conceptual Personae*. Lanham, MD.

Henao Castro, A. F. 2023. "From a Euromodern Biopolitical Antigone to Postmodern Necropolitical Antigones in Latin Americas." *Philosophy and Global Affairs* 3.1: 60–88.

Hiscock, M. 2018. "Sophoclean Suicide." *CA* 37.1: 1–30.

Holmes, B. 2012. *Gender: Antiquity and Its Legacy*. Oxford.

Honig, B. 2013. *Antigone, Interrupted*. Cambridge.

Honig, B. 2021. *A Feminist Theory of Refusal*. Cambridge, MA.

Honig, B. 2022. "A Method in the Madness: After *AFTR*, in Grateful Reply." *CA* 41.2: 34–49.

Hyacinthe, G. 2019. *Radical Virtuosity: Ana Mendieta and the Black Atlantic*. Cambridge, MA.

Jackson, S. 2022. *Back Stages: Essays across Art, Performance, and Public Life*. Evanston, IL.

Jackson, Z. I. 2020. *Becoming Human: Matter and Meaning in an Antiblack World*. New York.

James, J. 2016. "The Womb of Western Theory: Trauma, Time, Theft, and the Captive Maternal." *Carceral Notebooks* 12: 253–96.

Janan, M. 2004. "The Snake Sheds Its Skin: Pentheus (Re)Imagines Thebes." *CP* 99.2: 130–46.

Janicka, I. 2017. *Theorizing Contemporary Anarchism: Solidarity, Mimesis and Radical Social Change.* London.

Janko, R. 2022. "The Cult of the Erinyes, the Villa of the Mysteries, and the Unity of the Derveni Papyrus." In *Studies on the Derveni Papyrus*, vol. 2, edited by G. W. Most, 151–81. Oxford.

Jaschik, S. 2017. "Judith Butler on Being Attacked in Brazil." https://www.insidehighered.com/news/2017/11/13/judith-butler-discusses-being-burned-effigy-and-protested-brazil

Jebb, R., ed. 1900. *Sophocles: Antigone*. Cambridge.

Johnson, B. 1986. "Apostrophe, Animation, and Abortion." *Diacritics* 16.1: 28–47.

Julien, C. F. 2021. "Collapse." In *More Posthuman Glossary*, edited by R. Braidotti, E. Jones, and G. Klumbyté, 16–18. London.

Kapparis, K. 2002. *Abortion in the Ancient World.* London.

Keegan, C. M. 2020. "Transgender Studies, and How to Do Things with Trans*." In *The Cambridge Companion to Queer Studies*, edited by S. B. Somerville, 66–78. Cambridge.

Keeling, K. 2019. *Queer Times, Black Futures.* New York.

Kelley, L. 2014. "Tranimals." *TSQ* 1.1–2: 226–28.

Kelley, L. 2017. "Menagerie à Tranimals." *Angelaki* 22.2: 97–109.

Kilby, L. 2023. "Protest, Race and Grievability: What Does It Mean for Lives to Matter?" *Social and Personality Psychology Compass* (June 11): 1–12. https://compass.onlinelibrary.wiley.com/doi/10.1111/spc3.12805

Kirby, V., and J. Butler. 2006. "Butler Live." In V. Kirby, *Judith Butler: Live Theory*, 144–58. London.

Knadler, S. 2022. "Neurodiverse Afro-Fabulations: Pauline Hopkins's Counterintelligence." *American Literature* 94.2: 301–29.

Knox, B. 1964. *The Heroic Temper: Studies in Sophoclean Tragedy*. Cambridge, MA.

Kornbluh, A. 2024. *Immediacy: Or, The Style of Too Late Capitalism.* London.

Kramer, S. 2014. "Outside/In: Antigone and the Limits of Politics." In *The Returns of Antigone: Interdisciplinary Essays*, edited by T. Chanter and S. D. Kirkland, 187–203. Albany, NY.

Kwon, M. 1996. "Bloody Valentines: Afterimages by Ana Mendieta." In *Inside the Visible: An Elliptical Traverse of 20th Century Art in, of, and from the Feminine*, edited by M. C. de Zegher, 165–71. Cambridge, MA.

Lacan, J. 1992. *The Ethics of Psychoanalysis: The Seminars of Jacques Lacan (Book VII)*. Edited by J. A. Miller. Translated by B. Fink. New York.

Lather, A. 2018. "Olfactory Theater: Tracking Scents in Aeschylus's *Oresteia*." *Arethusa* 51.1: 33–54.

Lebeck, A. 1971. *The* Oresteia: *A Study in Language and Structure*. Washington, DC.

Lecznar, A. 2020. *Dionysus after Nietzsche*. Cambridge.

Leitao, D. 2012. *The Pregnant Male as Myth and Metaphor in Classical Greek Literature*. Cambridge.

Leonard, M. 2000. "Creating a Dawn: Writing through Antiquity in the Works of Hélène Cixous." *Arethusa* 33.1: 121–48.

Leonard, M. 2005. *Athens in Paris: Ancient Greece and the Political in Post-War French Thought*. Oxford.

Leonard, M. 2006. "Lacan, Irigaray, and Beyond: Antigones and the Politics of Psychoanalysis." In *Laughing with Medusa: Classical Myth and Feminist Thought*, edited by V. Zajko and M. Leonard, 121–40. Oxford.

Leonard, M. 2013. "Freud and Tragedy: Oedipus and the Gender of the Universal." *Classical Receptions Journal* 5.1: 63–83.

Leonard, M. 2015. *Tragic Modernities*. Cambridge, MA.

Leonard, M. 2016. "Freud and the Biography of Antiquity." In *Creative Lives in Classical Antiquity: Poets, Artists and Biography*, edited by R. Fletcher and J. Hanink, 305–26. Cambridge.

Leonard, M. 2018. "Arendt's Revolutionary Antiquity." *CP* 113.1: 53–66.

Leonard, M., and J. I. Porter, eds. 2014. "Forum on Bonnie Honig's *Antigone Interrupted*." *International Journal of the Classical Tradition* 21.3: 296–335.

Levinas, E. 1996. "Peace and Proximity." In *Basic Philosophical Writings*, edited by A. T. Peperzak, S. Critchley, and R. Bernasconi, 161–70. Bloomington, IN.

Lewis, S. 2021. *Full Surrogacy Now: Feminism against the Family*. London.

Lewis, S. 2022. *Abolish the Family*. London.

Lewis, S. 2023. "Paul Preciado's Uterine Politics: Abolish the Family or Reclaim Confiscated Queer Genetic Patrimony?" *Paragraph* 46.1: 74–89.

Lewis, S., and A. Seresin. 2022. "Fascist Feminism." *TSQ* 9.3: 463–79.

Lipari, G., and F. G. Sirna. 2023. "Laughing Waves in Ancient Greek." *CP* 118.3: 317–50.

Littlewood, C. 1997. "Seneca's *Thyestes*: The Tragedy with No Women." *MD* 38: 57–86.

Lloyd, M. 2005. "Butler, Antigone and the State." *Contemporary Political Theory* 4: 451–68.

Lloyd-Jones, H., and N. G. Wilson, eds. 1990. *Sophoclis Fabulae*. Oxford.

Loebl, N. G. 2022. "Reading Judith Butler's *Gender Trouble* in the Age of Ron DeSantis." https://www.thenation.com/article/society/judith-butler-gender-trans-1990s?

Loraux, N. 1990. "La métaphore sans métaphore à propos de l'*Orestie*." *Revue Philosophique de la France et de l'Étranger* 8: 247–68.

Loraux, N. 2002. *Mothers in Mourning*. Ithaca, NY.

Lorde, A. 1981. "A Poem for Women in Rage." *The Iowa Review* 12.2–3: 220–22.

Lorde, A. 1984. *Sister Outsider*. Trumansburg, NY.

Lorde, A. 2020. "The Uses of Anger: Women Responding to Racism" In *The Selected Works of Audre Lorde*, edited by R. Gay, 53–65. New York.

Lyman, P. 2004. "The Domestication of Anger: The Use and Abuse of Anger in Politics." *European Journal of Social Theory* 7.2: 133–47.

Manning, E. 2013. *Always More Than One: Individuation's Dance.* Durham, NC.

Manning, E. 2019. "Fugitively, Approximately." *The Fibreculture Journal* 30: 10–23.

Marder, M. 2009. "Breathing 'to' the Other: Levinas and Ethical Breathlessness." *Levinas Studies* 4: 91–110.

Marder, M. 2016. *Dust*. London.

Marriott, D. S. 2021a. *Lacan Noir: Lacan and Afropessimism*. London.

Marriott, D. S. 2021b. "On Revolutionary Suicide." *Diacritics* 49.4: 101–33.

Martin, E. D. 1920. *The Behavior of Crowds: A Psychological Study*. New York.

Martínez Ruiz, R. 2019. *Eros: Beyond the Death Drive.* New York.

Mason, F. 2020. *The Viscous: Slime, Stickiness, Fondling, Mixtures*. Goleta, CA.

McDonald, M. 2010. "A Hero for our Time: Bernard Knox." *Arion* 18.2: 131–46.

McEleney, C. 2021. "The Resistance to Overanalysis." *differences* 32.2: 1–38.

McIvor, D. W. 2016. *Mourning in America: Race and the Politics of Loss*. Ithaca, NY.

McNeilly, K. 2013. "Framing Wrongs and Performing Rights in Northern Ireland: Towards a Butlerian Approach to Life in Abortion Strategising." *Journal of International Women's Studies* 14.4: 95–108.

McRobbie, A. 2003. "Mothers and Fathers: Who Needs Them?" *Feminist Review* 75.1: 129–36.

Memmi, D. 2011. *La seconde vie des bébés morts*. Paris.

Miller, P. A. 2007. "Lacan's Antigone: The Sublime Object and the Ethics of Interpretation." *Phoenix* 61.1–2: 1–14.

Miller, P. A. 2021. *Foucault's Seminars on Antiquity: Learning to Speak the Truth*. London.

Morales, H. 2020. *Antigone Rising: The Subversive Power of the Ancient Myths.* New York.

Morales, H. 2022. "Bonnie Honig's *A Feminist Theory of Refusal* with Kehinde Wiley's *After John Raphael Smith's 'A Bacchante after Sir Joshua Reynolds'*." *CA* 41.2: 25–33.

Morin, F. F. 2017. "Ego Hippo: The Subject as Metaphor." *Angelaki* 22.2: 87–96.

Morrison, T. 1955. "Virginia Woolf's and William Faulkner's Treatment of the Alienated." Cornell M. A. Thesis.

Morrison, T. 2007. *The Bluest Eye.* New York.

Moten, F. 2003. *In the Break: The Aesthetics of the Black Radical Tradition.* Minneapolis.

Moten, F. 2008. "The Case of Blackness." *Criticism* 50.2: 177–218.

Moten, F. 2013. "Blackness and Nothingness (Mysticism in the Flesh)." *SAQ* 112.4: 737–80.

Moten, F. 2018a. *Stolen Life.* Durham, NC.

Moten, F. 2018b. "Ensemble: An Interview with Fred Moten." https://micemagazine.ca/issue-four/ensemble-interview-dr-fred-moten

Moten, F., and S. Harney. 2013. *The Undercommons*. New York.

Muñoz, J. E. 1999. *Disidentifications*. Minneapolis.

Muñoz, J. E. 2011. "Vitalism's After-Burn: The Sense of Ana Mendieta." *Women and Performance* 21.2: 191–98.

Murnaghan, S. 1999–2000. "The Survivors' Song: The Drama of Mourning in Euripides' *Alcestis*." *ICS* 24–25: 107–16.

Murnaghan, S., ed. 2023. *Sophocles: Antigone.* New York.

Nancy, J.-L. 1989. "Beheaded Sun *(Soleil cou coupé)*." *Qui Parle* 3.2: 41–53.

Nancy, J.-L. 1992. "*La Comparution**/The Compearance: From the Existence of 'Communism' to the Community of 'Existence'." *Political Theory* 20.3: 371–98.

Nancy, J.-L. 1994. *The Birth to Presence*. Stanford, CA.

Nancy, J.-L. 1997. *The Gravity of Thought*. Atlantic Highlands, NJ.

Nancy, J.-L. 2009. *The Fall of Sleep.* New York.

Nancy, J.-L. 2016. *Ego Sum: Corpus, Anima, Fabula*. New York.

Nancy, J.-L. 2023. *Corpus III:* Cruor *and Other Writings*. New York.

Nestor, H. 2021. "Tracing Mendieta, Mendieta's Trace: The Silueta Series (1973–1980)." *MAI: Feminism and Visual Culture* (June 14): 1–23. https://maifeminism.com/tracing-mendieta-mendietas-trace-the-silueta-series/

Neyra, R. E. 2020a. "Queer Poetics: Deviant Swerves, in Three." In *The Cambridge Companion to Queer Studies*, edited by S. Somerville, 125–41. Cambridge.

Neyra, R. E. 2020b. *The Cry of the Senses: Listening to Latinx and Caribbean Poetics*. Durham, NC.

Njoya, W. 2020. "The Progress of Law: Aeschylus's *Oresteia* in Feminist and Critical Theory." *Political Theory* 48.2: 139–68.

Nooter, S. 2017. *The Mortal Voice in the Tragedies of Aeschylus.* Cambridge.

Nooter, S., and M. Telò, eds. 2024. *Radical Formalisms: Reading, Theory, and the Boundaries of the Classical.* London.

North, P. 2021. *Bizarre-Privileged Items in the Universe: The Logic of Likeness.* New York.

O'Donnell, E., and J. Talbot-Jones. 2018. "Creating Legal Rights for Rivers: Lessons from Australia, New Zealand, and India." *Ecology and Society* 23.1: 1–10.

Okiji, F. Forthcoming. "Billie's Bent Elbow/Subjunctive, Semblant, Spectral."

Oliensis, E. 2019. "Ovid's Niobe." Unpublished abstract.

Olsen, S. E. 2016. *Solo Dance in Archaic and Classical Greek Literature*. Cambridge.

Olson, G. A., and L. Worsham. 2000. "Changing the Subject: Judith Butler's Politics of Radical Resignification." *JAC* 20.4: 727–65.

O'Neill, E. G. 1941. "The Prologue of the *Troades* of Euripides." *TAPA* 72: 288–320.

Ormand, K. 2003. "Oedipus the Queen: Cross-Gendering without Drag." *Theatre Journal* 55.1: 1–28.

Orrells, D. 2023. "Queer Oedipus After Freud?" Keynote Lecture at the International Conference "Tragedy Queered," University of Reading (6–7 July).

Osmundson, J. 2022. *Virology: Essays for the Living, the Dead, and the Small Things in Between*. New York.

Padel, R. 1992. *In and out of the Mind: Greek Images of the Tragic Self.* Princeton.

Padel, R. 1995. *Whom Gods Destroy: Elements of Greek and Tragic Madness.* Princeton.

Panagia, D. 2018. *Rancière's Sentiments.* Durham, NC.

Pauly, E. 2023. "The Roaring God and an Everything Bagel: Queer Rage and Rejection in *Bacchae* and *Everything Everywhere All at Once.*" Paper presented at the International Conference "Tragedy Queered," University of Reading (6–7 July).

Peppiatt, M. 1996. *Francis Bacon: Anatomy of an Enigma*. New York.

Peradotto, J. J. 1964. "Some Patterns of Nature Imagery in the *Oresteia*." *AJP* 85.4: 378–93.

Peradotto, J. J. 1969. "The Omen of the Eagles and the ΗΘΟΣ of Agamemnon." *Phoenix* 23.3: 237–63.

Perera, S., and J. Pugliese. 2011. "Introduction: Combat Breathing: State Violence and the Body in Question." *Somatechnics* 1.1: 1–14.

Pezaro, S., Crowther, R., Pearce, G. et al. 2023. "Perinatal Care for Trans and Nonbinary People Birthing in Heteronormative 'Maternity' Services: Experiences and Educational Needs of Professionals." *Gender & Society* 37.1: 124–51.

Pickens, T. A. 2016. "The Verb Is No: Towards a Grammar of Black Women's Anger." *CLA Journal* 60.1: 15–31.

Podlecki, A. J., ed. 1989. *Aeschylus: Eumenides*. Warminster.

Porter, J. I. 1990. "Patterns of Perception in Aeschylus." In *Cabinet of the Muses: Essays on Classical and Comparative Literature in Honor of Thomas G. Rosenmeyer*, edited by M. Griffith and D. J. Mastronarde, 31–56. Atlanta.

Porter, J. I. 2000. *The Invention of Dionysus*. Stanford, CA.

Porter, J. I. 2005. "Nietzsche and Tragedy." In *A Companion to Tragedy*, edited by R. Bushnell, 68–87. Malden, MA.

Porter, J. I. 2006. "Love of Life: Lucretius to Freud." In *Erotikon: Essays on Eros, Ancient and Modern*, edited by S. Bartsch and T. Bartscherer, 113–41. Chicago.

Porter, J. I. 2024. "Foucault, Kant, and Antiquity." *Representations* 165: 120–43.

Powers, M. 2018. *Diversifying Greek Tragedy on the Contemporary Stage*. Oxford.

Prahlad, A. 2017. *The Secret Life of a Black Aspie*. Fairbanks, AK.

Preciado, P. B. 2008. *Testo Junkie: Sex, Drugs, and Biopolitics in the Pharmacopornographic Era.* New York.

Preciado, P. B. 2018. *Countersexual Manifesto.* New York.

Preciado, P. B. 2021. *Can the Monster Speak? Report to an Academy of Psychoanalysts.* Los Angeles.

Prins, Y. 1991. "The Power of the Speech Act: Aeschylus's Furies and Their Binding Song." *Arethusa* 24: 177–95.

Prins, Y. 2017. *Ladies' Greek: Victorian Translations of Tragedy*. Princeton.

Pugliese, J. 2023. "Intercorporeity of Animated Water: Contesting Anthropocentric Settler Sovereignty." *Angelaki* 28.1: 22–35.

Pyne, J. 2021. "Autistic Disruptions, Trans Temporalities: A Narrative 'Trap Door' in Time." *SAQ* 120.2: 343–61.

Quashie, K. E. 2021. *Black Aliveness, or a Poetics of Being.* Durham, NC.

Quint, D. 2011. "Virgil's Double Cross: Chiasmus and the *Aeneid*." *AJP* 132.2: 273–300.

Rabinowitz, N. S. 2014. "Melancholy Becomes Electra." In *Sex in Antiquity: Exploring Gender and Sexuality in the Ancient World*, edited by M. Masterson, N. S. Rabinowitz, and J. Robson, 214–30. London.

Radcliffe, B. 2024. "Niobe's People: Ambiguous Violence and Interrupted Labor in *Iliad* 24." In *Niobes: Antiquity Modernity Critical Theory*, edited by M. Telò and A. Benjamin, 54–68. Columbus, OH.

Radi, B. 2020. "Reproductive Injustice, Trans Rights, and Eugenics." *Sexual and Reproductive Health Matters* 28.1: 396–407.

Raine, A. 1996. "Embodied Geographies: Subjectivity and Materiality in the Work of Ana Mendieta." In *Generations and Geographies in the Visual Arts: Feminist Readings*, edited by G. Pollock, 228–52. New York.

Rancière, J. 1992. "Politics, Identification, and Subjectivization." *October* 61: 58–64.

Rancière, J. 2004. *The Flesh of Words: The Politics of Writing*. Stanford, CA.

Rancière, J. 2009. *The Aesthetic Unconscious.* Cambridge.

Rancière, J. 2011. *Mute Speech: Literature, Critical Theory, and Politics.* New York.

Rancière, J. 2014. *The Intervals of Cinema*. London.

Rancière, J. 2017. *The Lost Thread: The Democracy of Modern Fiction*. London.

Rapp, R. 2000. *Testing Women, Testing the Fetus: The Social Impact of Amniocentesis in America.* New York.

Reynolds, A. 2021. "Thinking the Ghost: Tragedy and the History of Theory." *Derrida Today* 14.1: 49–66.

Ricco, J.-P. 2023. "Incongruity." *differences* 34.1: 156–64.

Richie, B. 2012. *Arrested Justice: Black Women, Violence, and America's Prison Nation.* New York.

Rifkin, M. 2022. "Beyond Family: Kinship's Past, Queer World Making, and the Question of Governance." In *Queer Kinship: Race, Sex, Belonging, Form*, edited by T. Bradway and E. Freeman, 138–58. Durham, NC.

Rimell, V. 2024. "Philosophers' Stone: Enduring Niobe." In *Niobes: Antiquity Modernity Critical Theory*, edited by M. Telò and A. Benjamin, 69–84. Columbus, OH.

Roane, J. T. 2021. "Spitting Back at Law and Order: Donnetta Hill's Rage in an Era of Vengeance." *Signs* 46.4: 853–82.

Roane, J. T. 2022. Talk at "Mad Blackness*: Rage, Resistance, Refusal." https://bcrw.barnard.edu/event/mad-blackness-rage-resistance-refusal/

Rose, J. 2023. *The Plague.* London.

Rose, P. W. 1992. *Sons of the Gods, Children of Earth: Ideology and Literary Form in Ancient Greece.* Ithaca, NY.

Rosen, R. M. 2004. "Aristophanes' *Frogs* and the Contest of Homer and Hesiod." *TAPA* 134.2: 295–322.

Rosenberg, J. 2014. "The Molecularization of Sexuality: On Some Primitivisms of the Present." *Theory & Event* 17.2.

Rosenbloom, D. 2002. "From *Ponêros* to *Pharmakos*: Theater, Social Drama, and Revolution in Athens, 428–404 BCE." *CA* 21.2: 283–346.

Rossi, L. E. 1971. "Il *Ciclope* di Euripide come *κῶμος* mancato." *Maia* 23: 10–38.

Roynon, T. 2013. *Toni Morrison and the Classical Tradition: Transforming American Culture*. Oxford.

Rudnytsky, P. L. 1987. *Freud and Oedipus*. New York.

Ruffell, I. 2022. "*Bacchae*—'An Excessively High Price to Pay for Being Reluctant to Emerge from the Closet'?" In *Queer Euripides: Re-Readings in Greek Tragedy*, edited by S. Olsen and M. Telò, 239–48. London.

Ruti, M. 2017. *The Ethics of Opting Out: Queer Theory's Defiant Subjects*. New York.

Saha, P. 2022. "Queering the Womb: Surrogacy and the Economics of Reproductive Feeling." In *Queer Kinship: Race, Sex, Belonging, Form*, edited by T. Bradway and E. Freeman, 119–37. Durham, NC.

Said, E. 2006. *On Late Style: Music and Literature Against the Grain*. New York.

Salih, S. 2003. "Judith Butler and the Ethics of 'Difficulty.'" *Critical Quarterly* 45.3: 42–50.

Sanyal, D. 2019. "Humanitarian Detention and Figures of Persistence at the Border." *Critical Times* 2.3: 435–65.

Sanyal, D. 2020. "The Social Contract and the Game of Monopoly: Listening to Kimberly Jones on Black Lives." https://ctjournal.org/2020/06/29/the-social-contract-and-the-game-of-monopoly-listening-to-kimberly-jones-on-black-lives/

Sanyal, D. Forthcoming. *Arts of the Border: Fugitive Bodies at Europe's Edges*. New York.

Sanyal, D., M. Telò, and D. R. Young. 2022. "Proximities." In *Proximities: Reading with Judith Butler*, edited by D. Sanyal, M. Telò, and D. R. Young. *Representations* 158: 1–16.

Savarese, R. J. 2014. "I Object: Autism, Empathy, and the Trope of Personification." In *Rethinking Empathy through Literature*, edited by M. M. Hammond and S. J. Kim, 74–92. London.

Saxonhouse, A. W. 1984. "Aeschylus's *Oresteia*: Misogyny, Philogyny, and Justice." *Women & Politics* 4.2: 11–32.

Scheler, M. 1954. "On the Tragic." *CrossCurrrents* 4.2: 178–91.

Schiesaro, A. 2003. *The Passions in Play:* Thyestes *and the Dynamics of Senecan Drama*. Cambridge.

Schroeder, J. L. 2000. "The *Eumenides*: The Foundation of Law in the Repression of the Feminine." *Cardozo Public Law & Legal Theory Working Paper* 2.

Scodel, R. 1980. *The Trojan Trilogy of Euripides.* Göttingen.

Seaford, R., ed. 1996. *Euripides: Bacchae.* Warminster.

Seaford, R. 2005. "Death and Wedding in Aeschylus' *Niobe*." In *Lost Dramas of Classical Athens: Greek Tragic Fragments*, edited by F. McHardy, J. Robson, and D. Harvey, 113–27. Exeter.

Secomb, L. 2007. "Words That Matter: Reading the Performativity of Humanity through Butler and Blanchot." In *Judith Butler in Conversation: Analyzing the Texts and Talk of Everyday Life*, edited by B. Davies, 145–63. London.

Segal, C. 1978. "Pentheus and Hippolytus on the Couch and on the Grid: Psychoanalytic and Structuralist Readings of Greek Tragedy." *CW* 72.3: 129–48.

Segal, C. 1997. *Dionysiac Poetics and Euripides'* Bacchae. Princeton.

Shirazi, A. 2022. "Glimpses of Gesture: Refusing and Recovering Loss in Honig and Euripides." *CA* 41.2: 16–24.

Siegel, H. 1980. "Self-Delusion and the *Volte-Face* of Iphigenia in Euripides' *Iphigenia at Aulis*." *Hermes* 80: 300–21.

Sjöholm, C. 2002. "Family Values: Butler, Lacan, and the Rise of Antigone." *Radical Philosophy* 111 (January/February): 24–32.

Sjöholm, C. 2009. "Fear of Intimacy? Psychoanalysis and the Resistance to Commodification." In *Psychoanalysis, Aesthetics, and Politics in the Work of Julia Kristeva*, edited by K. Oliver and S. K. Keltner, 179–94. Albany, NY.

Sloterdijk, P. 2016. *Spheres* vol. 3 (*Foams*). South Pasadena, CA.

Sommerstein, A, ed. 1989. *Aeschylus: Eumenides*. Cambridge.

Sparrow, M. 2013. *No You Don't: Essays from an Unstrange Mind.* Green Cove Springs, FL.

Spillers, H. 1987. "Mama's Baby, Papa's Maybe: An American Grammar Book." *Diacritics* 17.2: 64–81.

Stanescu, J. 2012. "Species Trouble: Judith Butler, Mourning, and the Precarious Lives of Animals." *Hypatia* 27.3: 567–82.

Stanley, E. A. 2021. *Atmospheres of Violence: Structuring Antagonism and the Trans/Queer Ungovernable*. Durham, NC.

Steinbock, E., M. Szczygielska, and A. Wagner. 2017. "Thinking Linking." *Angelaki* 22.2: 1–10.

Stewart-Steinberg, S. 2011. *Impious Fidelity: Anna Freud, Psychoanalysis, Politics*. Ithaca, NY.

Stocking, D. 2008. "Antigone, *désoeuvrée*: Tragedy, Finitude, and Community." *Mosaic* 41.3: 153–68.

Stocking, D. 2014. "The Ruin of Song: Community and Autoimmunity in Sophocles' *Antigone*." In *The Returns of Antigone: Interdisciplinary Essays*, edited by T. Chanter and S. D. Kirkland, 69–85. Albany, NY.

Stryker, S. 2008. "Dungeon Intimacies: The Poetics of Transsexual Sadomasochism." *Parallax* 14.1: 36–47.

Stryker, S. 2015. "Transing the Queer (In)Human." *GLQ* 21.2–3: 227–30.

Stryker, S., and P. Currah. 2015. "General Editors' Introduction." *TSQ* 2.2: 189–93.

Sullivan, N. 2006. "Transmogrification: (Un)Becoming Other(s)." In *The Transgender Studies Reader*, edited by S. Stryker and S. Whittle, 552–64. New York.

Sullivan, N. 2014. "Somatechnics." *TSQ* 1.1–2: 187–90.

Szendy, P. 2023. "Conspiring (Sympnea and Dyspnea)." *SubStance* 52.1: 108–16.

Taplin, O. 1972. "Aeschylean Silences and Silences in Aeschylus." *HSCP* 76: 57–97.

Taplin, O. 2007. *Pots & Plays: Interactions between Tragedy and Greek Vase-Painting of the Fourth Century B.C.* Los Angeles.

Taussig, M. 1999. *Defacement: Public Secrecy and the Labor of the Negative*. Stanford, CA.

Taxidou, O. 2004. *Tragedy, Modernity and Mourning*. Edinburgh.

Telò, M. 2017. "Reperformance, Exile, and Archive Feelings: Rereading Aristophanes' *Acharnians* and Sophocles' *Oedipus at Colonus*." In *Imagining Reperformance in Ancient Culture*, edited by R. Hunter and A. Uhlig, 87–110. Cambridge.

Telò, M. 2019. "Iambic Horror: Shivers and Brokenness in Archilochus and Hipponax." In *The Genres of Archaic and Classical Greek Poetry: Theories and Models*, edited by M. Forster, L. Kurke, and N. Weiss, 271–96. London.

Telò, M. 2020a. *Archive Feelings: A Theory of Greek Tragedy*. Columbus, OH.

Telò, M. 2020b. "Laughter, or Aristophanes' Joy in the Face of Death." In *Aristophanic Humour: Theory and Practice*, edited by P. Swallow and E. Hall, 53–68. London.

Telò, M. 2022a. "Ancientmodern Objects: Viewing Freud's Oedipus Complex." In *Freud's Antiquity: Object / Idea / Desire*, edited by R. Armstrong, M. Leonard, D. Orrells, T. DeRose, and K. Heller, 79–90. London.

Telò, M. 2022b. "Foucault, Oedipus, and Virality." *symplokê* 30.1–2: 383–94.

Telò, M. 2023a. *Greek Tragedy in a Global Crisis: Reading through Pandemic Times*. London.

Telò, M. 2023b. *Resistant Form: Aristophanes and the Comedy of Crisis*. Goleta, CA.

Telò, M. 2023c. "Improvisational Solidarity: A Conversation with Judith Butler." In *Wayne Shorter and esperanza spalding's (. . .Iphigenia): Interdisciplinary Approaches*, edited by H. Morales and M. Telò. *Ramus* 52.1: 13–20.

Telò, M. 2023d. "Medea in the Courtroom: Foucault, Alice Diop, and Abolition." *Arethusa* 56.3: 413–39.

Telò, M. 2024a. "Introduction: Critical Encounters with Niobe." In *Antiquity, Modernity, Critical Theory*, edited by M. Telò and A. Benjamin, 1–22. Columbus, OH.

Telò, M. 2024b. "Fear of Flaying: Sontag, Language, Animality." In *Susan Sontag's Tangential Classics*, edited by L. Jansen. Oxford.

Thompson, C. 2005. *Making Parents: The Ontological Choreography of Reproductive Technologies*. Cambridge, MA.

Thompson, D. 2017. "An Exoneration of Black Rage." *SAQ* 116.3: 457–84.

Thompson, M. A. 2022. "Choosing Threat, Embodying the Viral: Trans* Endemics in Times of Pandemic." *TSQ* 9.3: 480–87.

Toscano, A. 2015. "Taming the Furies: Badiou and Hegel on *The Eumenides*." In *Badiou and Hegel: Infinity, Dialectics, Subjectivity*, edited by J. Vernon and A. Calcagno, 193–206. Lanham, MD.

Toscano, A. 2022. "Tragedy and Juridical Forms." *SAQ* 121.4: 777–94.

Toscano, A. 2023. *Late Fascism: Race, Capitalism and the Politics of Crisis*. London.

Toze, M. 2018. "The Risky Womb and the Unthinkability of the Pregnant Man: Addressing Trans Masculine Hysterectomy." *Feminism and Psychology* 28.2: 194–211.

Tralau, J. 2016. "The Justice of the Chimaira: Goat, Snake, Lion, and Almost the Entire *Oresteia* in a Little Monstrous Image." *Arion* 24.2: 41–67.

Tremblay, J.-T. 2022. *Breathing Aesthetics*. Durham, NC.

Uhlig, A. 2021. "Satyrs in Drag: Transvestism in Ion's *Omphale* and Elsewhere." In *Reconstructing Satyr Drama*, edited by A. P. Antonopoulos, M. M. Christopoulos, and G. W. M. Harrison, 455–75. Berlin.

Uribe, S. 2016. *Antígona González*. Los Angeles.

Vaccaro, J. 2014. "Handmade." *TSQ* 1.1–2: 96–97.

Walker, D. 2000. *Appeal to the Coloured Citizens of the World*. Edited with an Introduction and Annotation by P. P. Hinks. University Park, PA.

Weil, A. 2017. "Trans*versal Animacies and the Mattering of Black Trans* Political Life." *Angelaki* 22.2: 191–202.

Weiner, J. J., and D. Young. 2011. "Introduction: Queer Bonds." *GLQ* 17.2–3: 223–41.

Weinmann, F. 2018. *"Je suis mort": essai sur la narrative autothanatographique*. Paris.

Weismann, A. 1892. *Das Keimplasma: Eine Theorie der Vererbung*. Stuttgart.

Weiss, N. 2017. "Noise, Music, Speech: The Representation of Lament in Greek Tragedy." *AJP* 138.2: 243–66.

Wiener, J. 2015. "Antigone in Juarez: Tragedy, Politics, and Public Women on Mexico's Northern Border." *Classical Receptions Journal* 7.2: 276–309.

Williams, J. H. 2018. "'Unlike the Average': Mental Disability as Narrative Form and Social Critique in Morrison's *The Bluest Eye*." *SAF* 45.1: 91–117.

Wilson, P. 2006. "*Dikên* in the *Oresteia* of Aeschylus." In *Greek Drama III: Essays in Honour of Kevin Lee*, edited by J. Davidson, F. Muecke, and P. Wilson, 187–201. London.

Wohl, V. 1998. *Intimate Commerce: Exchange, Gender, and Subjectivity*. Austin, TX.

Wohl, V. 2002. *Love Among the Ruins: The Erotics of Democracy in Classical Athens*. Princeton.

Wohl, V. 2005. "Beyond Sexual Difference: Becoming Woman in Euripides' *Bacchae*." In *The Soul of Tragedy: Essays on Athenian Drama*, edited by V. Pedrick and S. M. Oberhelman, 137–54. Chicago.

Wohl, V. 2009. "Sexual Difference and the Aporia of Justice in Sophocles' *Antigone*." In *Bound by the City: Greek Tragedy, Sexual Difference, and the Formation of the* Polis, edited by D. McCoskey and E. Zakin, 119–48. Albany, NY.

Wohl, V. 2015. "How to Recognize a Hero in Euripides' *Electra*." *BICS* 58.1: 61–76.

Wohl, V. Forthcoming. "Intelligent Air."

Wolin, S. S. 1994. "Fugitive Democracy." *Constellations* 1.1: 11–25.

Wong, S. 1990. "Trangression as Poesis in *The Bluest Eye*." *Callaloo* 13.3: 471–81.

Woolf, V. 1925. "On Not Knowing Greek." In *The Common Reader*, 39–59. London.

Worm, S. 2021. "The Eyes of Others." https://openspace.sfmoma.org/2021/09/the-eyes-of-others/

Worman, N. 2012. "Cutting to the Bone: Recalcitrant Bodies in Sophocles." In *A Companion to Sophocles*, edited by K. Ormand, 351–66. Malden, MA.

Worman, N. 2018. *Virginia Woolf's Greek Tragedy*. London.

Worman, N. 2020. *Tragic Bodies: Edges of the Human in Greek Drama*. London.

Wynter, S. 1979. "Sambos and Minstrels." *Social Text* 1: 149–56.

Yancy, G. 2023. "Judith Butler: Palestinians Are Not Being 'Regarded as People' by Israel and US." *Truthout* (October 31). https://truthout.org/articles/judith-butler-palestinians-are-not-being-regarded-as-people-by-israel-and-us/

Yergeau, M. 2018. *Authoring Autism: On Rhetoric and Neurological Queerness*. Durham, NC.

Yi, S.-H. 2015. "Democratic Inclusion and 'Suffering Together' in *The Eumenides*: Duality of Immigrants." *Political Theory* 43.1: 30–53.

Yoon, H. 2017. "Feral Biopolitics: Animal Bodies and Border Technologies." *Angelaki* 22.2: 135–50.

Zakin, E. 2009. "Marrying the City: Intimate Strangers and the Fury of Democracy." In *Bound by the City: Greek Tragedy, Sexual Difference, and the Formation of the Polis*, edited by D. E. McCoskey and E. Zakin, 177–96. Albany, NY.

Zaman, H. A. 2023. "Furry Acts as Non/Human Drag: A Case Study Exploring Queer of Colour Liveability through the Fursona." *Queer Studies in Media & Popular Culture* 8.1: 99–114.

Zeitlin, F. I. 1985. "Playing the Other: Theater, Theatricality, and the Feminine in Greek Drama." *Representations* 11: 63–95.

Zeitlin, F. I. 1996. *Playing the Other: Gender and Society in Classical Greek Literature*. Chicago.

Zeitlin, F. I. 2005. "Dionysus in 69." In *Dionysus Since 69: Greek Tragedy at the Dawn of the Third Millennium*, edited by E. Hall, F. Macintosh, and A. Wrigley, 49–76. Oxford.

Žižek, S. 1992. *Enjoy Your Symptom! Jacques Lacan in Hollywood and Out*. London.

Žižek, S. 2004. "From Antigone to Joan of Arc." *Helios* 31.1–2: 51–62.

Žižek, S. 2005. *Interrogating the Real*. London.

Žižek, S. 2012. *Less Than Nothing: Hegel and the Shadow of Dialectical Materialism*. London.

Žižek, S. 2015. *Antigone*. London.

Zupančič, A. 2023. *Let Them Rot: Antigone's Parallax*. New York.

Index